West Bengal has the longest ruling democratically elected Communist government in world history. Since 1977 the Left Front has governed a population
of 68 million people and has received considerable world-wide attention as a
positive example of Third World development and change. In this book,
Dr. Ross Mallick convincingly challenges this view of the Left Front government, arguing that it has been a failure in terms of redistributive development
reforms.

Using interviews with government officials and ruling party members as
well as internal government and party documents, the author concentrates upon
the Left Front's rural development policy and compares and contrasts this with
their policy towards industrial labor, the state bureaucracy and big business.
He explores the role of different classes in formulating and directing the
Communist party's policies and explains why communism developed in
Bengal, but not in neighboring states. The author also assesses why the
communism that has developed is not of a revolutionary character, but of the
most minimal type of reformism in which the lower classes have had a
peripheral role and which has not significantly improved their standard of
living. Mallick concludes that, although the powers and policy options of the
state government were necessarily limited, a great deal more could have been
achieved had the ruling party not been impeded by the elitist nature of its
political base.

*Development policy of a Communist government* will be widely read by
students and specialists of South Asian studies, Third World development and
comparative communism.

T0371487

*Cambridge South Asian Studies*

# Development policy of
# a Communist government

# Development policy of a Communist government:

## West Bengal since 1977

Ross Mallick

CAMBRIDGE
UNIVERSITY PRESS

CAMBRIDGE UNIVERSITY PRESS
Cambridge, New York, Melbourne, Madrid, Cape Town, Singapore, São Paulo

Cambridge University Press
The Edinburgh Building, Cambridge CB2 8RU, UK

Published in the United States of America by Cambridge University Press, New York

www.cambridge.org
Information on this title: www.cambridge.org/9780521432924

First published 1993
This digitally printed version 2008

*A catalogue record for this publication is available from the British Library*

*Library of Congress Cataloguing in Publication data*

Mallick, Ross.
Development policy of a Communist government: West Bengal since 1977/
Ross Mallick.
    p.   cm. – (Cambridge South Asian studies)
Includes bibliographical references (p.   ).
ISBN 0 521 43292 8
1. West Bengal (India) – Economic policy. 2. Communism – India-West Bengal.
I. Title. II. Series.
HC437. W44M35 1993
338.954' 14' 009047 – dc20                              92-20010 CIP

ISBN 978-0-521-43292-4 hardback
ISBN 978-0-521-04785-2 paperback

# Contents

# Figures and maps

# Tables

# Acknowledgements

This book would not have been completed without the help of a number of people who wish to remain anonymous. I would particularly like to thank my Cambridge doctoral thesis supervisor, Geoffrey Hawthorn, without whom the study would never have come to fruition. My relations who looked after me at their expense during my trips to India and whose contacts proved extremely useful, were indispensable to the research. My work was funded by a Social Sciences and Humanities Research Council of Canada Doctoral Fellowship, a United Kingdom Committee of Vice-Chancellors and Principals Overseas Research Students Award, and grants from the Beit Fund and Smuts Memorial Fund.

# Glossary

| | |
|---|---|
| AIKS | All-India Kisan Sabha (CPM Peasant Organization) |
| *Bargadar* | Sharecropper |
| *Benami* | Property transferred to another only nominally |
| *Bhadralok* | Literally "gentleman," normally refers to high caste upper class Bengali |
| *Biga* | 1/3rd of an acre in Bengal |
| CADP | Comprehensive Area Development Program |
| CC | Central Committee |
| CITU | Centre of Indian Trade Unions (CPM Trade Union) |
| Class 1–IV employees | Grades of Government employees with Class 1 being the highest |
| CPC | Communist Party of China |
| CPI | Communist Party of India (previously "pro-Soviet") |
| CPM, CPI (M) | Communist Party of India, (Marxist), independent |
| CPI (M-L) | Communist Party of India (Marxist-Leninist), Maoist commonly referred to as Naxalites |
| CPSU | Communist Party of the Soviet Union |
| *Crore* | Ten million |
| FB | Forward Bloc |
| Hectare | 2.47 acres |
| IAS | Indian Administrative Service |
| ICS | Indian Civil Service |
| IPS | Indian Police Service |
| IRDP | Integrated Rural Development Program |
| *Lakh* | One hundred thousand |
| Panchayat | Village Council |
| PB | Politburo (CPM) |

| | |
|---|---|
| RSP | Revolutionary Socialist Party |
| Scheduled Castes | Untouchable castes listed or "scheduled" in the constitution of India |
| SFI | Student Federation of India (CPM) |
| SUC | Socialist Unity Centre |
| WBCS | West Bengal Civil Service |
| Writers Building | Secretariat, seat of West Bengal government |
| Zamindar | Landlord and colonial revenue collector |

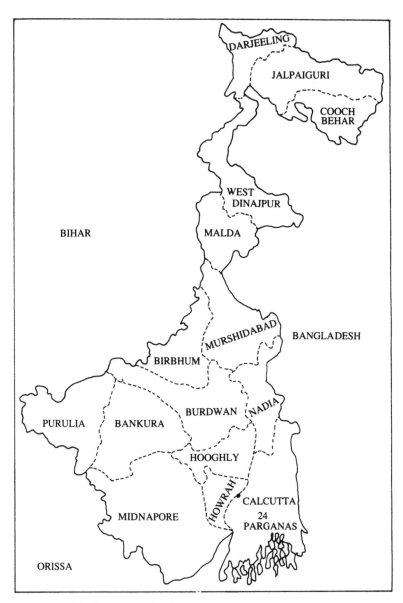

District map of West Bengal

# 1    A problematic legacy

West Bengal has the longest ruling democratically elected Communist government in world history. Since 1977 the Communists have governed a population
larger than that of Britain or France. Its 68 million people re-elected the
Communists repeatedly, indicating a continuing popularity and longevity not
found by Marxists in any other democracy. The Communist takeover of one of
India's most industrialized and strategically important states predictably created
considerable interest and controversy over its performance in office.

Though development policy implementation was not the only Left Front
endeavor, it was the most critical in providing a working example for the rest
of India, and in consolidating Communist power. Electorally the rural areas with
74 percent of the state population would be critical in maintaining Communist
influence. For this reason rural development had priority over urban industrial
development in determining the success of the Left Front government. It was
also the area where the Communists had greatest constitutional authority as
agrarian reform fell largely within state jurisdiction. Rural development has
therefore taken up most of the present work, with industrial and trade union
policies providing analogous urban examples. Administrative reforms have
been covered to indicate the policy instruments available to the Left Front for
reform implementation. The emphasis is on development policies that might be
attempted by any provincial Third World government trying to alter socio-
economic conditions in favor of the lower classes.

The task facing the Left Front government on assuming office in 1977
was fraught with difficulties, despite its massive majority in the Legislative
Assembly. The problems posed by the transition to socialism in the conditions
of West Bengal were hardly amenable to easy solutions. The United Fronts of
the late 1960s, under pressure from the Maoist left, had attempted rapid radical
change only to be brutally repressed. This radical activity helped gain the
Communist Party of India–Marxist (CPM) a larger base, but the party's inability
to stand up to state repression exposed its weakness in the face of a dictatorial
government. Only the return of democracy after the Emergency enabled the
CPM to show that its popular following had been enhanced during the years of
"semi-fascist terror."

Though the central Janata government formed in 1977 was not hostile to the Left Front, it could hardly be expected to countenance revolutionary change in a state government, nor was a successful revolution possible in one province alone. Having won the election, the Left Front could use its power either for radical polarization of class forces, or for a more gradual incremental change designed to give longevity to the government: a longevity sufficient for its base to survive till revolutionary conditions in the rest of India caught up with West Bengal. These revolutionary conditions however would likely take decades to come if they came at all. A state government intent on remaining in power for decades could hardly be expected to keep up a tempo of popular revolutionary fervor.

Surprisingly even the Communists never expected to win all but sixty-three of the 293 assembly seats when they ran for election in 1977. They had gone to great lengths to form a seat adjustment with the non-Communist Janata Party then ruling the central government, but when rebuffed contested on their own and won a landslide victory. Their unexpected victory left them without an articulated strategy for directing their new-found power. However, their *ad hoc* reactions to problems indicated where their interests lay and the groups they were most oriented to promoting. It was these policies which insured their popularity and consolidated their base in the state.

Perhaps the most frank statement of Left Front government policy was made by its Chief Minister Jyoti Basu in setting forth West Bengal as an example for the rest of India.

The Left Front Government in the State of West Bengal has limited powers. It has to operate within a capitalist feudal economy. The Constitution, contrary to federal principles, does not provide for the needed powers for the States and we suffer from a special disability because the Union Government is ill disposed towards our Government. In such a situation, we have been explaining to the people why we cannot bring about fundamental changes even though the ideology and character of our Government are different from those that characterise the Government at the Centre. But we do hold that by forming the Government through elections it is possible for us to rule in a manner which is distinctly better and more democratic than the way followed by the Congress party at the Centre and in many other States. It is also possible to give relief to the people, particularly the deprived sections, through the minimum programme adopted by the Left Front. We have been attempting to do so by motivating the people and enlisting their support and sympathy. Our objective is to raise their political consciousness along with giving them relief so that they can distinguish between truth and falsehood and friends and enemies, and realise the alternative path which will free them from the shackles of Capitalism and Feudalism and usher in a new modern progressive society. This is a difficult task and we have to traverse a long path. But we visualise success in our objective when large masses all over India will be imbued with the correct political consciousness and free themselves from *bourgeois* influence and ideology, particularly the working masses. They will arrive at the truth through experience and continuous struggles. The left and democratic State Governments can help and expedite this process even with their limited powers. It is with such a perspective and objective that we are functioning in West Bengal.[1]

This Communist transitional strategy takes place in two stages. The first stage would create governments at the state level opposed to the ruling Congress, breaking its virtual monopoly of power, and enabling other popular parties including the Communists to make inroads. In such fluid conditions the Communists could eventually attain a dominant position in coalition governments at the state level. When dominance was achieved at a national level, the Communist takeover would be complete.

The first stage involving Communist participation in state governments would attempt reforms only as a means of developing a Communist political base. In its political practice, however, the reforms would not be much different from what Social Democratic parties might be expected to deliver, but which the establishment parties had proved unable or unwilling to implement. Therefore, the Communist state governments could not be expected to implement an immediate revolutionary program. Rather their policy implementation could only be considered on the basis of (1) whether it used all avenues for reform available within the constitutional system, and (2) whether these reforms contained a potential for further radicalization and expansion of the Communist movement towards the ultimate goal of a Communist revolution. A failure to implement reforms could be due to the constitutional system's allowing insufficient scope for reform along lines conducive to Communist growth, or because of inadequacies with Communist policy implementation. The final possibility is that while the reforms may succeed in their immediate objectives, they create interests inimical to more radical alternatives and supportive of a new status quo. This book will argue that while there was sufficient scope within the Indian constitution for reforms conducive to Communist growth in a revolutionary direction, these reforms were not undertaken. Furthermore what reforms were implemented furthered class and group interests hostile to more radical change, making the development of a revolutionary conjuncture less likely. As a result reforms ground to a halt, and their continued stay in office has become counterproductive from a revolutionary Communist viewpoint, but helpful to the establishment they aimed at overthrowing.

The Communist state government had limited jurisdiction over many institutions and departments, having to operate within the constitutional constraints of the central government, which had the power to remove it from office by Presidential decree. With these limitations in mind, the policy implementation of the Left Front government has been analyzed to determine its success in

[1] Jyoti Basu, Chief Minister of West Bengal, *Left Front Government's Industrial Policy: Some Aspects* (Calcutta: Information and Cultural Affairs Department, 1985), p. 5.

bringing about social and economic change, and to indicate groups that benefited from these reforms. Their electoral success was due to following policies
that promoted rural middle- and upper-class interests, while distributing palliatives to the lower classes. In the urban areas the interests of the government
clerical staff were promoted, as well as of those corporations still willing to
invest in the state (ch. 5). The industrial and rural working class received few
if any benefits from Left Front rule, and might have been better off had the
Communists remained in opposition where they could have led strikes in pursuit
of wage demands.

It will be argued that the Left Front failed, not primarily because of the
limitations on its power and resources, but because it did not make appropriate
use of the powers and resources that it had at its disposal. Rather than promoting
the interests of the rural and urban lower classes, it gave primacy to the
traditional rural and urban middle-class base of the Communist movement,
which ultimately proved an obstacle to the further advancement both of lower-
class interests, and those of the revolutionary Communist movement as a whole.
The ruling Communist Party of India – Marxist (CPM) which had been founded
as a revolutionary alternative to the old "revisionist" Communist Party, became
through its experience in office, no different from its parent party. It thus ceased
to be revolutionary in its practice, and even to call it reformist would be
overstating its achievements in office. The rural and urban vested interests
which the Left Front promoted will likely make further change in both reformist
and revolutionary directions more difficult, as these interests are more firmly
entrenched than ever, and are opposed to any change in the status quo which
would threaten the newly created privileges the Left Front provided them with.
While this distribution of patronage has enabled the Communists to be an
electoral success, it is proving detrimental to the advancement of revolutionary
communism: an impasse out of which it is unlikely to emerge in the foreseeable
future. By promoting various propertied class interests, it has given these groups
a stake in the status quo, and made them more hostile to reforms that would
benefit the society as a whole. These classes have been transformed from being
the traditional advocates of reform, to being its most vociferous opponents. With
4/5ths of the state budget going to pay the salaries of government employees
whose support has been fostered by Left Front pay increments, and with
additional revenues from agriculture being blocked by its rural landowner
supporters, the Left Front has little left for development expenses. In pursuit of
short-term electoral gains, it has sacrificed both its revolutionary and its reformist options, and can do nothing but cling to office through the distribution of
largesse, much of it supplied by the central government.

To understand why these middle-class interests played such a vital role in
formulating and directing Communist policies in office, it is necessary to look at
the history of Bengal and the role this class played in its politics. This will indicate

the reasons communism developed in Bengal but not in neighboring states, and why the communism that did develop was not of a revolutionary character, but of the most minimal type of reformism, in which the lower classes had a peripheral role. Chapters 2–4, dealing with different aspects of rural development, argue that Left Front policies have in practice favored those landed and middle classes that formed the politically active base of the Left Front. The analysis also deals with policy towards industrial labor, the state bureaucracy and big business. While the Left Front insured support from the lower levels of the bureaucracy with pay bonuses, it alienated the officer cadre by its factional manipulation and political interference. Its attempt at encouraging corporate investment, while winning the support of big business, has failed to give a boost to the state economy, and in the process there has been a slower increase in wages during this period than when the Communists were in opposition. In short, the beneficiaries of the Left Front have been the rural landed middle class, the lower-level government employees, and the capitalist class. The book will show that the lower classes largely received what had already been available to them under previous governments, or was being simultaneously offered in other states under central government-funded programs.

### Research methodology

The development reforms in West Bengal have received considerable praise in the foreign academic development literature. The most detailed foreign studies endorsing the West Bengal development programs have been conducted by Atul Kohli (Princeton) and T.J. Nossiter (LSE), but their views have been shared by James Manor, Paul Brass, and the Rudolphs[2]. It will be argued that this literature is based on misleading West Bengal government statistics which have been insufficiently scrutinized by the development specialists. Despite efforts to find at least one successful program, in the end I found that all the major development programs provided only marginal benefits to the poorer classes. Where programs were part of national development programs, the West Bengal performance was mediocre and often considerably worse than that of other states. The Left Front could not be credited with successful implementation of any program.

In assessing development programs scholars often use some combination of

---

[2] Paul R. Brass, *The Politics of India Since Independence: The New Cambridge History of India IV. 1* (Cambridge: Cambridge University Press, 1990); Atul Kohli, *The State and Poverty in India: The Politics of Reform* (Cambridge: Cambridge University Press, 1987); James Manor, "Tried, then Abandoned: Economic Liberalisation in India," *IDS Bulletin*, vol. 18, no. 4 (1987), pp. 39–44; T.J. Nossiter, *Marxist State Governments in India* (London: Pinter Publishers, 1988); Lloyd I. Rudolph and Susanne Hoeber Rudolph, *In Pursuit of Lakshmi: The Political Economy of the Indian State* (Chicago: The University of Chicago Press, 1987).

Table 1.1. *Total agricultural land leased-in and leased-out estimated through listing and agriculture schedules (acres)*

| Schedule type | Leased-in | Leased-out |
|---|---|---|
| Listing | 4,645 | 1,408 |
| Agriculture | 4,436 | 312 |

*Source:* Maitra (1982), p. 9.

ruling party members, civil servants, and development beneficiaries as informants in their program evaluations. Statistical data is collected either through their
own surveys or through those of colleagues and governments. What weight is
given to the often conflicting evidence determines the conclusions reached.
Informants inevitably have personal biases as well as restraints on their freedom
of expression. Party members and civil servants must publicly defend the
government position while beneficiaries may fear that criticism will result in
the withdrawal of aid or in even worse sanctions. The West Bengal development
literature illustrates this problem. Atul Kohli, in interviewing sixty West Bengal
Gram Panchayat (village council) members, states: "Because these interviews
were always carried out in group situations, which included members of the
local community, it was difficult for the respondents to hide the length of their
party involvement, as well as their ownership of land and the mode of land use."[3]
However the American anthropologist James M. Freeman states: "To be polite,
Indian villagers often provide answers that they think the investigator wants to
hear. Their replies usually bear little relation to the way they live their lives or
view the world."[4] In one of my meetings with a Gram Panchayat, the elected
members all assured me that they were landless agricultural laborers. The local
government official who had arranged the meeting stated later that this was not
the case, as was obvious from their appearance. Public statements cannot
therefore be taken at face value. Under-reporting of landholdings is more clearly
revealed by an ILO study in West Bengal where leased-in land was virtually
identical in two surveys but leased-out land was 1/3 to 1/14 this size, though the
figures should have been nearly identical, as there was virtually no landowner
absenteeism (table 1.1)[5]. The discrepancy in the leased-out land between the
two surveys was attributed to the threat of sharecropper rights' being recorded.

---

[3] Kohli, *The State*, p. 110.

[4] James M. Freeman, *Untouchable: An Indian Life History* (Stanford: Stanford University Press, 1979), p. 11.

[5] Tares Maitra, *Expansion of Employment Through Local Resource Mobilisation: Study of a Cluster of Villages in West Bengal* (Bangkok: Asian Employment Programme, International Labour Organisation, 1982), pp. 9–10.

Only those living in a village are likely to uncover the reality behind all the deceptions. However, among academics only anthropologists generally live in villages, though the villages selected may not be typical, and this will not reveal state-level decision-making problems. Much the same difficulty arises with civil servants and ruling party members who are obliged to defend the government record. Only private conversations are likely to result in truthful responses and even then frankness is not always advisable. To achieve frankness a period of often prolonged confidence-building is required. In an anonymous questionnaire sent to West Bengal Indian Administrative Service (IAS) officers, 45.65 percent would not even respond to the question of whether political pressure on officers had increased under the Left Front government.[6] Obtaining accurate surveys in such circumstances is extremely difficult. Generally, however, it is fair to say that the respondent's property will be understated and confidence in the government overstated.

The same caution must be exercised with West Bengal government statistics which are presented in Left Front publications to give a positive impression. Nossiter implicitly accepts these statistics as do other writers who praise the Left Front experiment. These statistics need comparison with earlier periods and require verification through interviewing administrators familiar with how these statistics were collected. This does not appear to have been done, as possible inaccuracies in the statistics cited are not mentioned in their publications. West Bengal IAS administrators critical of the Left Front performance have not been given credibility by either Kohli or Nossiter. Kohli states in the footnotes that the "senior civil servants like D. Bandopadhyay and B. Sarkar," in asserting the landed supporters of the CPM were blocking agrarian reform, followed what "almost appeared to be the bureaucratic line."[7] Though Dr. Sarkar's thesis/book on West Bengal land reform is the definitive work on the subject and D. Bandopadhyay subsequently became all-India Rural Development Secretary, their views, gained from years of experience in the field, have been discounted despite their access to material far exceeding that available to scholars.[8] Whether to accept the "bureaucratic line" or a Communist party one is a difficult judgment call. Though Nossiter and Kohli, along with a number of other scholars have essentially accepted the party line, in fact, even many CPM members privately do not accept the party line on the success of their policies, as will be indicated later.

The academic literature on the performance of the Left Front government is composed of two opposing Indian Marxist views and the non-Communist

6 Ratna Bhattacharya, *Administrators in a Developing Society: West Bengal* (Bombay: Himalaya Publishing House, 1989), p. 149.

7 Kohli, *The State*, p. 127.

8 Bikram Sarkar, *Land Reforms in India: A Study of Legal Aspects of Land Reforms Measures in West Bengal* (New Delhi: Ashish Publishing House, 1989).

scholarship. The Marxist academics divide into supporters and opponents of the Left Front. The CPM economists Biplab Dasgupta and Ashim Dasgupta take the official view, while the Marxist critics Ashok Rudra, Profulla Roy Choudhury, and Ajit Roy are consistently critical. They have engaged in a rather acrimonious debate which is most readily available in the *Economic and Political Weekly*. The positions of the authors are entirely predictable reflecting stands adhered to long before the Left Front came to power. The CPM economist Biplab Dasgupta criticizes Ashok Rudra and others of his view as "academics with Left-wing pretensions." Rudra, rejecting the whole Left Front experience in office, says "… it is futile for any left party to form a government at the state level and expect to serve the cause of the toiling masses."[9] He criticizes the privileges enjoyed by Left Front academics, and points to the difficulties of non-Left Front supporters doing research in the state.

My means of transportation has been the ramshackle overcrowded buses, where no seats can be reserved, and equally overcrowded second class train compartments (I refuse to travel first class while conducting surveys among the rural poor!) and I have had often to travel standing all the way … Dasgupta and his academic colleagues in the service of the government travel, as a matter of rule, in chauffeur-driven saloon cars. For spending nights, I had to depend on *mofussil* hotels and nobody who has not travelled in West Bengal countryside will know how miserable their conditions can be. Biplab Dasgupta and his friends enjoy such luxurious accommodation as is provided by Circuit Houses and bungalows of the different Departments meant for touring government officials. Indeed, in contemporary West Bengal, academics with Leftist "commitments" (meaning thereby support to the Front government) stand to gain ample rewards for their leftism. For, whatever else the Left Front government may lack resources for, the Finance Minister has always more than enough funds for distributing perquisites and patronage amongst all those intellectuals who are prepared to lend their support to the regime. And in this one respect the state government has outdone the Central government.[10]

This critical position is disputed by C.N. Ray who claims that "within the limited scope of political and financial power alloted to the state government, the performance of the Left Front government is quite satisfactory." The non-Communist scholar, Atul Kohli, has taken the view that the Left Front government has been a success or at least successful relative to other Indian states. He considered West Bengal to have the best rural development program of the three states he studied. Though the CPM government is not "without its share of failings, problems, and critics" its "redistributive programs are nevertheless impressive."[11] The CPM has become reformist and part of the constitutional system, which in his view is a positive development.

[9] Ashok Rudra, "Agrarian Policies of Left Front Government in West Bengal," *Economic and Political Weekly*, vol. 20, no. 23, June 8, 1985, p. 1016.
[10] *Ibid.*
[11] Kohli, *The State.*

Clearly, how one assesses the Left Front depends very much on one's philosophy. What is positive for Kohli is anathema to Rudra. The Left Front experiment is too controversial for unanimity to be expected, however by examining development performance a program evaluation is possible. This has been done by analyzing the Left Front government's own statistics and interviewing its officials at all levels of the administration. This has not been easy. Fear of the "foreign hand," though a national concern, is understandably acute with a Communist government, particularly when the previous Communist-dominated government was destabilized through CIA funding of the rival Congress Party. Fixed appointments were generally not honored and eventually the direct approach had to be abandoned in favor of less formal contacts.[12] State-level administrators implementing government programs usually proved to be more objective and forthcoming than senior party officials in interviews, and better placed in providing government statistics.

That the Left Front can still be considered a success raises the question as to how such an impression could be created. Only a few private conversations with the people implementing the Left Front programs should have quickly revealed what was happening. However, interviewing top party leaders only provides good examples of party line, as published interviews have shown. On the other hand, civil servants will not talk critically of their government in front of staff, and never for the record. In private, however, both government officials and middle-level party members are often much more forthcoming and very critical of their leaders. Despite these criticisms, the Communists were able to achieve noticeable success in obtaining favorable media coverage. The West Bengal government was able to get a favorable press from normally anti-Communist media who found the Left Front moderation reassuring. This support is understandable considering the innocuousness of the Left Front policies, which do not represent a threat to any major class. As the CPM has ceased to be a reformist party, much less a revolutionary one, its media public relations successes are hardly surprising. Though its rhetoric maintains some of its old Communist revolutionary flavor, this is no longer taken seriously by anyone aside from the party faithful.

---

[12] Another reason suggested for this non-cooperation was the lack of the CPM leadership's understanding of socialist transition theory. They claimed few CPM leaders had any conception of Gramsci's theories and more recent debates in Marxism had completely passed them by. CPM theory has an ideological time warp where the old 1951 Statement of Policy is adhered to and the cult of personality followed with Stalin calendars and penholders. The CPM may be the only significant non-Maoist party in the world still having a Stalin personality cult. This does not mean that its policies in government are Stalinist, however. Though capable of murder, defalcation of state funds, and tolerating police torture, its policies are a model of moderation. The gap between theory and practice in the CPM is extremely wide; in fact there is no fully elaborated theory of the transition to socialism, and what determines policy is short-term political expediency and *ad hocism*.

The Left Front justified any inaction as due to the impossibility of achieving genuine reform under capitalism. However, its claim to be taking reforms to the constitutional limits is doubtful. When compared with other states the Bengal achievement is average at best and often well below the national average, though a Communist government would have been expected to surpass all other states in reform implementation. A visit to the most backward district in Maharashtra confirmed this impression. One Maharashtra government official observed that while the Bengal Left Front government publicized all their achievements, in his own state they had achieved better results without the fanfare. The achievements appear less impressive when compared with international experiences. A Secretary of the West Bengal government on returning from a British posting realized that the CPM was less radical than the British Labour Party which at least had an orientation towards lower-class problems that the Left Front lacked. The Left Front parties are less radical than many European Social Democrats, the CPM having been transformed from a party for change to that of the status quo. This is a major transformation for a party formed in 1964 as a revolutionary alternative to the "reformist" CPI, but which is now no longer reformist. As there are no revolutionary or Social Democratic national parties, however, the lack of a serious radical alternative to the CPM enables it to maintain its inert position unchallenged from the left.

This transformation of a revolutionary Marxist party into a reformist and finally an establishment party is not unique in history. The transformation of the German Social Democratic Party was only the classic example. However, in an underdeveloped nation with about half the population below the most minimal poverty line and a third of the population suffering from malnutrition, the existence of a Communist movement subservient to the interests of big business and landowners is unparalleled. In no other Third World nation has the Communist movement so neglected the interests of the lower classes and been so accommodative of the "class enemy." When a Secretary of the Indian government said the Left Front experience in West Bengal would set back the Indian Communist movement fifty years he may have made an accurate prediction. Certainly it is difficult to see how the Communist movement can recover from its failure in West Bengal and regain its original radicalism. The trend is entirely in the opposite direction towards greater accommodation with the establishment. In the immediate post-independence years the CPI was India's main opposition party. Today the Communists can hardly consider themselves a national force and other parties have overtaken them from the right.

This abandonment of a radical strategy was not readily apparent when the Left Front first took power in 1977. A number of potentially significant reform programs was undertaken and existing ones revitalized, leading to the view that significant changes were underway in West Bengal. This was the view I shared on beginning my research. It was only slowly over four visits since 1977 that these assumptions gave way to a more realistic assessment of the Left Front government. Though in the government's first term the rural reforms were running into difficulty, it took a number of years to realize that all the reform programs were failing to achieve their objectives. The Communists' continuing electoral success was rooted less in growing enthusiasm for the Left Front than in the corruption of the Congress governments and the oppositions' continuing failure to act as a viable alternative. The reform and development policies had consolidated electoral support for the Left Front from new elites hostile to radical reforms favoring the poorest classes. My field research ended in a futile attempt to find at least one significant reform program that was successful, if for no other reason than to provide a more balanced and constructive view of development programs in West Bengal. The list of policy failures that ultimately emerges from the research was unedifying in not providing any positive examples for development programs. To the extent that program failure can illustrate the obstacles to incremental development, the book may show the difficulties that have to be overcome should future attempts at development be anticipated.

### Communist Party history.

To understand Left Front government policies it is necessary to study the Communist Party–Marxist (CPM). A detailed account of the CPM history has been presented elsewhere; but the themes that bear on the conduct of the Left Front government will be briefly examined.[13]

The Bengali, M.N. Roy, founded the Communist Party of India (CPI) at Tashkent in the Soviet Union in 1921.[14] However, it was not till the 1930s that it developed a significant base inside the country. The debate between Lenin and M.N. Roy at the second Communist International Congress on whether Communists should support national elites struggling against colonialism, which Lenin supported, or oppose them as basically reactionary, as Roy wanted, was never resolved by the Indian Communist Party. The faction which was closest to Roy's original position in opposing collaboration with the Congress

---

[13] Sudipta Kaviraj, "The Split in the Communist Movement in India" (Jawaharlal Nehru University Ph.D. thesis, 1979); Marcus Franda, *Radical Politics in West Bengal* (Cambridge, Massachusetts: The MIT Press, 1971); K.S. Subramanian, "The Ideological Evolution of the Indian Communist Movement in the Post-Independence Period" (Karnataka University Ph.D. thesis, 1983); Ross Mallick, *Indian Communism: Opposition, Collaboration and Institutionalization* (Oxford University Press, 1993).

[14] G. Adhikari, editor, *Documents of the History of the Communist Party of India*, vol. I, 1917–1922 (New Delhi: People's Publishing House, October 1971), p. 231.

Party, eventually left the party to form the Communist Party of India – Marxist (CPM) in 1964.

The CPM is the product of the split of the left and centrist factions from the Communist Party of India (CPI). The CPM contained two factions: a centrist group which was opposed to splitting the party but joined the splitters when the breakup became inevitable, and a left wing which was itself divided between radicals and Maoists. When the CPM entered the coalition United Front government of West Bengal in 1967, the Maoists refused to support the new government and formed their own party.[15] The splitting of the Communist movement into three parties was to have a profound impact on the conduct of the Left Front government, because the Maoists gave the left wing leverage over the centrist group. With the departure of the Maoists the centrists gradually came to dominate party policy and the non-Maoist radicals were marginalized.

When the CPM first entered the West Bengal government in 1967 the CPM's Maoists launched a peasant soviet in Naxalbari. They probably expected that the new reformist government would not repress a peasant movement led by members of the CPM on whom the United Front government depended to stay in office. However, rather than side with their own Maoist members in opposition to the other parties in the coalition, the CPM decided to remain in office and acquiesced in the government's repression of the peasant movement. The use of police to defeat a Communist peasant movement showed the Marxist leadership were determined to remain in office and utilize the parliamentary system. The Maoist uprising was undoubtedly premature but it had the backing of China which was then in the Cultural Revolution. The Naxalbari uprising served to give the Bengal Maoist leadership ascendancy over the national Maoist movement, whose most important leader, T. Nagi Reddy, was opposed to immediate armed struggle. Reddy was leader of the opposition in the Andhra state assembly and had the support of half the Andhra CPM members. The Bengal Maoists by contrast were led by only a district level CPM leader with the support of about 15 percent of Bengal party members. The Bengal Maoist Charu Mazumdar, however, by first launching the armed struggle was able to undermine Reddy's leadership and launch an equally unsuccessful uprising in Andhra. The CPM leadership eventually used police and paramilitary forces to put down the Maoist uprising and the Maoists retaliated by murdering the CPM members. Eventually the Maoist CPI-ML and the CPM indulged in mutual mass killing. With the central and state governments as well as the CPM killing thousands of Maoists they were virtually wiped out as a political force in West Bengal politics. Thereafter the CPM led the left in West Bengal politics from the early 1970s on, without having to worry about a left opposition.

[15] Sumanta Banerjee, *In the Wake of Naxalbari* (Calcutta: Subarnarekha, 1980); Amiya K. Samanta, *Left Extremist Movement in West Bengal* (Calcutta: Firma KLM, 1984).

There remained two factions in the CPM. One faction of old centrists led by the Kerala leader E.M.S. Namboodiripad and the Bengal leader Jyoti Basu were initially opposed to the formation of the CPM. They eventually joined out of political expediency since the party cadre were mostly in the left faction, and because of personal and ideological differences with the rightist faction. Initially their centrist faction was the minority as the Maoists and other radicals dominated the party. Gradually this radical faction, to accommodate the centrists in the party, compromised their policies and the centrists slowly expanded their influence. When the Maoists left, over this turn to moderation, the remaining radicals were significantly weakened and eventually lost control over the direction of party policy.

It seems extraordinary that the centrists, the weakest of the three factions at the time of the CPI split in 1964, eventually came to dominate CPM party policy and the Left Front government of West Bengal from the 1970s. They did so due to Indian political events favoring a centrist position, the death or expulsions of some radical leaders, and the conservatism of the CPM's class base. The development of this centrist approach into the dominant position in the CPM went through three phases, culminating in the policies of the present Left Front government.

In the first stage, EMS and Basu were clearly in the minority and in obvious disagreement with the party line. In the second phase, the rise of a more militant Naxalite ultra left made for reconciliation between the two sections of the leadership. In the third phase, after the Naxalite left had gone out of the party, and after the CPC started open ideological attacks on the CPI (M), the exact reverse of the first process happened. Originally, the EMS–Basu section had conceded to the other section of the CPI(M). Historical circumstances made the main leadership gradually shift to the EMS position ten years later.[16]

Rather than the Communist Party leading the middle and poor peasantry together through a united front towards a transition to socialism, the Party split over what strategy should be followed. The Maoists demanded that the poor peasant class interests have priority while the CPM wished to create multi-class alliances, and in effect postpone radical class struggle to a more opportune time. This conflict between former comrades escalated into all-out murder of each other's cadre. The Maoists were decimated and the CPM survived as an even more moderate party with a rural base more closely tied to the middle peasantry than before. The centrists' position came to dominate the party. There was a dynamic interaction between the Communist Party and its class base. Both influenced each other but in separate directions. Radical Maoist cadre influenced their peasant bases into armed struggle, whose initial success spurred the Maoists to greater acts of militancy. The CPM on the other hand, when faced

[16] Kaviraj, "The Split," p. 216.

with Congress repression, recoiled into inactivity only to return after a fortuitous election victory in 1977. In the party split there was no exact correlation dividing the middle and poor peasantry along CPM and Maoist lines but the tendencies were there. By the time the Left Front came to power the CPM had lost much of its impetus to press poor peasant interests.

The middle peasantry by contrast was not revolutionary at all, but reformist. It had nothing to gain by revolution that could not be acquired by a few reforms. To expect the middle peasantry to support a revolutionary program when a reformist one would do as well was unrealistic in a competitive democratic environment, where there were other more moderate parties offering reformist solutions. Alavi's warning that as the revolution advances the middle peasants may move away from the movement did not happen.[17] Rather than lose a middle-peasant base the CPM moved away from the revolution. Thus the CPM stayed with its class base rather than pursue revolutionary goals. A party that in the 1950s seemed to have much potential as the official opposition and expected successor to the Congress government at the national level, lost this position to communal, regional, and rightist parties. The Congress Party lost a subsequent general election and a coalition government supported by Communists came to power, but the Communists are no longer in a position to achieve hegemony in national government.

In retrospect the critical period in the change from a revolutionary to a reformist orientation in the CPM was during the United Front governments from 1967 to 1970. The Communists formed a coalition government with anti-Congress parties that were actually little different in class orientation from the ruling party, which they had left as dissident factions tired of Congress Party corruption. The first major dissident Congress faction in West Bengal was the Bangla Congress. After the Congress Party was defeated in 1967 all the opposition parties formed a United Front government, with the CPM as a major participant and the Bangla Congress holding the top post of Chief Minister. In this nine-month government and a subsequent thirteen-month United Front government in 1969–70, the CPM became the dominant party in the state through mass mobilization and splitting its opposing coalition partners. Since then the primary political conflict has been between the Congress and the CPM with other parties dissolving, as in the case of the Bangla Congress, or playing only peripheral roles in opposition or government. A period of Presidential Rule was followed by the 1972 election in which Congress ballot rigging enabled it to return to power. With the CPM boycotting the assembly and being driven underground in many areas, the left movement became largely ineffectual. After the lifting

---

[17]  Hamza Alavi, "Peasants and Revolution" reprinted from *The Socialist Register 1965* (Boston: New England Press), p. 275.

of the Emergency in 1977, the CPM again returned to power but this time with its own party in an absolute majority and in a Left Front coalition composed only of Marxists.

When faced with a Maoist radical left alternative, the CPM in 1967–70 had been obliged to use its power in government to achieve hegemony in the coalition through radical mass movements. This radicalism helped it to increase its mass base and push aside its coalition partners. The Maoists were wiped out and when the CPM returned to power in 1977 it no longer had to worry about a threat to its base from the left. There was no alternative pole to keep it from sliding into moderation as radicals still in the CPM had no other party to turn to. The 1967–70 United Front governments enabled the CPM to achieve a hegemonic position in the anti-Congress opposition, through radical mass movements.[18] This was also, as it later turned out, the last radical action of the CPM. The radicals still in the CPM subsequently lost influence and their leaders in Bengal, Muzaffar Ahmed and Harekrishna Konar, died. The radical national leader Sundarayya resigned as CPM General Secretary and has also passed away. The ground was thus cleared for the old centrists to consolidate their control of the Party and turn it towards an increasingly moderate electoral path.

While the absence of a revolutionary left may now be viewed as increasing the stability of Indian democracy, the drift of the Communists to constitutional reformism has not helped the lower classes. It could be argued that by not promoting their interest as a class, the Communists have effectively disenfranchised the lower classes. In the absence of any other national party willing to pursue their class interests as its top priority, the lower classes have been effectively left out of politics, the franchise being of limited value without party candidates willing to promote the real class interests of the poor. It is for this reason that the CPM has been so vociferous in opposing the Naxalites. Any popular independent organization of the poor would threaten the CPM at the polls. Hence the CPM insistence on a poor and middle peasant alliance under the dominance in practice of the middle peasantry.

The CPM felt the old CPI had collaborated too closely with the ruling Congress Party in the futile hope of promoting progressive government policies, and instead claimed the Congress government should be destabilized in order to enable a coalition of opposition parties to take power. These alternative popular governments with Communist participation could facilitate the advancement of the Communist movement towards a revolutionary conjuncture. However, as these opposition coalitions were dominated by parties to the right of the ruling Congress, any subordinate role given to the CPM would hardly be conducive to expanding its influence nationally in the face of conservative coalition

---

[18] Sally Ray, "United Front Government and the Politics of Agrarian Struggle in West Bengal, 1967 and 1969–70," *Australian Outlook*, August 1971, p. 214.

partners. Whereas in Bengal the Communists had the electoral base as the leading anti-Congress party to marginalize more conservative partners in the United Fronts, nationally it would be the subordinate partner. While supporting an Indian government might ease pressure on the Bengal government, its participation at the national level was bound to be limited given its regional following in Kerala and Bengal. That such a strategy was developed at all amounted to a tacit admission of Communist weakness, and its inability to make headway nationally. As the alternate CPI strategy of pushing the Congress to adopt more progressive policies had also failed and subsequently been abandoned, there seemed no strategy likely to produce success in the foreseeable future. Only long hard grass-roots work needed to build up a base could produce results, though probably not for the present generation of leaders. Though there was discussion of developing into contiguous areas from existing bases, the cadre available for this were limited. Bengalis were generally disliked in neighboring states, which they had often historically dominated, making geographical expansion difficult. The Bengali Communist experiment was therefore not easily translated into a following elsewhere.

This does not mean that the Communists will be unable to play a significant role in Indian society. Though the signs are all negative, one cannot preclude the rise of a more radical faction within the CPM and CPI. However, if such a movement were to arise, it would need a better sense of direction than the Indian Communist movement has so far exhibited. The movement has gone from one political extreme to another without ever finding a clearly defined road to socialism. The switch from armed struggle to reformism within a few short years is only symptomatic of the Communist failures of policy analysis when confronted with Indian realities. Though the Communists have split in two opposing directions, neither has found a viable strategy. The oscillation between revolutionary "adventurism" and reformist "opportunism" has left the middle ground untested. The Polish economist Oskar Lange writing in 1936 argued:

A socialist government really intent upon socialism has to decide to carry out its socialization program at one stroke, or to give it up altogether. The very coming into power of such a government must cause a financial panic and economic collapse. Therefore, the socialist government must either guarantee the immunity of private property and private enterprise in order to enable the capitalist economy to function normally, in doing which it gives up its socialist aims, or it must go through resolutely with its socialization program at maximum speed. Any hesitation, any vacillation and indecision would provoke the inevitable economic catastrophe. Socialism is not an economic policy for the timid.[19]

The problem in West Bengal is that both these alternatives have been tried and

---

[19] Oskar Lange, *On the Economic Theory of Socialism*, edited by B.E. Lippincott (New York: McGraw-Hill, 1964), pp. 124–5.

found wanting. The United Front and the Maoists attempted the radical socialization program only to be repressed and driven underground. In their present tenure in office they learned from their mistakes and avoided precipitous actions that had caused the previous flight of capital, but in so doing they abandoned the socialist path, as Lange predicted was likely, with the avoidance of immediate socialization. His formulation, however, assumed a national transition to socialism. Such a transition is impossible in one province, which inevitably lacks control of the armed forces and the economic levers normally exercised by national governments. Socialism in one province therefore necessitates the development of a new strategy that takes into account the regional nature of socialist influence. Such a strategy does not exist in the literature on the transition to socialism. The studies either assume an advanced capitalist state or an underdeveloped country without democratic traditions, but with socialist control of national policy.

The transition to socialism in advanced capitalist countries offers few comparisons with India. According to Adam Przeworski, the European working class has always been a minority of the population, necessitating socialist appeals to other groups on the basis of reformist demands which have nothing to do with changing the ownership of production.[20] This problem, however, does not exist in the same way in India, since a substantial majority of the population is clearly exploited or at least would benefit from property redistribution.

The literature on the socialist transition in the Third World is also inapplicable to West Bengal or even to India as a whole. Clive Thomas's *Dependence and Transformation* is aimed at small underdeveloped countries which he argues have few prospects for capitalist development, unlike India where he concedes such a route may still be possible.[21]

Sweezy and Bettelheim argue that "a comparative study of transitions can be extremely valuable" but concede that "each transition is a unique historical process which must be analysed and explained as such."[22] The West Bengal analysis, however, has been so focused on partisan party positions as to be of limited value. Those who argue for immediate radical action, such as Ashok Rudra, oppose those endorsing the CPM practice, such as Biplab Dasgupta. But neither the Maoist nor the CPM strategy has led to a transition to socialism. Each side uses statistics to discredit their opposition, rather than for creative policy formulation.

---

[20] Adam Przeworski, *Capitalism and Social Democracy* (Cambridge: Cambridge University Press), 1985, p. 23.

[21] Clive Y. Thomas, *Dependence and Transformation: The Economics of the Transition to Socialism* (New York: Monthly Review Press, 1974), pp. 299–300.

[22] Paul M. Sweezy and Charles Bettelheim, *On the Transition to Socialism* (New York: Monthly Review Press, 1971), p. 107.

The West Bengal experiment is best seen as what Lange calls one of the
special situations where a socialist government, even if it has not the power to achieve
a comprehensive socialization, may have a useful task to fulfil, a task which a capitalist
government may be unable to carry out ... In such circumstances the socialists might
form a government with a "labor plan" to attack unemployment and the depression. If
the labor plan is carried out successfully the popularity of the socialists will be greatly
increased ... But even a socialist government whose purposes are confined within the
limits of such a labor plan needs boldness and decision in carrying out its program;
otherwise it degenerates into a mere administrator of the existing capitalist society.[23]

Though the Left Front came to power with just such a "labor plan" in mind,
it ended up being "a mere administrator of the existing capitalist society." Its
labor plan was purely theoretical and rhetorical; its practice was that of administrator of a capitalist system.

## Center–state relations

In circumstances where power at the national level was unlikely, the Communists gave prominence to centrifugal tendencies by demanding greater state
autonomy that would thereby increase their own influence. It gave first billing
in the Second Left Front Government Program to its demand for more provincial
autonomy: even though the center alone could fulfil the demands, which it was
hardly likely to do in the foreseeable future. In an ethnically and linguistically
distinct state, devolution of power was likely to be a popular issue. The
Communists were early proponents of these state demands against an allegedly
discriminatory central government. With the Indian Communists lacking any
prospect of controlling the central government it was understandable they
should try to gain as much as they could in those states they controlled. This
power could only be achieved at the expense of the central government, which
was a convenient scapegoat for provincial problems. The central government
through politically motivated interference in the state and dismissal of previous
Communist governments only played into the hands of the Communists. Their
interventions served to justify Communist complaints in the public view, and
thereby helped to return the Communists to power with even bigger majorities.
Presidential Rule only increased Communist support in the long term, however
effective it appeared at the time in suppressing the Communists. Communist
opposition to central interference, since it played on multi-class ethnic grievances, was a particularly effective issue. Since the central government was
controlled by the Congress Party which was also the main rival of the Communists in Bengal, the state Congress Party was at a disadvantage in taking up

---

[23] Lange, *Economic Theory*, pp. 126–9.

grievances against the central government as these complaints reflected on themselves as well. As Bengal was politically less important than some other states which returned more MPs, it was only to be expected that undue favors would be provided elsewhere, particularly to those states ruled by the Congress Party. The Communists could only hope to get around this inherent disadvantage if power was devolved to a state level where they would be able to control it.

These demands for state autonomy were transparent attempts to acquire more power in Communist hands. It was hardly surprising the Left Front demands were widely supported by rightist politicians from other states also wishing to acquire provincial powers. In the Indian nation where both the central and provincial governments are democratically elected, neither is inherently more legitimate or democratic than the other. It is therefore a question of delegating power to different levels of government. Despite Left Front claims, Indian unitary powers are roughly equivalent to those of other major nations.[24] No nation has delegated to a provincial level the types of powers demanded by the Left Front government. To have acceded to Left Front demands would have left minority groups in every province vulnerable to communal rioting which the central government would have been powerless to stop without state government permission. Though the central government has also not been above playing on communal divisions, giving states a veto over central actions while hindering the overthrow of Communist provincial governments would also protect communal forces which are never far below the surface in Indian politics.

It is doubtful these extreme demands for devolution were taken as serious possibilities by the Left Front governments. Rather they were probably seen as populist demands and bargaining positions for more allocation of central revenues and some increase in areas of provincial jurisdiction. As India has been put under growing pressure from internal secessionists and external threats, power has been placed increasingly in central government hands. The army and central police have had to be called in to put down domestic disturbances repeatedly, while the central government has put most of the revenue income in its own coffers. However, beyond general agreement on these trends the problems of center–state relations is in dispute, with positions dependent on whether the observers see India as a unitary or federal state. As such the issue is inherently difficult to resolve and a consensus is problematic.

The Left Front claims of discrimination against Bengal, however, are more easily determined. It has been a perennial complaint of the Left Front and

[24] Department of Information and Cultural Affairs, *Reply to Questionnaire: Commission on Centre–State Relations* (Calcutta: Government of West Bengal, July 1984), p. 2.

Table 1.2. *Gross Budgetary transfers from the center, 1956–81*

| | Rupees per capita | | | | Index numbers | | | |
|---|---|---|---|---|---|---|---|---|
| | Stat-utory | Plan | Discre-tionary | Total | Stat-utory | Plan | Discre-tionary | Total |
| High income | 471 | 338 | 449 | 1,248 | 91 | 77 | 118 | 94 |
| Punjab | 405 | 443 | 604 | 1,452 | 78 | 101 | 159 | 109 |
| Haryana | 389 | 498 | 490 | 1,377 | 75 | 113 | 129 | 103 |
| Maharashtra | 461 | 291 | 397 | 1,149 | 89 | 66 | 104 | 86 |
| Gujarat | 466 | 355 | 398 | 1,219 | 90 | 81 | 105 | 91 |
| West Bengal | 524 | 314 | 486 | 1,324 | 102 | 71 | 128 | 99 |
| Middle income | 542 | 436 | 386 | 1,364 | 105 | 99 | 102 | 102 |
| Tamil Nadu | 446 | 350 | 274 | 1,070 | 86 | 80 | 72 | 80 |
| Kerala | 611 | 445 | 335 | 1,391 | 118 | 101 | 88 | 104 |
| Orissa | 708 | 536 | 476 | 1,720 | 137 | 122 | 125 | 129 |
| Assam | 742 | 675 | 659 | 2,076 | 144 | 153 | 173 | 155 |
| Karnataka | 465 | 374 | 384 | 1,223 | 90 | 85 | 101 | 92 |
| Andhra Pradesh | 504 | 427 | 381 | 1,312 | 98 | 97 | 100 | 98 |
| Low income | 459 | 398 | 332 | 1,189 | 89 | 90 | 87 | 89 |
| Uttar Pradesh | 446 | 390 | 264 | 1,100 | 86 | 89 | 69 | 82 |
| Rajasthan | 553 | 461 | 734 | 1,738 | 107 | 103 | 193 | 130 |
| Madhya Pradesh | 428 | 434 | 248 | 1,110 | 83 | 99 | 65 | 83 |
| Bihar | 456 | 363 | 318 | 1,137 | 88 | 83 | 84 | 85 |
| Special category | 1,701 | 1,902 | 1,086 | 4,689 | 330 | 432 | 286 | 351 |
| Himachal Pradesh | 1,102 | 1,405 | 498 | 3,005 | 214 | 319 | 131 | 225 |
| Jammu and Kashmir | 1,304 | 2,058 | 1,466 | 4,828 | 253 | 468 | 386 | 361 |
| Tripura | 1,519 | 1,125 | 381 | 3,025 | 294 | 256 | 100 | 226 |
| Manipur | 2,302 | 1,331 | 925 | 4,558 | 446 | 303 | 243 | 341 |
| Nagaland | 6,080 | 3,896 | 2,758 | 12,734 | 1,178 | 885 | 726 | 963 |
| Meghalaya | 1,702 | 1,764 | 845 | 4,311 | 330 | 401 | 222 | 323 |
| Sikkim | 722 | 3,271 | 1,071 | 5,064 | 140 | 743 | 282 | 379 |
| All states | 516 | 440 | 380 | 1,336 | 100 | 100 | 100 | 100 |

*Source:* West Bengal Information and Cultural Affairs Department, *Reply to Questionnaire: Commission on Centre–State Relations*, July 1984, p. 22, citing K.K. George, "Centre–State Financial Flows and Inter–State Disparities in India," University of Cochin (mimeographed), 1982.

Bengalis that the state is a net revenue contributor to the central government which has in return been very parsimonious in rendering aid to the state. The Left Front has used this as a reason for their shortcomings and thereby placed the blame on the central government. However, the West Bengal government's own reply to the Commission on Centre–State Relations indicates West Bengal has received an average share of central budgetary transfers to the states (table 1.2). Aggregate central transfers to the states represented 41.6 percent of total state disbursements in 1979–84. During the same period total resource transfers from the center to the states were 32.6 percent of the center's aggregate resources. The states raised 38.9 percent of the total taxation from 1974–79.[25] The revenue-raising powers of state governments are therefore considerable. Though the Left Front claims that centrally owned public sector lending institutions discriminate in loan disbursements, its own statistics appear not to support this as far as West Bengal is concerned (table 1.3).

Central politicians may be able to influence the location of particular projects to their own states and therefore away from Bengal, but this does not normally reach the level of influencing central government revenue disbursements to the state. The resource allocations are done on an administrative basis according to set formula and regulations, which are usually not interfered with by politicians directly. Apart from anything else, too direct an interference in routine allocations would result in a provincial backlash which would reduce the chances of the central ruling party returning to power in the state. In practice Left Front conflicts with the center never extended to mobilization of a mass movement, being mostly oriented to obtaining greater central funding.

### Social milieu

The Indian Communist movement is unique in operating within the institutions of a parliamentary democracy not unlike that of the industrialized West, while trying to develop a base in conditions of extreme poverty and exploitation. India combines many of the institutions of an advanced capitalist state with cultural and economic conditions often not far removed from feudalism. Thus it is unlikely Communists can take power in the same way as in China or Russia, both of which lacked the tradition of parliamentary democracy. Indian communism, through its policies, has become a part of the Indian parliamentary system and has attempted to adapt to these Indian traditions. This has required mobilization of class forces somewhat different from those traditionally associated with Communist movements elsewhere in the world. The Bengal Communist movement grew as a primarily middle-class movement. This urban and rural middle-class involvement has shaped the policies of the Left Front, in a way that is unique in India.

The economic downturn in Bengal created new underprivileged classes out of the traditional landed elite, providing an impetus for the spread of Communism. The old elite classes lost their landed property with the creation of Pakistan after the partition of India, becoming refugees in West Bengal. At the same time the expansion of education beyond the capacity of a sluggish economy to absorb it created acute unemployment and frustration for an aspirant

---

[25] *Ibid.*, pp. 20, 23; Government of India, Planning Commission, *Draft Five Year Plan, 1978–83*, vol. II, p. 89.

Table 1.3. *Per capita center–state financial flows 1973–83 – budgetary and institutional*

| State | Budgetary | Commercial Banks | | | Development Banks | ARDC | Total Institutional (4+5+6) | Rupees per capita — Institutional and Budgetary | Share of Institutions finance total |
|---|---|---|---|---|---|---|---|---|---|
| **High income** | | | | | | | | | |
| Punjab | 491 | 734 | 42 | 776 | 78 | 87 | 941 | 1,432 | 65.7 |
| Haryana | 447 | 446 | 74 | 520 | 113 | 123 | 756 | 1,203 | 62.9 |
| Maharashtra | 412 | 618 | 49 | 667 | 151 | 30 | 848 | 1,260 | 67.3 |
| Gujarat | 471 | 323 | 69 | 392 | 219 | 27 | 638 | 1,109 | 57.5 |
| West Bengal | 498 | 321 | 49 | 370 | 70 | 9 | 449 | 947 | 47.4 |
| **Middle income** | | | | | | | | | |
| Tamil Nadu | 402 | 327 | 38 | 365 | 97 | 19 | 481 | 883 | 54.5 |
| Kerala | 504 | 316 | 69 | 385 | 67 | 14 | 466 | 970 | 48.0 |
| Orissa | 659 | 85 | 35 | 120 | 31 | 18 | 169 | 828 | 20.4 |
| Assam | 749 | 92 | 40 | 132 | 35 | 6 | 175 | 922 | 18.8 |
| Karnataka | 388 | 315 | 34 | 349 | 122 | 35 | 506 | 894 | 56.6 |
| Andhra Pradesh | 492 | 213 | 30 | 243 | 59 | 45 | 347 | 839 | 41.4 |
| **Low income** | | | | | | | | | |
| Uttar Pradesh | 500 | 121 | 28 | 149 | 37 | 28 | 214 | 714 | 30.0 |
| Rajasthan | 559 | 168 | 51 | 219 | 60 | 26 | 305 | 864 | 35.3 |
| Madhya Pradesh | 424 | 111 | 27 | 138 | 26 | 32 | 196 | 620 | 31.6 |
| Bihar | 445 | 83 | 26 | 109 | 23 | 20 | 152 | 597 | 25.5 |
| **Special category** | | | | | | | | | |
| Himachal Pradesh | 1,741 | 144 | 61 | 205 | 58 | 8 | 271 | 2,012 | 13.5 |
| Kashmir | 2,087 | 163 | 74 | 237 | 77 | 1 | 315 | 2,402 | 13.1 |
| Tripura | 1,904 | 100 | 49 | 149 | 17 | 2 | 168 | 2,072 | 8.1 |
| Manipur | 2,886 | 50 | 91 | 141 | 5 | 8 | 154 | 3,040 | 5.1 |
| Nagaland | 7,052 | 84 | 280 | 364 | 35 | 4 | 403 | 7,455 | 5.4 |
| Meghalaya | 2,488 | 55 | 127 | 182 | 86 | – | 268 | 2,756 | 9.7 |
| All states | 521 | 252 | 40 | 292 | 73 | 28 | 393 | 914 | 43.0 |

*Source:* West Bengal Information and Cultural Affairs Department, *Reply to Questionnaire: Commission on Centre–State Relations,* July 1984, p. 52, citing K.K. George, "Center–State Financial Flows and Inter-State Disparities in India," University of Cochin (Mimeographed), 1982.

middle class. These conditions in Bengal have been developing for some time. The decline has taken place over a number of decades, and in fact the highpoint of Bengal's influence in India was in the nineteenth century. Bengal was the springboard for the expansion of British domination of the sub-continent and the first to experience the impact of Westernization. The opportunities of Western education provided Bengali Hindus with a head start in adapting to and serving the British Raj. This educated Bengali middle class worked throughout India under the colonial government and in the service sector. Though originally tied to landed interests, by the 1920s it "contained a very large proportion whose only sources of livelihood, real or prospective, were entirely urban – in administration, small trade and commerce, education or the professions."[26] Thus early penetration of British colonialism enabled the growth of an overdeveloped Bengali middle class dependent not on land, but on serving the colonial state or the various Western-modeled institutions it had created. This employment base was removed in East Bengal by partition creating East Pakistan and reduced in the rest of India by competing local educated elites. The Bengali middle class no longer had an economic or employment base capable of absorbing its now surplus educated manpower. This was to have important political ramifications. "It was this class which provided the organising cadres of the new parties of mass mobilisation."[27] "A new generation of *bhadralok* youth, predominantly urban in cultural outlook and shorn of the former ties binding the class to fragmentary remnants of landed property, now sought to forge new links with the masses in militant trade unionism, more radical programs of agrarian reform and a new vanguardism in political organization."[28] This was the base for the emerging Communist movement in Bengal, and has formed its cadre and leadership ever since.

The flowering of Bengali culture under the impact of Western ideas, became known as the Bengal Renaissance. This took increasingly nationalist forms, with Bengalis playing a leading role in the Congress movement. In response, the British detached Assam, Orissa, and Bihar from Bengal and transferred the capital from Calcutta to Delhi. By the 1920s, the centre of the nationalist leadership under Gandhi, Patel, and Nehru shifted from Bengal, and its political leadership in India was permanently lost. Inevitably with the spread of modernity and education, new groups asserted their cultural identity, and closed the cultural and economic gap between Bengal and the rest of India. In Bengal the dominant Hindus were a minority and with the expansion of the electoral rolls, were reduced to an oppositional role from 1927. From then till independence,

---

[26] Partha Chatterjee, *Bengal 1920–1947: The Land Question* (Calcutta: K.P. Bagchi & Co., 1984), vol. I, p. 179.

[27] *Ibid.*, p. 210.

[28] *Ibid.*, pp. 179–80.

there was a gradual erosion of Bengali Hindu power and influence in India. After losing a dominant political base in their own state, they had only a secondary role in the Gandhian independence struggle. Gandhi never had as strong a following in Bengal as elsewhere. Bengali nationalists tended to take a more radical approach to the nationalist struggle, and a section of them resorted to terrorism. The militant alternative led by Subhas Chandra Bose, however, came to naught.

Communal tension and riots led to the decision to partition India, creating East Pakistan (now Bangladesh) out of eastern Bengal. The two halves of Bengal were complementary to each other. Calcutta had been the *entrepot* for the rural hinterland in East Bengal which provided raw materials for Calcutta mills and a market for their finished products. Of greater political importance was the loss of the Bengali elite's landed property in East Bengal which had to be abandoned in their flight to Calcutta.

Partition marked the ending of any illusion Bengal might have had of playing a leading role in India. With most of its electorate in the newly created East Pakistan, West Bengal returned only forty-two MPs, less than several other states. Its role as the leading industrial center fell behind Bombay and recently other states. Four million refugees from all walks of life flooded West Bengal. Politically, however, the landed and middle classes were to have greater influence on the course of Bengali politics which had always centered around them and their demands. The wealthier Zamindars could retreat to their town houses in Calcutta and some exchanged property with Muslims moving east, but few could survive without employment after the loss of their land. Their downward mobility was often rapid. Reduced to living in penury in Calcutta, they now had to work for a living and were forced to sell their antiques to make ends meet. From the point of view of social justice it may be all they deserved for exploiting the peasants for generations, but for the individuals concerned, their experience was traumatic. Attitudes were inevitably slower in adapting to the new economic reality. They became a classic case of an uprooted social group. The Bengali elite was relatively small and close knit and many refugees eventually obtained employment through relatives and friends who helped them resettle. The East Bengalis in Calcutta came to have great influence in the professions and in bureaucracy. Perhaps out of desperation they tended to be more successful and ambitious than the West Bengal residents who often still had landed property to fall back on. There developed a certain antagonism between the East and West Bengalis. Many, however, did not have the requisite skills required by an industrialized Calcutta and had to live off employed relatives or resort to proletarian occupations.

The importance of the refugees was related by Professor Zagoria:

In the urban areas of West Bengal, Communist strength does not appear to be based on any particular caste or community. Rather, one of the main bases seems to be the several million "declassed" Hindu refugees who fled their homes in East Bengal after partition. These refugees constitute about one-fourth of the West Bengal population and a substantial portion of the Calcutta population. They apparently vote for the Communists overwhelmingly. Here, it would seem is a classic example of uprooted and declassed individuals supporting an extremist party in accordance with the model put forth by the proponents of the concept of mass society. The uprootedness of the Hindu refugees in Calcutta is aggravated by the fact that many of them occupied positions of considerable power and influence in East Bengal, but are denied power or status in West Bengal. The absence of an effective and large Jana Sangh in Calcutta is probably the main reason why the Hindu refugees there have chosen left-wing rather than right-wing extremism. At least one Communist leader frankly admitted to the author that many of the followers of his party in Calcutta were the kind of declassed *petit bourgeois* who in the North belonged to the militantly communal Hindu party, the Jana Sangh.[29]

This raises a fundamental question as to whether the Communists simply filled in a political vacuum which more or less accidentally happened to fall to them. A definitive answer is not possible but the problem cannot readily be dismissed. It has often been said that the social basis of communism in West Bengal is the urban middle class, ranging from clerks to professionals and dispossessed Zamindars. These Communist supporters are often superficially progressive, being casteist and communal in attitude. This is particularly revealed in cases of marriage. Though social mixing is acceptable, in marriage the only thing worse than marrying an untouchable is marrying a Muslim. Nevertheless, they have an intellectual tradition of the Bengal Renaissance which would more naturally lead to a Communist rather than a communal orientation.

The traditional industries of Bengal such as jute, cotton, coal, tea, steel, and paper tended to employ rural migrant labor from Bihar and Uttar Pradesh. With the opening of new industries in the mid 1950s requiring higher levels of skill, Bengalis, and particularly refugees, tended to be employed in the new engineering, electronic, and chemical industries.[30] In contrast to the traditional peasant-based working class in Bengal, these refugees had acquired skills through the expanding educational system. While half of jute workers were peasants or sons of previous employees, only 1/5th of engineering workers came from peasant stock. Half belonged to white-collar families engaged in professions, business, and government. The new literate worker had entrenched middle-class aspirations. "The leftist parties were more strong in such work places where the work force comprised new workers drawn from refugee families."[31] The educated

---

[29] Donald S. Zagoria, "The Social Bases of Indian Communism" in *Issues in the Future of Asia* edited by Richard Lowenthal (New York: Praeger, 1969), p. 115.

[30] K.N. Vaid, *Gheraos and Labour Unrest in West Bengal* (New Delhi: Shri Ram Centre for Industrial Relations and Human Resources, 1972), p. 141.

[31] *Ibid.*, p. 140.

East Bengal refugees thus eventually became part of a wide range of social classes from the professional elite to the industrial working class and lumpen-proletariat. The wealthier refugees tended to adapt themselves to the new professional avenues of employment their higher education offered, but the general trend was of a downturn in income and status, with great variation in income and success even within families.

The dominant influence of the Communist Party had been in East Bengal and its ideological influence was carried over by the refugees into West Bengal. Most of the Communist members and their strongest bases were in East Bengal. The CPM noted that, "The main base and influence of our united party before partition lay in East Bengal. Apart from the peasant movement, the majority of party members were from this region."[32]

Thus, whatever Hindu cadre the Communists had in the east, came over with the refugee influx and continued their political work. The refugees felt neglected by the central government, which tended to devote more effort to the rehabilitation of refugees from West Punjab than from East Bengal.[33] Bengalis had never been satisfied with the Gandhian Congress leadership, and under C.R. Das and later Subhas Chandra Bose had challenged Gandhi's and Nehru's leadership of the movement. Political marginalization and the defeat of Bengal's more militant brand of nationalism created a strong regional anti-center attitude which all political parties in the state had to come to terms with. This combined with a Bengali feeling of intellectual and cultural superiority over the rest of India, which the economic downturn did little to alter. Bengalis thus found little in common with the central government. Their harking back to a golden age of the Bengali Renaissance did nothing to improve their adjustment to the present reality. Partition increased the competition for limited jobs and resources, making them unpopular in Orissa and Assam where their numbers were greatest. However, West Bengal was economically linked to India and their political aspirations were tuned to an all-India solution of their problems rather than towards secession. Gokhale's saying that "what Bengal thinks today, India thinks tomorrow" continued to appeal to Bengali sentiments long after it had ceased to be true.

A number of factors thus contributed to making Bengal a fertile area for the growth of Communism. An economic and political decline in Bengal's importance coupled with the influx of refugees from the partition of the state created an atmosphere of Bengali alienation in the Indian Union. The influx of refugees and their loss of land eliminated a large class of Zamindars and landowners who

---

[32] Communist Party of India (Marxist), Central Committee Statement, "The Party and the Struggle of the Bangladesh People," *People's Democracy*, supplement (February 13, 1972), p. 19.

[33] Ranajit Roy, *The Agony of West Bengal* (Calcutta: New Age Publishers, 1973), p. 57.

would otherwise have proved a serious impediment to land reform and the growth of Communist influence among the middle class.

The loss of the Hindu landed interests combined with the absence of a Bengali bourgeoisie. Bengalis had preferred to invest in land rather than in industry and commerce and as a result this field had been occupied by Marwaris, other non-Bengali businessmen, and foreign corporations. West Bengal, therefore, lacked an indigenous industrial bourgeoisie. None of the Indian big business houses was Bengali-controlled, and Bengalis showed little interest in business. What business existed provided scope for anti-foreign and anti-non-Bengali sentiments as Bengalis were not identified with them. The Bengali class structure with few exceptions never rose beyond the professional and manage-rial upper middle class. This provided an opportunity for Bengali regionalism to combine with anti-capitalism and communism, without creating a split along class lines. The Communists could thus find support from virtually all classes of Bengalis. Since Bengal was completely dependent on non-Bengali entrepre-neurship, they lacked the ability to shape their own destiny. The non-Bengalis' lack of interest in the civic improvement of Calcutta only made matters worse.

Those Bengalis nearest the top of the business world are in a minority. Only 38.4 percent of managers in the Calcutta Management Association are Bengali. Even in the Bengali-dominated Calcutta Branch of the Indian Institute of Per-sonnel Management, which has a more broad-based membership, non-Bengalis dominate in the categories of advisers and decision-making managers. Only at the implementation levels do Bengali executives outnumber non-Bengalis. This causes "several serious repercussions for social harmony in the area."[34] The disparity may be due to corporate ownership and control being in the hands of non-Bengalis, who tend to hire people from their own community.

Non-Bengali businessmen appeared to be pursuing a policy of non-invest-ment. Between 1965 and 1975, industrial production in West Bengal declined by 16.13 percent as against an all-India increase of 40.55 percent. During this period, the average daily employment in the registered working factories in West Bengal declined by 4.65 percent as against an all-India increase of 6.14 percent.[35]

This was accompanied by an increase in the urban population below the poverty line from 31.48 percent in 1961–62 to 35.7 percent in 1972–74. The increase was even more dramatic in the rural population where it increased from 40.4 percent to 66 percent during the same period.[36]

---

[34] Vaid, *Gheraos*, pp. 178–9.
[35] Commerce and Industries Department, *A Review of Industrial Growth in West Bengal* (Calcutta: Government of West Bengal, March 1979), p. 23.
[36] Development and Planning Department, *West Bengal Draft Five Year Plan 1978–83* (Calcutta: Government of West Bengal), p. A7.

The government service and public sector has traditionally provided employment opportunities for educated Bengalis, and as a result, it is dominated by them. This has not given the bureaucracy a stake in the maintenance of the status quo beyond their narrow professional interests, for they lack direct links with the propertied classes in Bengal.

The middle and upper rungs of bureaucracy in West Bengal have hardly any connection with land unlike in most other states. Recruits come from the urban middle class, many of whom are migrants from erstwhile East Pakistan. The coalescing of interests of rural landed gentry and the bureaucracy, which happens in other states is not a common feature in this state.[37]

The richest class of Bengalis are the professional elite, mainly doctors and lawyers. Thus, aside from West Bengali landowners, there is no class in Bengali society which would have an economic interest in opposing communism. With the partition of Bengal the Hindus were able to assert their domination of West Bengal. The communal factors that divided the old Bengal were eliminated as the dominant political features of state politics. After independence the main opposition to Congress came not from the right but from the left in the form of the Communist Party. The Communists were the inheritors of the most radical wing of the nationalist movement, and also constituted the most effective vehicle for opposition to the Congress Party in West Bengal.

[37] D. Bandyopadhyay, Land Reforms Commissioner, *Land Reforms in West Bengal* (Calcutta: Information and Cultural Affairs Department, Government of West Bengal, 1980), p. 10.

# 2    Agrarian reform

### Land distribution

Despite periodic electoral setbacks in the urban areas, the rural vote has re-elected the Communists for subsequent terms. This has led to considerable debate as to the reasons for this electoral success. While the existence of rural support is evident, the causes for it are controversial. It will be argued that, while agrarian reforms have not been outstanding compared to the rest of India or even past state achievements, in the political sphere power has shifted from the traditional pro-Congress elite to a new middle landed class. This class, while lacking the wealth of the traditional elite, is more numerous, and now with state patronage more powerful, than the rural Congress Party supporters. Though the socio-economic condition of the lower classes and their influence on policy have seen little or no improvement, the Left Front programs with partial funding from the central government, have provided more aid than under previous regimes. This has helped maintain a Left Front lower- and middle-class voting bloc in which the lower-class influence has remained decidedly subordinate. The structural reforms that might have altered this situation were not undertaken, partly for fear of central government intervention, but mainly due to the influence of this new middle-class landed elite on the Communists who feared loss of their electoral support.

Land reform is potentially the most significant program the Communist government might be expected to undertake. As it is a state subject under the Indian constitution it is within the jurisdiction of the Communist government. Though court challenges are open to plaintiffs and new legislation is subject to Presidential approval, the legal and extra-legal powers open to a state government are considerable. These include use of the state police and administration, as well as Communist party peasant organizations. Central government dismissal of a state government is constitutionally allowed, and has been used to dismiss previous Communist governments, placing limits on how far revolutionary methods can be undertaken.

At a macro level the radical objectives of the state land reform program appeared unambiguous in their devotion to helping the lower classes. According to the West Bengal government's Seventh Five Year Plan:

The basic reason for initiating rural development through the poor is as follows. There is a remarkable evidence, available from all the districts of the State, that the highest record of production, taking into account per acre yield of the crops and also the cropping intensity is obtained not from the land of the big or the middle farmers but from the poor farmers. What these poor farmers do not have by way of implements and other inputs, they over-compensate by fuller application of their labour. It follows therefore that if the ceiling surplus land is distributed to the poorer farmers and then they are assisted in terms of non-land inputs, then not only the inequality between the farmers gets lessened, but a definitive move is also initiated to increase the level of production.[1]

By the time the Left Front came to power there had already been a gradual lowering and tightening of land ceiling laws to the point where the small minority of Zamindars and big landlords had been eliminated. Any further expropriation of progressively smaller landholding units will antagonize increasing numbers of villagers in the large and middle peasant category. Any equalization of land holdings would therefore result in a very large minority of villagers being deprived of some of their land, thus threatening the Communists' rural base. Greater political mobilization of agricultural laborers and marginal cultivators with enforcement of land expropriations by the state government would increase polarization in rural society, resulting in a backlash which might drive the Communists from power. Since organization of the lowest strata is weak or non-existent, the safe option for the Communists is to soft-pedal serious and meaningful attempts at land redistribution. The radical alternative would be collectivization of land. However, experiences in China and the Soviet Union indicate decreased productivity under this system, aside from the violence that would be required to implement it. Some economists argue that with provision of credit and agricultural inputs, small peasants are more efficient and productive than their larger counterparts, thereby rendering collectivization unnecessary and counter-productive. However, in Bengal this small peasant class lacks the financial resources to implement improvement schemes and the State's resources are limited. The land–person ratio will continue to deteriorate as cultivable area cannot be significantly increased, and population growth continues unabated. Between 1961 and 1971 the land–person ratio decreased by 28 percent from .444 acres to .321 acres.[2]

Any possible solution is bound to adversely affect a sizeable class in rural Bengal. The villages are not homogeneous and peasant unity only artificial if it

---

[1] West Bengal, Development and Planning Department, *Draft Seventh Five Year Plan 1985–90 and Annual Plan 1985–86*, vol. I (Calcutta: mimeographed, January 1985), p. VI.

[2] Biplab Dasgupta, "Gram Banglar Sreni Binyas" ("Class Relations in Rural Bengal"), *Deshhitaishee*, annual Puja issue, 1980, p. 86.

can be developed at all. It is no longer possible to benefit the many by sacrificing the few large landowners as happened previously. Complete or even partial expropriation will antagonize a large number of people, many of them not particularly well off. The difficulty of choosing the expropriators from the expropriated was illustrated by the West Bengal Board of Revenue's analysis of the antagonisms among the different strata of the Bengal peasantry.

The old straight forward classification of the landed as one group or class and the landless as another group or class no longer holds good. As a matter of fact it is often the 3rd and 4th strata (less than 1 hectare to three hectares or slightly more) that now find themselves in deadly antagonism to the 5th stratum of sharecropper or the 6th landless stratum. Even the share cropping sections in stratum 5, particularly if they are engaged in multiple-cropping, identify their destinies with stratum 3 and 4 and not with the pure agricultural landless labour or the single-cropping sharecroppers of the stratum 5. The battle for finely graded security or the absence of it is sharpening class or interest antagonisms, further complicating the problems of area planning, decentralised decision taking, bureaucratic and political accessibility and efficiency, extension activity and the distribution of institutional benefits ... Questions of what administrative or fiscal action benefits whom, how, why and where have grown in complexity and so have the consequences of these actions on shifting interest alignments and conflicts within the rural structure.[3]

While Marxists tend to classify the peasantry as exploiters and exploited according to whether or not they employ labor, in West Bengal there is a wide variation of employment patterns with a large intermediate class which simultaneously hires labor, works on their own land and hires themselves out as laborers. According to Utsa Patnaik, a class breakdown by land holdings in Bengal would classify poor peasants as owning less than 1.60 acres, lower middle between 1.61 and 4.60, upper middle as between 4.61 and 9.80, and the rich peasants and landlords as over 9.81 acres.[4] With the decreasing land–man ratio and the increasing use of high-yielding varieties this might be considered slightly on the high side. For Bengal, P. Sundarayya's upper limit of 5 acres for the middle peasantry would seem more accurate at the present time.[5]

With varied local conditions any categorization can only be an approximation rather than a definite classification. Even within West Bengal there are seven different agro-climatic regions resulting in wide variations in land productivity and cropping patterns (see table 2.1). Any classification of landownership would have to take these productivity variations into account in a land reform program. Another factor that must be kept in mind is the small absolute sizes

[3] West Bengal, Board of Revenue, *Dynamics of the Rural Situation in West Bengal – Panchayati Raj* (Calcutta: West Bengal Government Press, 1979), p. 13.
[4] Utsa Patnaik, "Class Differentiation within the Peasantry: An Approach to Analysis of Indian Agriculture," *Economic and Political Weekly*, Review of Agriculture, September 1976, p. 193.
[5] P. Sundarayya, *An Explanatory Note on the Central Committee Resolution on Certain Agrarian Issues*, adopted March 8–15, 1973 (Calcutta: Communist Party of India – Marxist, 1973), p. 44.

Table 2.1. *Districtwise area under principal crops*

| District | Gross cropped area (000 hec) | Paddy | Maize | Wheat | Barley | Gram | Tur | Other pulses | Sugar-cane | Ragi | Other oilseed | Mesta | Jute | Tea | Misc |
|---|---|---|---|---|---|---|---|---|---|---|---|---|---|---|---|
| Bankura | 417 | 382 (92) | 1 (.2) | 4 (1) | 0 | 1 (.2) | 2 (.5) | 9 (2) | 2 (.5) | | 4 (1) | 2 (.5) | 0.4 (.1) | | 9 (2) |
| Purulia | 312 | 260 (83) | 8 (2) | .4 (.1) | | 1 | 5 (2) | 21 (7) | 1 (.3) | 1 | 4 (1) | 3 | .1 | | 7 (2) |
| Nadia | 511 | 217 (43) | | 26 (5) | 3 (1) | 68 (13) | 14 (3) | 67 (13) | 7 | | 26 (5) | 11 (2) | 66 (13) | | 6 (1) |
| Murshidabad | 647 | 291 (45) | 4 (.1) | 57 (9) | 16 (3) | 42 (6) | 11 (2) | 97 (15) | 9 (1) | | 30 (5) | 6 (1) | 73 (11) | .4 (.1) | 10 (1) |
| Burdwan | 563 | 472 (84) | .4 | 17 (3) | .4 | 7 (1) | 2 | 23 (4) | 4 (1) | | 5 (1) | 2 (.4) | 13 (2) | | 17 (3) |
| Birbhum | 445 | 334 (75) | .4 | 43 (10) | 1 (.3) | 10 (2) | 1 (.4) | 32 (7) | 4 (1) | | 6 (1) | .2 | .2 | | 12 (3) |
| Malda | 425 | 213 (50) | 8 (.2) | 10 (2) | 24 (6) | 18 (4) | 2 (.4) | 77 (18) | 3 (1) | 2 (1.4) | 20 (5) | 6 (2) | 24 (6) | 1 (.2) | 10 (2) |
| West Dinajpur | 646 | 455 (70) | 2 (.3) | 10 (2) | 17 (3) | 3 (.5) | 2 (.3) | 32 (5) | 2 (.3) | .1 | 27 (4) | 14 (2) | 67 (10) | | 14 (2) |
| 24 Parganas | 836 | 637 (76) | .4 (.1) | 9 (1) | | 12 (1) | 1 (.1) | 53 (6) | 2 (.2) | | 9 (1) | 6 (1) | 47 (6) | | 60 (7) |
| Hooghly | 305 | 211 (69) | | 13 (4) | | 1 (.4) | | 13 (13) | 1 (.4) | | 4 (1) | .4 | 38 (13) | | 24 (8) |
| Howrah | 120 | 94 (78) | | 4 (3) | | .1 (.1) | | 6 (5) | | | 2 (1) | .8 (.1) | 6 (5) | | 8 (8) |
| Midnapur | 1030 | 902 (88) | 1 (.1) | 8 (3) | | .4 | 2 | 52 (5) | 4 (.3) | | 7 (1) | 3 (.3) | 11 (1) | .2 | 38 (4) |
| Darjeeling | 117 | 40 (34) | 27 (23) | .4 (.4) | .4 (.3) | | .1 (.1) | 2 (5) | .1 (.1) | 6 (5) | 1 (1) | | 3 (3) | 28 (24) | 8 (7) |
| Cooch-Behar | 357 | 261 (73) | .2 | 5 (1) | 2 (.4) | | .2 | 12 (3) | .4 (.1) | | 7 (2) | 4 (1) | 48 (13) | | 17 (6) |
| Jalpaiguri | 376 | 253 (67) | 2 (.5) | 1 (.2) | 1 (.2) | | .4 (.1) | 4 (1) | .4 (.1) | .1 | 6 (2) | 2 (.5) | 40 (11) | 59 (16) | 7 (2) |

Note: (1) Percentage figures have been rounded off so gross totals do not add up to 100. (2) Figures in brackets are percentages to gross cropped area.
Source: *Rainfall and Cropping Patterns: West Bengal*, vol. XVI, National Commission on Agriculture 1979, Government of India, p. 13.

Table 2.2. *Percentage number and area of operational holdings in West Bengal, 1970–71 and 1976–77*

| Category | Hectares size-class | Percentage number of holdings | | Percentage area | |
|---|---|---|---|---|---|
| | | 1970–71 | 1976–77 | 1970–71 | 1976–77 |
| Marginal | Below – 0.5 | 36.94 | 43.54 | 7.52 | 10.27 |
| | 0.5 – 1.0 | 23.03 | 22.94 | 14.01 | 16.88 |
| | Below – 1.0 | 59.97 | 66.48 | 21.53 | 27.15 |
| Small | 1.0 – 2.0 | 22.33 | 20.55 | 25.72 | 28.54 |
| | 2.0 – 3.0 | 9.78 | 8.05 | 19.14 | 19.13 |
| | 3.0 – 4.0 | 3.45 | 2.33 | 9.80 | 7.96 |
| Semi medium | 2.0 – 4.0 | 13.23 | 10.38 | 28.94 | 27.09 |
| | 4.0 – 5.0 | 2.32 | 1.54 | 8.40 | 6.72 |
| | 5.0 – 7.5 | 2.06 | 0.85 | 10.83 | 5.12 |
| | 7.5 – 10.0 | – | 0.16 | – | 1.41 |
| Medium | 4.0 – 10.0 | 4.38 | 2.55 | 19.23 | 13.25 |
| | 10.0 – 20.0 | 0.07 | 0.03 | 0.70 | 0.35 |
| | 20.0 – 30.0 | N | N | 0.05 | 0.04 |
| | 30.0 – 40.0 | 0.01 | N | 0.02 | 0.02 |
| | 40.0 – 50.0 | – | N | – | N |
| | 50.0 & Above | 0.01 | 0.01 | 3.81 | 3.56 |
| Large | 10.0 & Above | 0.09 | 0.04 | 4.58 | 3.97 |
| Total | | 100.00 | 100.00 | 100.00 | 100.00 |

N = Negligible
*Source: Agricultural Census 1976–77*, Board of Revenue and Directorate of Agriculture (Socio-Economic and Evaluation Branch), Government of West Bengal, 1979, p. 10.

Table 2.3. *Percentage and cumulative percentage distribution of households and of area owned by size class of household ownership holding in West Bengal*

| Size class of household ownership holding | | Average area owned by household | Percentage of | | Cumulative Percentage of | |
|---|---|---|---|---|---|---|
| Acres | Hectares | Hectares | Households | Area owned | Households | Area owned |
| 0 | — | — | 9.78 | — | 9.78 | — |
| 0.01 – 0.49 | 0.002 – 0.20 | 0.05 | 37.31 | 2.52 | 47.09 | 2.52 |
| 0.50 – 0.99 | 0.21 – 0.40 | 0.32 | 9.43 | 4.31 | 56.52 | 6.83 |
| 1.00 – 1.24 | 0.41 – 0.50 | 0.43 | 4.86 | 3.02 | 61.38 | 9.85 |
| 1.25 – 2.49 | 0.51 – 1.00 | 0.75 | 16.24 | 17.43 | 77.62 | 27.28 |
| 2.50 – 4.99 | 1.01 – 2.02 | 1.42 | 12.64 | 25.69 | 90.26 | 52.97 |
| 5.00 – 7.49 | 2.03 – 3.03 | 2.39 | 5.38 | 18.39 | 95.64 | 71.35 |
| 7.50 – 9.99 | 3.04 – 4.04 | 3.41 | 1.92 | 9.34 | 97.56 | 80.69 |
| 10.00 – 12.49 | 4.05 – 5.05 | 4.44 | 1.28 | 8.16 | 98.84 | 88.85 |
| 12.50 – 14.99 | 5.06 – 6.07 | 5.47 | 0.43 | 3.39 | 99.27 | 92.24 |
| 15.00 – 19.99 | 6.08 – 8.09 | 6.77 | 0.49 | 4.58 | 99.76 | 96.82 |
| 20.00 – 24.99 | 8.10 – 10.12 | 8.88 | 0.19 | 2.48 | 99.95 | 99.30 |
| 25.00 – 29.99 | 10.13 – 12.14 | 10.69 | 0.05 | 0.70 | 100.00 | 100.00 |
| 30.00 – 49.99 | 12.15 – 20.24 | — | — | — | 100.00 | 100.00 |
| 50.00 & above | 20.25 & above | — | — | — | 100.00 | 100.00 |

*Source: National Sample Survey*, No. 215, 26th Round, July 1971 – September 1972, Department of Statistics, Ministry of Planning, Government of India, p. 66.

Table 2.4. *Household income sources and consumption of industrial goods*

| Type of household | Estimated income (Rs. millions) | | | Labor income as percent of total | Use of industrial consumption goods as a percentage of total income |
|---|---|---|---|---|---|
| | Labor | Property ownership | Total | | |
| 1. (a) Landless agricultural | | | | | |
|     laborer | 25.6 | – | 25.6 | 100.0 | 23.1 |
|   (b) Landless sharecropper | 4.2 | 2.1 | 6.6 | 68.2 | |
| 2. Marginal farmer | 18.6 | 39.7 | 58.3 | 31.9 | 25.1 |
| 3. Small farmer | 6.8 | 18.6 | 25.4 | 26.8 | 28.7 |
| 4. Other farmer | 2.7 | 8.0 | 10.7 | 25.2 | 29.2 |
| 5. Artisans | 7.4 | 3.0 | 10.4 | 71.2 | 27.6 |
| 6. Others | 14.4 | 14.0 | 28.4 | 50.7 | |
| 7. Total | 79.7 | 85.4 | 165.4 | | |

Note: Marginal farmer is defined as owning less than 1 hectare; small farmer 1–2; other farmer over 2 hectares.
*Source:* A.N. Bose, "Intersectoral Linkage in a Comprehensive Area Development Approach: The Case of West Bengal," World Employment Programme Research Paper, International Labour Office, Geneva, 1983, p. 55, 62.

Table 2.5. *Percentage distribution of cash credit received by cultivators by sources*

| Source | 1951 | 1961 | 1971 |
|---|---|---|---|
| Government | 1.8 | 25.0 | 16.3 |
| Co-operatives | 1.3 | 4.7 | 15.1 |
| Commercial banks | 0.0 | 0.0 | 1.3 |
| Other institutions | 0.0 | 0.0 | 0.3 |
| Landlords | 3.2 | 0.7 | 3.7 |
| Agriculturist money-lenders | 2.1 | 33.8 | 12.5 |
| Professional money-lenders | 58.9 | 6.8 | 15.6 |
| Traders | 0.5 | 10.8 | 9.4 |
| Friends and relatives | 32.1 | 9.4 | 24.1 |
| Others | 0.1 | 8.8 | 1.7 |

Source: Ajit Kumar Ghose, *Agrarian Reform in West Bengal*, ILO Working Paper, May 1980, p. 14.

Table 2.6. *Percentage of holdings where agricultural work is done with or without hired labor*

| Size–class (Hectares) | Work by household | Bulk of work by household | Bulk of work by hired out | Total No. of holdings |
|---|---|---|---|---|
| Below 0.5 | 86.39 | 7.37 | 6.24 | 1,557,696 |
| 0.5 – 1.0 | 82.10 | 9.03 | 8.87 | 970,789 |
| 1.0 – 2.0 | 77.99 | 10.97 | 11.04 | 941,753 |
| 2.0 – 3.0 | 70.52 | 13.39 | 16.09 | 412,530 |
| 3.0 – 4.0 | 64.65 | 12.79 | 22.56 | 146,493 |
| 4.0 – 5.0 | 63.24 | 14.33 | 22.43 | 97,690 |
| 5.0 – 10.0 | 56.05 | 14.92 | 29.03 | 86,766 |
| 10.0 – 20.0 | 32.46 | 10.16 | 57.38 | 3,134 |
| 20.0 – 30.0 | 44.31 | 20.45 | 35.24 | 103 |
| 30 and Above | 38.04 | 2.17 | 59.79 | 373 |
| Total | 80.05 | 9.64 | 10.31 | 4,216,327 |

*Source: World Agricultural Census 1970–71*, Board of Revenue and Directorate of Agriculture (Socio-Economic and Evaluation Branch), Government of West Bengal, 1975, p. 92.

involved (table 2.2). In an equitable land reform, a third of an acre per person would have to be the maximum allowable. Supplementary income through outside work is very common in rural India and would have to be taken into consideration. Many small farmers must work elsewhere to make a living while leasing out their land (table 2.9). One Bengal survey found that marginal farmers (defined as owning less than 1 hectare) derived 68.9 percent of their income from property rather than from their own or family labor (table 2.4). Integration into the market economy is also considerable. Even landless agricultural laborers, according to this survey, spend 23.1 percent of their income on industrially produced consumption goods (table 2.4). Some crops such as jute are produced exclusively for market while food crops are also traded extensively. Though private money-lenders remain the major source of rural credit, institutional sources have increased significantly, giving the state an increased role in the rural economy (table 2.5).

Most spectacular of all has been the green revolution, which has produced significant increases in fertilizer and High Yielding Variety use as well as in irrigation and output (table 2.7). Though not as early and rapidly as in the Punjab, the 1970s showed substantial increases in these inputs. This resulted in increased productivity and market surplus, which, because of the strength of the surplus farmer lobby, the government has had to subsidize with higher food procurement prices than a free market might provide. Food self-sufficiency had been achieved but at a gain to the dominant segment of rural society.

The increasing integration of the rural economy with the urban and state sector makes social science analysis more complex than the more isolated village economy of the past required. Today only the government and senior academics can obtain the funding required for statistically significant sample surveys. The surveys which are conducted have no common set of definitions which would make them strictly comparable, at least from their published results. With a myriad of classifications presented such as rich peasant, landlord, and middle peasant etc., the studies are not really comparable. The most that can be done is to define common trends and attributes.

As the preceding analysis indicates no strict income or size definitions in and of themselves would be adequate to deal with the range of sample surveys conducted and examined. This is especially true when it comes to correlating such categories as land ownership with political attitudes. Political opinion surveys in West Bengal are almost non-existent despite decades of electoral politics, and rarely include occupational criteria. The much more numerous economic surveys, even when conducted by politically committed academics such as Ashok Rudra, contain little that is conducive to political analysis. Statistically verified surveys such as the National Sample Survey are conducted too infrequently to make them readily usable for a time series analysis of the Left Front government's policy implementation.

In categorizing rural social classes the landless agricultural labor category is straightforward, but many minute landowners lease out land to bigger landowners and vice versa (table 2.9). If one uses the employment of hired labor, rather than size of landholdings, as a definition of class, then by this definition

Table 2.7. *Variations in West Bengal agrarian structure*

| | Tenancy (percentage of operated area) | | | Agricultural laborers (percentage of labor force in agricultural sector) | | Fertilizer intensity (nutrient-kg per hectare per crop) | | HYV intensity (percentage of area under HYV's) 1978 | |
|---|---|---|---|---|---|---|---|---|---|
| | 1939 | 1951 | 1981 | 1951 | 1981 | 1970–72 | 1978–80 | Aman | Aus |
| West Bengal | 22.7 | 28.6 | 16.5 | 21.4 | 44.4 | 13.1 | 37.3 | 24.0 | 34.0 |
| Burdwan | 25.2 | 31.1 | 21.2 | 25.0 | 56.4 | 21.2 | 59.6 | 46.0 | 100.0 |
| Hooghly | 30.5 | 31.2 | 20.9 | 23.3 | 53.2 | 42.9 | 101.5 | 46.1 | 81.1 |
| Birbhum | 24.8 | 26.2 | 18.6 | 32.0 | 50.0 | 21.8 | 42.9 | 29.7 | 100.0 |
| 24 Parganas | 22.3 | 26.7 | 17.8 | 26.9 | 49.6 | 10.9 | 33.4 | 19.7 | 100.0 |
| Nadia | 24.1 | 22.9 | 9.6 | 20.9 | 46.9 | 11.9 | 49.3 | 37.7 | 38.3 |
| Murshidabad | 25.8 | 26.9 | 11.6 | 23.9 | 48.7 | 9.4 | 33.8 | 35.0 | 23.5 |
| Bankura | 29.2 | 26.6 | 10.2 | 23.8 | 45.4 | 15.8 | 33.7 | 17.4 | 53.7 |
| Midnapore | 17.1 | 25.2 | 12.1 | 16.5 | 36.3 | 8.1 | 24.1 | 16.1 | 52.5 |
| Howrah | 23.4 | 32.3 | 22.7 | 33.1 | 57.4 | 23.9 | 176.8 | 20.6 | 100.0 |
| Jalpaiguri | 25.9 | 50.9 | 45.1 | 2.5 | 31.9 | 3.7 | 11.2 | 18.1 | 23.3 |
| Darjeeling | NA | 16.3 | 15.9 | 5.6 | 24.3 | 15.5 | 47.6 | 45.2 | 65.5 |
| Malda | 9.6 | 30.1 | 19.0 | 17.3 | 46.2 | 8.3 | 31.9 | 18.0 | 13.6 |
| West Dinajpur | 14.5 | 37.2 | 13.0 | 12.1 | 42.0 | 2.4 | 18.7 | 18.1 | 19.2 |
| Cooch Behar | NA | 28.4 | 35.1 | 8.4 | 34.0 | 2.0 | 14.0 | 19.8 | 8.6 |
| Purulia | NA | NA | NA | NA | 32.6 | 4.7 | 18.7 | 18.5 | 100.0 |

*Source:* James K. Boyce, *Agricultural Growth in Bangladesh and West Bengal,* Oxford University, D. Phil Thesis 1984, pp. 275, 345.

there would be little land left to give to the tillers since only landholdings over 10 hectares use hired labor for most farm work (table 2.6). Production of a surplus for a market is even more difficult to define as a class category since some crops like jute or sugar cane are only for the market, while rice, wheat, and potatoes can be for both, and the portion sold depends on seasonal prices and productivity. Furthermore, peasants with as little as 2 or 3 hectares are often connected to urban employment and have relatives completely integrated into the urban sector. A single criterion, even the most commonly used one of landownership, is therefore in itself inadequate. The use of hired labor and land leasing must also be taken into account as well as additional sources of income. A small farmer might be defined as having land or equivalent sources of income around the 0.321 acre per land–man ratio or about 2 acres per household, anything less than half this being defined as marginal farming. The middle peasantry, as commonly suggested, would be those who work their own land without normally employing non-family labor. This would be placed somewhat arbitrarily at 5 acres. The current law of 12 to 17 irrigated acres is more than this. Confiscation of land over 5 acres, which could be defined as rich peasant, and over the current ceiling limit as landlord, would provide 44 percent of cultivable land for redistribution and leave 87 percent of agricultural households either the gainers or unaffected by the reform (tables 2.2 and 2.3). This should be the minimal first step towards land reform, a short-term goal to be followed at an opportune time by equalization of land as the medium-term goal. As seen from table 2.2 this categorization differs from the agricultural census definition, but has the advantage of including use of hired labor as a criterion as well as providing a workable guideline for a land reform program that would allow large-scale land redistribution without alienating the vast majority of the agricultural population. The use of the 5-acre limit is chosen because the number of households with more land than this is significantly less than those with less than 5 acres. There will therefore be less opposition to implementation than would arise from a lower ceiling limit.

According to the Communist Party – Marxist (CPM) Land Reforms and Land Revenue Minister Benoy Choudhury, only the complete confiscation of all holdings over 10 acres would enable the agricultural laborers and marginal farmers to receive 1.5 acres per household. According to him only 4.2 percent of households own over 10 acres, controlling 33.3 percent of agricultural land or 4.53 million acres. With 3,751,000 landless and marginal farmer households, equalization of landholdings at 1.5 acres per household would require complete confiscation of all land held by these largest landowners. The Land Reforms Minister states that the biggest lacuna is allowing the landlords to retain land up to the ceiling limit. The basic land reform slogan should be taking over all the land from feudal and capitalist landlords without compensation and distributing it among landless laborers free. All the land must be taken from the landlords, otherwise the *Ceiling Act* would end up as a farce and not enough land would be available to distribute.[6] This is precisely what has happened. The ceiling being too high, there is insufficient land available for a significant land redistribution, and whatever may be the Land Reforms Minister's view on the subject, the CPM government has shown no intention of changing the status quo in this regard or the Minister of implementing his own recommendations. When the CPM first published Benoy Choudhury's booklet in May 1977 on the eve of the election of the CPM to power, his position could be taken as a statement of party policy, but by its fifth reprinting in January 1981 it had ceased to have any meaning except to show how far short the political practice had fallen from its original policy.

The original CPM position as formulated in the resolution of the Central Committee on *Tasks on the Kisan Front* of 1967 and on *Certain Agrarian Issues* in 1973 is far different from the current CPM policies in the Left Front government.[7] This difference reflects part of the general trend towards moderation in the CPM. The 1967 and 1973 documents bear the orientation of the then General Secretary P. Sundarayya who subsequently resigned from the party leadership and Politburo, when his positions were no longer being accepted in the drift towards moderation. Though these resolutions have since been repudiated they illustrate the change that has taken place in party policy, resulting in the present West Bengal Government position. The difference on the agrarian question between the former Central Committee position and that of some West Bengal Party members which later became the state government and CPM policy is brought out in P. Sundarayya's explanatory note on *Certain Agrarian Issues.* Sundarayya's critique of the Bengal position is only a thinly disguised accusation of reformism in the West Bengal Party and by implication of the current Party position which now advocates the policy.[8] "Some comrades in West Bengal argue that the ownership right to the tenants should not be campaigned for now ... as it would antagonise these sections" of landowners "and they would go away from the democratic alliance." That "these critics have gone to the extremely ridiculous position" of hesitating to raise popular demands when "the Congress itself is forced to come forward to satisfy ... the masses with such legislation, though only to cheat them, is something queer ... This attitude, if logically extended, would mean that we should formulate and advance the demands of tenants in such a way as would be acceptable to the

---

[6]  Benoy Choudhury, *Banglar Bhumibyabasthar Ruprekha* ("Outline of the Land Settlement of Bengal") (Calcutta: National Book Agency, fifth edition, January 1981), pp. 30–1.

[7]  Communist Party of India – Marxist, Central Committee, *Tasks on the Kisan Front* (Calcutta: April 1967); Communist Party of India – Marxist, Central Committee, *Resolution on Certain Agrarian Issues* (Calcutta: 1973).

[8]  Sundarayya, *Explanatory Note*, p. 30.

landlords."[9] Sundarayya rejected the position of some West Bengal peasant leaders that a ceiling of 25 acres would be "a very big step." "With such an amount of ceiling ... no land will be available for distribution."[10] He reiterated the Central Committee policy of expropriating all the land of the landlords including that below the ceiling. To allow retention of land below the ceiling would only perpetuate landlordism, "cheating the agricultural labour and poor peasants", leaving the CPM policy of distributing land free to the landless as an "empty slogan."[11]

The reason for this wrong position in the CPM lies, according to Sundarayya, in the rich and middle peasant composition of the party and in their orientation to these classes.[12] The CPM Central Committee itself had earlier admitted peasant unity in the party was erroneously "based upon the middle and rich peasantry, instead of building it round the rural labour and the poor and ... organising these sections as the main backbone and driving force of the movement."[13] The Central Committee admitted this task would not be easy as the rich and middle peasant orientation was "deeprooted and long-accumulated" and because "the bulk of our leading *kisan* activists come from the rich and middle peasant" class rather than the poor peasants and agricultural labor.[14] Harekrishna Konar took the same position, noting that "today the old practice of building peasant unity based on the middle peasants is not useful for agrarian revolution but this old outlook still holds the activists of the peasant movement back." Though he argued "particular emphasis" had to be "laid on the task of organising the agricultural labourers and poor peasants and making them conscious," this was almost totally absent from the policy implementation of the Left Front government.[15]

Given the acute land shortage and the elimination of the larger landowners over the years through land reforms, the only options left are collectivization, which is politically untenable, or lowering the land ceiling, which would antagonize many of the Communist Party's own supporters in the villages. When the CPIML leader Santosh Rana suggested lowering the land ceiling, the CPM Land Reforms Minister described this as a provocation, which it certainly would have been, even among the CPM's supporters.[16] Faced with the choice

---

[9] *Ibid.*, pp. 8–9, 30.
[10] *Ibid.*, pp. 11–12.
[11] *Ibid.*, pp. 1–2.
[12] Communist Party of India – Marxist, 1967, *Tasks*, pp. 5–6.
[13] *Ibid.*, p. 16.
[14] Harekrishna Konar, *Agrarian Problems of India* (Calcutta: Gour Sabha, 1977), p. 47.
[15] Santosh Rana, "Left Front Government in West Bengal: Appraisal," *For a New Democracy*, special issue, October–February 1981–82 (Calcutta: Provisional Central Committee, Communist Party of India – Marxist–Leninist, 1982), p. 43.
[16] Bhabani Sen Gupta, "Time to take Stock," *India Today*, December 31, 1982, p. 115.

between implementing significant land reforms to help the landless and poor peasantry, or helping the middle and rich peasantry by doing nothing of significance, the Left Front chose the latter approach, thereby preserving its most important rural base. The CPM "Central leadership wanted to abandon political action that would polarise the rich and middle peasants on the one hand and the poor and marginal peasants and landless workers on the other. They practically abandoned meaningful struggle for land reforms."[17] "In their eagerness to preserve all peasant unity in rural West Bengal the Government is probably shifting away from potentially the most active agents of agrarian reorganisation" namely agricultural labor and the poor peasantry.[18] This all-peasant unity could only be preserved by keeping the potentially most revolutionary classes inactive or subordinate, as they represented the greatest potential threat to the Communists' own vested interest in the middle and rich peasantry.

As a result, all the Left Front could offer the lowest classes were minor concessions and palliatives, often through laws passed by the previous Congress regime but never implemented. The agency for this implementation was the existing state bureaucracy, with all the deficiencies that entailed. Unlike the Panchayats where the parties at least had to put up slates of candidates and participate politically, in the land reform program, party participation was optional. Though the Communist peasant organizations were requested to assist the administration, the administration carried out the work at every step of the process.

In the Land Reforms Department the officials were about evenly divided between those originating from East Bengal and those from West Bengal. Though only those from West Bengal were often landowners, some of the East Bengalis retained a landed ideological orientation. In these circumstances the dedicated officers found it difficult to work in the administration. The few dedicated senior officials, often of leftist inclination, could not easily carry through land reform when junior officials in department offices and in the field were lacking in motivation and would not cooperate. The junior staff in the Land Reforms Department who often had the most contact with the common people also had the least sympathy with them. A publication of the Directorate of Land Records and Surveys even stated, that "the entire gamut of land reforms implementation is an open sesame for the dishonest employees is a widely known fact of life."[19] Though the legislation that the department was implementing had

---

[17] Ranjit Kumar Lahiri, "Land Reforms in West Bengal – Some Implications" in *Land Reforms in Eastern India* edited by Manjula Bose (Calcutta: Planning Forum, Jadavpur University, 1981), p. 120.

[18] B.K. Sarkar and R.K. Prasannan, *What Happened to the Vested Land?* (Calcutta: Directorate of Land Records and Surveys, West Bengal, March 1976), p. 6.

[19] D. Bandyopadhyay, Land Reforms Commissioner, *Land Reforms in West Bengal* (Calcutta: Information and Cultural Affairs Department, Government of West Bengal, 1980), pp. 10–11.

usually been in effect from the Congress period, the Left Front claimed greater dedication in carrying the program through. The laws had been introduced by Congress but till the Left Front government came to power, they had largely been observed in the breach.

The Land Reforms Commissioner noted the deficiencies of the bureaucracy as an agency of social change.

Generally the Bureaucracy maintains a stance of hostile neutrality to the entire issue of land reforms. The reason lies in the age-old tradition of the administration of maintaining order, with or without law. The main burden of administrative ethos and procedure, general civil and original laws, judicial pronouncements and practices is the maintenance and safeguarding of existing property relationship in the rural areas. Hence it is natural for the bureaucracy to develop a bias against any action or an isolated law which aims at altering the existing socio-economic arrangements.[20]

The "reactionary" rulings of the allegedly Congress-oriented Calcutta High Court resulted in 20,000 civil injunctions centering around land reforms, and the Land Revenue Courts had 27,000 cases pending, resulting in 180,779 acres being hit by court injunctions.[21] The acreage increased slightly from 164,733 acres under injunction at the end of 1978, indicating the backlog of cases was not being cleared. This was alleged to be with the connivance of Marxist lawyers who for personal gain prolonged cases at government expense.[22] Between 1977 and 1980, the Left Front government spent about Rs. 1.20 crores as fees to official lawyers, yet these suits were not cleared.[23] Those retaining their land through court injunctions and pending cases were earning over Rs. 4 crores per year.[24]

The Indian Supreme Court, by contrast, proved to be more progressive in its orientation.[25] The Supreme Court Judgement of May 9, 1980 noted that "there is no substantial decrease in the limit" of ceiling land under current West Bengal law. The ceiling limit of "6.18 acres in the case of an individual, and 12.35 to 17.29 acres of irrigated land, in the case of a family ... in the Gangetic plains

---

[20] Timir Basu, *Bhumi Sanskarer Swarup* ("A Picture of Land Reforms") (Calcutta: Abaniranjan Rai, February 1982), p. 17; West Bengal, "Statement of Vested Agricultural Land Hit by Injunction up to 31st December, 1984" (mimeographed), 1985.

[21] Basu, *Bhumi*, p. 17.

[22] Profulla Roy Choudhury, "Land Reforms: Promise and Fulfilment", *Economic and Political Weekly*, December 27, 1980, p. 2172.

[23] *Ibid.*

[24] Communist Party of India – Marxist, *Political Resolution*, adopted by the Eleventh Congress, Vijayawada, January 26–31, 1982 (New Delhi: March 1982), pp. 33–4.

[25] West Bengal, Board of Revenue, *Supreme Court Judgement* dated the 9th May 1980 Upholding Ceiling on Land Prescribed under the West Bengal Land Reforms Act, 1955 (Calcutta: Government of West Bengal, 1981), p. 13.

of West Bengal, is not small by any standard."[26] Such land reforms would leave all but the biggest landlords untouched and even they would be able to retain up to the ceiling, enabling them to remain in the landlord class. The surplus land above the ceiling was available for distribution to the landless and poor peasantry.

To satisfy the largest number of people the Left Front distributed the surplus into pieces all below an acre and averaging .54 acres. While good for acquiring a political base and helping to meet immediate peasant aspirations, in the long run it will be counter-productive if collectivization is going to be employed later.

It is perfectly understandable that if we want to maintain the status quo – or any other social order – we should try to involve as many people as possible in it so that at least a majority of the population acquire a stake in the status quo or the system in question. Keeping this in view, it is perfectly reasonable to distribute small bits of land however uneconomic to land hungry peasants and/or agricultural labourers so that they never look for any radical alternative to the present property system and stay eager to acquire some property. However to call it socialism is a sad travesty of truth.[27]

The identification and distribution of this surplus land was almost entirely the work of the state bureaucracy. By 1982, 1,249,117 acres of agricultural land had been vested representing about 1/4 of the all-India total. The Left Front claimed that "West Bengal is the only state in India to have vested so much ceiling surplus agricultural land."[28] According to Nossiter:

The LF ministries' record on land redistribution is indubitably impressive, particularly when compared with other states in India. Some 4.4 million acres were "vested" (expropriated and held) in government nationwide. Of this West Bengal accounted for 1.2 million acres of which 800,000 acres have been redistributed to the landless (Election Manifesto of the LF, 1987).[29]

This uncritical acceptance of Left Front land reform statistics is surprising since it is well known among both the land reform officials in charge of the redistribution and Indian scholars of the subject that these figures are the result of inappropriately including redistribution figures from the Estates Acquisition Act (1,049,221 acres till 1985) with that under the Land Reforms Act (184,049). As only the latter is comparable with land reforms in other states, the former

---

[26] Asit Kumar Bhattacharyya, "An examination of Land Reforms with Special Reference to West Bengal" in *Land Reform in Eastern India*, edited by Manjula Bose (Calcutta: Jadavpur University, 1981), p. 185.

[27] West Bengal, Board of Revenue, Statistical Cell, *Land Reforms in West Bengal: Statistical Report VII* (Calcutta: 1982), p. 4.

[28] West Bengal State Committee, Communist Party of India – Marxist, *Significant Six Years of the Left Front Government of West Bengal* (Calcutta: CPM West Bengal State Committee, September 1983), p. 42.

[29] T.J. Nossiter, *Marxist State Governments in India* (London: Pinter Publishers, 1988), p. 140.

being part of the zamindari abolition program, "the performance of West Bengal with respect to ceiling laws cannot, therefore, be regarded as extraordinary" as indicated by table 2.8.[30] At the end of 1978 1,005,148 acres had been distributed under the Estates Acquisition Act and 117,428 under the Land Reforms Act. But by the end of 1984 only 1,049,220 acres and 184,049 had been vested indicating only 44,072 and 66,621 acres had been vested in the first six years of Left Front rule, a rate no better than under the previous Congress government.[31] The Land Reforms Minister stated in the assembly that from the election of the Left Front till mid 1982 150,000 acres had been vested and 120,000 distributed, which meant that 1 million acres had been vested before the Left Front came to power and 630,000 acres distributed already.[32] The 799,224 acres distributed by the end of 1984 went to 1,572,531 persons or about 1/2 acre per beneficiary.

Though a Left Front government annual publication continues to make the claim West Bengal has vested 1/6th of the all-India total and distributed 1/5th, the same publication admits only about 200,000 acres have been vested over the first twelve years of Communist rule, leaving the majority of land being vested by previous Congress regimes.[33] As the 200,000 acres vested over the twelve years of Communist rule is only .92 percent of the total state area and 1.2 percent of the cultivable area, Nossiter's claim that "the LF ministries' record of land redistribution is indubitably impressive" is open to serious doubt.[34] The West Bengal government blames this poor record on central government delays in giving Presidential assent to land reform legislation and on previous Marxist governments having already distributed land in the 1967 to 1969 period. It neglects to mention that in these previous radical Communist governments the peasants were encouraged by the Communists to seize the land themselves without waiting for the administration. It is a mark of the political distance the CPM has traveled from its early revolutionary phase of the 1960s that the state bureaucracy is now left to do everything and peasant movements are discouraged, even when legislation waiting for central government approval is delayed giving time for "unscrupulous" land owners "to formulate strategy to evade the new ceiling provisions."[35]

In contrast to the land grab movements of Communist peasants during the

---

[30] Nripen Bandyopadhyaya, "Evaluation of Land Reform Measures in West Bengal: A Report" (Calcutta: mimeographed by the Centre for Studies in Social Sciences, 1983), p. 23.

[31] Profulla Roy Choudhury, *Left Experiment in West Bengal* (New Delhi, Patriot Publishers, July 1985), p. 159.

[32] West Bengal, Board of Revenue, Statistical Cell, *Land Reforms in West Bengal*, VII, p. 7.

[33] Government of West Bengal, Department of Information and Cultural Affairs, *12 Years of Left Front Government* (Calcutta: Director of Information, June 1989), pp. 2–4.

[34] Nossiter, *Marxist State Governments*, p. 140.

[35] Government of West Bengal, *12 Years*, p. 4.

Table 2.8. *Land reform in Indian states*[a] *(in acres)*

| | Area declared surplus | Area taken possession | Area declared surplus but possession not taken | Area distributed | Area distributed as percentage of cultivable area |
|---|---|---|---|---|---|
| Andhra Pradesh | 1,014,050 | 456,021 | 558,029 | 331,976 | .88 |
| Assam | 450,918 | 376,445 | 74,473 | 373,020 | 5.21 |
| Bihar | 287,931 | 194,037 | 93,894 | 179,046 | .67 |
| Gujarat | 182,138 | 87,020 | 95,118 | 51,133 | .19 |
| Haryana | 30,757 | 22,796 | 7,961 | 22,591 | .24 |
| Himachal Pradesh | 283,994 | 281,403 | 2,591 | 3,335 | .12 |
| Jammu and Kashmir | 6,000 | — | 6,000 | — | |
| Karnataka | 296,355 | 152,317 | 144,018 | 115,661 | .38 |
| Kerala | 121,385 | 87,189 | 34,196 | 58,443 | 1.04 |
| Madhya Pradesh | 227,377 | 139,957 | 87,420 | 93,400 | .17 |
| Maharashtra | 390,040 | 304,884 | 85,156 | 304,894 | .62 |
| Orissa | 162,390 | 140,642 | 21,766 | 127,117 | .74 |
| Punjab | 27,444 | 15,235 | 12,209 | 14,140 | .13 |
| Rajasthan | 240,050 | 232,531 | 7,519 | 145,319 | .29 |
| Tamil Nadu | 94,762 | 89,008 | 5,754 | 77,835 | .39 |
| Uttar Pradesh | 301,561 | 275,226 | 26,341 | 244,208 | .51 |
| West Bengal | 182,157 | 126,743 | 55,414 | 80,639 | .55 |

[a] West Bengal Land Reforms Act or equivalent legislation in other states

*Source:* Government of India, Department of Rural Development, Ministry of Agriculture and Rural Development, "Proceedings of Conference of Revenue Ministers" held in New Delhi, May 1985, pp. 131–3.

Marxist governments of the 1960s, the present government has done practically nothing. According to CPM Central Committee member Biplab Dasgupta:

During the brief United Front rule by the left-wing parties in 1967 and 1969–70, the village level committees of poor peasants and landless labourers helped to identify such *benami* land (that is land held illegally in excess of the permitted limit), took over 300,000 acres of such land and distributed it among the landless. While the legality of such action was disputable there was no denying the effectiveness of bringing about a change in the land relations in rural West Bengal. The beneficiaries of such populist land reform formed the hard core of the support which the Left Front received during the 1977 and 1982 elections.[36]

Thus nineteen months of Communist rule in the 1960s achieved more through peasant land seizures than the twelve years of Communist rule since 1977 (300,000 acres versus 80,000 distributed till 1985). As this represents only 1.8 and .55 percent of cultivable land, the distribution of 2.35 percent of the land under all Communist governments does not indicate significant land reform. The redistribution can only be described as cosmetic, and in fact neither Congress nor Communist governments have carried out significant land reform since zamindari abolition. "With these land ceiling measures, and the abolition of landlordism and intermediaries, the power in the countryside was transferred to small landlords and rich peasants ... Their needs and priorities became, to the administrators and policy-makers, the needs and priorities of the village population as a whole."[37] Though Biplab Dasgupta refers here to the pre-Communist period, the limited land redistribution since then indicates that their elite class position remains unchanged. There are indications of the opportunist members in this class supporting the Left Front parties, though no reliable party-class membership survey exists. As the rest of the country is no better than Bengal in redistribution, the all-India land reform effort appears also to be cosmetic (table 2.8). The downsizing of reported land holdings is largely the result of generational subdivision and bogus transfers rather than state intervention.

Kohli and Nossiter, in specifically examining and then praising the West Bengal land reform, do not point out its insignificance in terms of total cultivable land. Kohli specifically mentions the percentage of cultivable land redistributed for the other two states he examined (Karnataka .2 percent and Uttar Pradesh .7 percent), thereby supporting his thesis of their poor land redistribution performance.[38] Nossiter and Kohli are aware of the importance of this figure

---

[36] Biplab Dasgupta, "Some Aspects of Land Reform in West Bengal" in *Land Reform: Land Settlement and Cooperatives*, no. 1/2 (United Nations Food and Agriculture Organization: 1982), p. 13.

[37] *Ibid.*, p. 14.

[38] Atul Kohli, *The State and Poverty in India: The Politics of Reform* (Cambridge: Cambridge University Press, 1987), pp. 166, 215.

but omitted to mention it for West Bengal. The redistribution in twelve years of only .55 percent of cultivable land makes their whole thesis of the Left Front's "spectacular," "indubitably impressive," and "truly remarkable accomplishment" in land reform untenable.[39] It will take the Left Front over a millennium at its present redistribution rate to distribute the land above the 5 acres as originally advocated. That this redistribution is no longer party policy is a measure of the political distance the CPM has traveled in the last quarter century.

The West Bengal government Third Workshop on land reforms noted that the "progress made up to date was rather tardy and unsatisfactory in almost all the districts."[40] Though recovery of ceiling surplus land was a priority item

it was felt that there was large scope for giving further attention to this matter at the field level and to speed up the vesting of surplus land ... It was pointed out that a very large quantity of ceiling surplus land was retained by the intermediaries by clandestine manner. The common *modus operandi* were *benami* transaction, creation of sham and fake tenancies, trusts and endowments.[41]

In 1981 3.74 lakh acres of vested land had not been distributed with little having been done in the previous three years to expedite distribution, thus earning their illegal occupants Rs. 14 crores annually.[42] The Third Workshop found that one of the reasons these acres of vested land could not be distributed was that the elected rural institutions described these lands as "unfit for agriculture."[43] Though peasants were expected to help in detecting surplus land, the policy was that vested land be taken possession of only after "quasi-judicial and administrative processes" were complete.[44] The CPM Land and Land Revenue Reforms Minister Benoy Choudhury concluded: "The achievement in the matter of distribution of vested land has not been satisfactory though highest priority was assigned to this job."[45] The Board of Revenue also found that they did not always get the desired degree of cooperation from the lower levels of the bureaucracy and the Panchayats. "It was thought that with their local knowledge the representatives of Panchayati Raj Institution would be able to make a breakthrough in the usual dilatory process of identification of vested plot and its occupier. The circular did not have the desired effect."[46] The Land Reforms Office in Burdwan stated that surplus land was not always being distributed

---

[39] *Ibid.*, p. 124; Nossiter, *Marxist State Governments*, pp. 140, 171, 184.
[40] West Bengal, Board of Revenue, *Third Workshop on Land Reforms: Operational Decisions*, September 15–16, 1980 (Calcutta: Government of West Bengal, October 1980), p. 3.
[41] *Ibid.*
[42] Roy Choudhury, "Land Reforms," p. 2172.
[43] West Bengal, Board of Revenue, *Third Workshop on Land Reforms*, p. 4.
[44] Roy Choudhury, "Land Reforms."
[45] West Bengal, Board of Revenue, Statistical Cell, *Land Reforms in West Bengal, VII*, p. 1.
[46] West Bengal, Board of Revenue, *Fourth Workshop on Land Reforms: Operational Decisions*, June 23–24, 1981 (Calcutta: Government of West Bengal, July 1981), p. 4.

according to the allocation priorities of the Government, implying that those less deserving but more influential were receiving the land. The Additional District Magistrate (Land Reforms) therefore instructed the Junior Land Revenue Officers to ensure proper distribution and to "pursue the Panchayats, where necessary, for making distribution accordingly."[47]

The problems were similar in another major effort at land reform, redistributing illegally acquired land. Under the Restoration of Alienated Land Act, land which had been acquired through distress sales or under coercion was legally entitled to be restored to the original owners. However, implementation was "extremely tardy and unsatisfactory" with disposal of cases having come to a "standstill." Only 15 percent of cases were disposed in favor of the aggrieved party, with an average area of 1 acre involved.[48] "It was found that not only restoration orders were passed in very few cases, but also most of these orders remained only in paper" with the party who had seized the land continuing to retain possession. Those disputes settled out of court also did not bring any benefit to the aggrieved party in a large number of cases.[49] The State Government Workshop on Land Reforms noted that the backlog of pending cases presented "a major problem specially in areas where there was concentration of Tribals. This might result in rural tension. It was imperative to dispose of all pending cases, particularly the cases involving alienation of Tribal Lands."[50] With over 200,000 cases pending representing a large area of land this will be difficult to achieve.[51] P. Roy Choudhury in an article in *Economic and Political Weekly* concludes:

the achievements of the Left Front Government in West Bengal in the matter of land reforms has not been such as warrant satisfaction. Whatever has been done, is to the credit of the much-maligned bureaucracy. The situation would have been far better had the political wing in the state been without link with land and landed interests.[52]

The dichotomy between theory and practice in land reform continued even within CPM publications. The CPM Kisan Sabha leader, Shantimoy Ghosh, in an article in the CPM theoretical journal "Marxbadi Path," wrote of the need to expropriate the land of landlords and distribute it to the tillers. When the inconsistency of this with the Left Front and Kisan Sabha's implementation

---

[47] West Bengal, Land Reforms Office (Management and Settlement Wings), Burdwan, *Land Reforms in the District of Burdwan* (Burdwan: Government of West Bengal, 1980) mimeographed, p. 15.

[48] West Bengal, Board of Revenue, *Fourth Workshop on Land Reforms*, p. 7.

[49] West Bengal, Board of Revenue, *Workshop on Land Reforms: A Few Operational Decisions*, June 23–24, 1978 (Calcutta: Government of West Bengal, 1978), p. 5.

[50] West Bengal, Board of Revenue, *Third Workshop on Land Reforms*, p. 9.

[51] Roy Choudhury, *Left Experiment*, p. 9.

[52] Roy Choudhury, "Land Reforms," p. 2173.

program was pointed out, Promode Das Gupta said that in West Bengal's current situation this "slogan was pure phrase mongering" but was valid in an all-India agrarian revolution.[53] Since land reform was a state subject the distinction between the two phases seems dubious, unless the purpose is to hold up agrarian reform in West Bengal till the political mobilization in the rest of the country catches up, thus preventing Bengal from being an example to the rest of India. Such radical reforms would presumably alienate landlords in the rest of the country, where the CPM would hope for their support until they are themselves expropriated after the revolution. The strategy of not undertaking radical reforms in Bengal against sectors of society which are potential allies in less-advanced parts of the country is an interesting anomaly. This is not the reason the CPM has given however. The party rather argues the limited powers of the state legislation as the reason for avoiding confrontational policies. The real reason, however, seems to be that the CPM's own mass base among the rural vested interests precludes a more radical strategy, so even in an area of its own jurisdiction with ample coercive forces at its disposal, it refrains from radical action.

Rather than making a radical redistribution of land, the Left Front was to put emphasis on ensuring security of tenure for sharecroppers, and providing them with a legally stipulated 3/4 share of crops. However, as the following section shows, these objectives were to prove illusory.

### Operation sharecropper

The agrarian reform program that has received the widest publicity is Operation Barga for recording tenancy rights to sharecroppers. That primary attention has been given to Operation Barga seems incongruous considering agricultural laborers outnumber sharecroppers and sharecropping is admitted, even by the proponents of Operation Barga, to be on the decline.[54] Why the West Bengal government chose not to give priority to the primary class in the rural areas can be surmised by the position agricultural labor holds *vis-à-vis* sharecroppers in rural Bengal. Agricultural labor is exclusively a dependent class, tied to the landlord for employment, debts, and social obligation. At best he owns too little land to make a living and therefore supplements it with wage labor. Thus he represents the most exploited class, but also the most difficult to organize.

The sharecropper on the other hand is in an intermediate class. At the higher end of the spectrum he can be a middle or even rich peasant, who supplements

[53]  Ashis Barman, "New Challenges for Left," *Link*, January 26, 1983, p. 38.
[54]  Dasgupta, "Gram Banglar," p. 89.

Table 2.9. *Distribution of households leasing-out and leasing-in on a crop-sharing basis and of sharecropped land (percentage) in West Bengal 1970–71*

| Size class of household ownership holding (acres) | Households leasing-out | Area leasing-out | Households leasing-in | Area leasing-in |
|---|---|---|---|---|
| 0.0 | — | — | 12.63 | 7.07 |
| 0.01 – 1.00 | 20.72 | 4.00 | 46.21 | 29.14 |
| 1.00 – 2.50 | 32.98 | 20.29 | 25.33 | 49.85 |
| 2.50 – 5.00 | 22.76 | 29.11 | 11.14 | 8.33 |
| 5.00 – 7.50 | 7.68 | 16.10 | 3.46 | 3.16 |
| 7.50 – 10.00 | 5.28 | 10.06 | 0.60 | 1.14 |
| Above 10.00 | 10.58 | 20.44 | 0.63 | 1.31 |
| All | 100.00 | 100.00 | 100.00 | 100.00 |

*Source: National Sample Survey.* Government of India, 26th round, Report No. 215 (West Bengal), vol. I pp. 67–8. Cited in Ajit Kumar Ghose, *Agrarian Reform in West Bengal: Objectives, Achievement and Limitations* (Geneva, International Labour Organisation, 1980), p. 35.

his own land by sharecropping on neighboring property. The number of landless sharecroppers is much less than those with some land, and in fact most sharecroppers own over half of the land they till.[55] The sharecropper aspires to be a landowner, and, by sharecropping several small plots as well as his own land, often has the economic status of the middle peasant. Even when poor, the very fact of having land to till, when 45 percent of the agriculturalists have nothing, gives him a status and landed interest that is the envy of nearly half the farming population. It is for this reason that landless agricultural labourers are always seeking land to cultivate on a sharecropping basis to improve their lot. Any land reform that cannot meet this desire of the landless for security of cultivation, if not ownership, can only be partial at best.[56]

Many large landowners are sharecroppers on land leased from small peasants. The ratio regarding sharecropping indicates a complex class division (see table 2.9). In the leasing of land for sharecropping or rent in Hooghly 90 percent of those who give land own less than 4.942 acres and 40 percent less than 1.23 acres while 90 percent of sharecroppers own less than 4.942 acres.[57] In this

---

[55] Ashok Rudra, *Paschim Banglar Bargadar* ("West Bengal's Bargadar") (Calcutta: Kalthasilpa, September 1981), p. 12.
[56] Govinda Chandra Mandal, "Land Reforms in the Context of Agricultural Development with Special Reference to West Bengal," in *Land Reforms in Eastern India* edited by Manjula Bose (Calcutta: Planning Forum, Jadavpur University, 1981), pp. 180–81.
[57] Rudra, *Paschim*, p. 20.

district 38 percent who lease out are salary earners.[58] Though the proximity of
Hooghly to Calcutta makes this atypical in having hardly any difference in land
ownership between those leasing in and out, other districts also have similar
patterns. In Hooghly, Birbhum, Bankura, and West Dinajpur only 47 percent of
landowners were better off than the sharecroppers and in 21 percent of cases
the sharecroppers were better off than the owner.[59] In Burdwan some sharecroppers employ agricultural labor.[60] The National Sample Survey reported that
21 percent of cultivable land belonged to sharecroppers and only 3.2 percent of
sharecroppers were landless.[61] Thus the conventional view of the exploited
sharecroppers according to Ashok Rudra is no longer valid and in fact rich
cultivator-sharecroppers "partially belong to capitalistic class."[62] Through
Operation Barga they could effectively increase their returns and become more
prosperous.

The normal pattern in West Bengal was for the crop to be equally shared
between owner and sharecropper when the latter provides the inputs. This equal
sharing occurred in 66.9 percent of cases according to one random sample
survey. Only in 6.4 percent of cases was the new law of 75 percent for the
sharecropper already in operation, while the owner received more than half the
crop in the remaining cases. When the owner provides inputs the ratio changes
in the owner's favor even more.[63]

About half of the land cultivated by sharecroppers was owned by landholders
possessing less than 5 acres; 16 percent of these landholdings of less than 5 acres
was *barga* cultivated. Even in the 0–1 acre category 16 percent of land was
given to *barga*, the proportion rising to 21 percent in the 4 to 5 acre category.
In the 5 to 10 acre category it was 25 percent and, when over 10 acres 1/3 to
over 1/2.[64] Rigorous implementation of the legislation would thus harm those
small landowners in the poor peasant category who gave some or all of their
land to *bargas*, due to their own incapacity to work the land themselves from
old age or the necessity of taking up urban employment. The legislation if
implemented would have had the effect of benefiting the *bargas* at the same
time as they adversely affected many poor peasant owners as well as middle
and rich peasants. The legislation contained the proviso for owners to resume
cultivation of their own lands, with compensation to the *bargas*, should they

[58] Debidas Ray, "The Small Lessor and the Big Lessee: Evidence From West Bengal," *Economic
and Political Weekly*, Review of Agriculture, December 1978, p. A121.
[59] Rudra, *Paschim*, p. 20.
[60] Bhattacharyya, "An examination of Land Reforms," p. 192.
[61] Rudra, *Paschim*, p. 33.
[62] *Ibid.*, pp. 22, 32.
[63] Rudra, *Paschim*, p. 2.
[64] P.K. Dutta, *Statistics of Bargadars and Extent of Barga Cultivation in West Bengal* (Calcutta:
Directorate of Land Records and Survey, West Bengal, May 1981), pp. 15–16.

desire, but those who could not do so would be adversely affected. The interests of the poor landowner and his poor sharecropper were as irreconcilable as those of their richer counterparts. If the new share was not enforced for those working the lands of poor landowners, the sharecroppers would suffer relative to their counterparts working for richer landowners who receive larger proportions. There was no way around this lacuna as long as the concept of private property in land was maintained, and collectivization would have alienated most landowning peasants, making this alternative politically untenable for the Left Front government.

The sharecroppers who have been most successful in resisting the landlords have been those viable sharecroppers who in some areas form the majority of the middle peasantry. They have taken part in Communist peasant organizations, and helped to shift the balance of power towards the middle peasantry from the landlords. Such middle peasant sharecroppers "are more independent than are completely propertyless labourers and, therefore, are more susceptible to radicalisation."[65] Their economic independence enables them to withstand the pressures of the landlord and get themselves registered as sharecroppers entitled to 3/4 of the produce. These middle peasant sharecroppers cultivating 2.5 to 7.5 acres are more politically active and influential, and as the prime beneficiaries of Operation Barga, support the Left Front.[66] Seemingly progressive programs like Operation Barga, in the context of the acute land shortage and landlessness, would turn the recorded *bargadars* into a vested interest, making further land reform even more difficult.[67] The larger *bargadars* would be in the best position to obtain credit and other inputs, and gain an additional crop share at the expense of both the large leasing landowners and the small lessors.[68] As 3/4 shareholders of the land they sharecrop, they have everything to lose by any generalized land reform that would equalize landholdings among the agriculturalists.

The poorer sharecroppers, with little or no land of their own, are more dependent on the landlord and therefore more afraid of being recorded as a *barga* from fear of eviction or simply not being able to borrow in time of need. The poorest *bargadars* are mostly from the scheduled castes and tribes who have never been able to form an effective organization of their own, and have generally been the ones left out of the *barga*-recording program due to fear and dependence on the propertied classes.[69]

[65] Donald S. Zagoria, "The Social Bases of Indian Communism" in *Issues in the Future of Asia* edited by Richard Lowenthal (New York: Praeger, 1969), p. 111.
[66] Ajit Kumar Ghose, *Agrarian Reform in West Bengal* (Geneva: International Labour Organisation, 1980), p. 24.
[67] Bhattacharyya, "An examination of Land Reforms," p. 192.
[68] Ghose, *Agrarian Reform*, p. 24.
[69] B.K. Sarkar, Director of Land Records and Surveys, West Bengal, "A Note on Barga Recording in West Bengal," October 23, 1979 (typewritten), p. 2.

From an organizational point of view mobilization of the middle peasantry and viable sharecroppers makes good sense, though from a Marxist point of view it should be secondary rather than primary, and only a stepping stone to later mobilization of agricultural labor. The basic problem of the rural CPM is that it has got stuck on the secondary front, and has become unwilling to push the struggle further to mobilize agricultural labor. The CPM and CPI were caught "between the alternatives: the ideological and tactical aim of organizing the landless laborers, or the politically expedient tactics of attempting to gain support of the small landholders."[70] Originally the CPM took the former position of attempting to give primacy to agricultural labor. However, this theory of Konar, Sundarayya, and the radicals was never fully implemented in practice, and with the ascendancy of the moderates was replaced by a middle and rich peasant orientation. Sundarayya denounced the tendency of the moderates to neglect agricultural labor in favor of maintaining a declining tenancy system of sharecropping.

We should not confuse this tenancy problem as if that is the predominant issue before the vast rural masses and ignore the tremendous growth of agricultural labour due to pauperisation on the one hand and due to the development of capitalism in agriculture itself. To go on exaggerating the problem of tenancy out of proportion and out of reality is in fact to ignore the need to concentrate on agricultural labour, their demands, their struggle and organisation.[71]

The actual implementation of Operation Barga is left to the bureaucracy and does not depend on party organization in the villages. Though they have been asked to assist, the program is not dependent on their cooperation. As a one time intervention, the program ends when the *barga* is recorded, the actual enforcement being left to the villagers and the administration. This was in contrast to the second United Front when Konar organized land-grab movements undertaken by the peasants themselves. The change in orientation was noted by the Maoists who claimed that the bureaucracy was being "asked to play the comic role of peasant leaders" and "pioneering cadres for building supportive peasant organisations."[72]

The Land Reforms Commissioner, D. Bandyopadhayay, who was at that time considered sympathetic to the Left Front, was energetic in implementing the program and forcing junior officials to fulfil their target quotas. As no updated

---

[70] Sally Ray, "United Front Government and the Politics of Agrarian Struggle in West Bengal, 1967 and 1969–70," *Australian Outlook*, August 1971, p. 214.

[71] Sundarayya, *Explanatory Note*, p. 36.

[72] CPI, "The Left Front Government in West Bengal: From Class Collaboration to Class Capitulation," *For a New Democracy*, vol. 1, no. 10–12, December 1978–February 1979 (Calcutta: Provisional Central Committee of the Communist Party of India – Marxist–Leninist), p. 84.

settlement record of holdings was available, the junior officials had to go into the field and depend on local knowledge of the land tenure holdings. Under pressure from their superiors to fulfil targets, the recordings were done in a summary fashion depending often on the local Left Front cadres to select the appropriate Barga beneficiaries. As a result a lot of legitimate sharecroppers were not recorded and Left Front supporters were recorded in their place. The local bureaucrats were intimidated into accepting the Left Front Barga applicants as this was the easiest method and the most beneficial to their own career prospects. As a result a lot of injustices were done to legitimate sharecroppers. One senior IAS officer who had complaints of improper recording investigated, and found the complaints justified, tried to get the Land Reform officials to review the cases. The officials said they had been instructed that reviews of cases were not to be entertained and that there was nothing they could do. As a result of their inability to appeal, the plaintiffs went to court, resulting in a backlog of cases that will continue into the twenty-first century. The injustices resulting from Operation Barga are not likely to be quickly if ever rectified, and in that sense the delay alone represents an injustice. By forcing recordings without doing the groundwork of an updated land settlement survey the officials were overdependent on the local party leaders to select beneficiaries, resulting in injustices which could not be easily changed. With the Left Front not knowing how long it would be in power, the temptation to record as many sharecroppers as quickly as possible without waiting for a laborious land survey, was undoubtedly present. In retrospect a land survey should have been undertaken first, given the length of time the Left Front remained in office; but at the time more political dividends could accrue from faster recording even at the expense of many wrong recordings.

The government initially stated that the recording of *bargadars* would be completed within a year.[73] However, four years later, on the completion of the Left Front first five year term in office, only half had been recorded. Though the program had only envisaged recording about 3/4 of the total *bargadars*, by 1982, the CPM Minister of Land and Land Reforms, Benoy Choudhury, admitted that 1,125,826 *bargas* or only 55 percent of this target group had been recorded.[74] Nearly a year later the total of recorded *bargas* stood at 1,198,000 as of November 1982, indicating from the recording of only an additional 73,000 that the program was slowing down without fulfilling the target.[75] By September 1985 the figure stood at 1,329,087, indicating the program had slowed down even further and had virtually come to a halt, as seen from the

[73] West Bengal, Board of Revenue, *Workshop on Land Reforms*, p. 1.
[74] West Bengal, Board of Revenue, Statistical Cell, Land Reforms in West Bengal, VII, p. 1.
[75] *The Statesman*, February 22, 1983.

Number of
sharecroppers
recorded

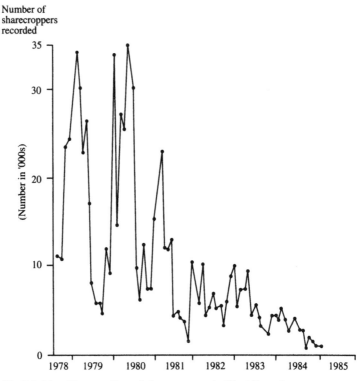

Fig 2.1. Monthly recording of sharecroppers in West Bengal

*Source:* West Bengal, Research & Training Cell, Directorate of Land Records & Surveys, *Statistical Handbook on Bargadars of West Bengal* (Calcutta, mimeographed, April 1985), pp. 26–8

graph of recordings (figure 2.1). Government statistics indicate an average landholding of .97 acres with a total statewide area of 2.5 million acres under *barga* cultivation. Therefore the *bargas* should number over 2,500,000.[76] The Land Revenue Minister has spoken of there being 3 million *bargas* in West Bengal, while the Commissioner for Agriculture and Community Development in West Bengal says there are 3.3 million.[77] Land Reforms officials think the figure closer to 3 million. The Left Front government has since claimed there are only between 1.5 and 2 million sharecroppers, but this seems to be a case

[76] West Bengal, Board of Revenue, Statistical Cell, *Land Reforms in West Bengal: Statistical Report – IV* (Calcutta: 1980), p. 1.
[77] S.K. Ghosh, "Land and Agricultural Development" in *Land Reforms in Eastern India*, edited by Manjula Bose (Calcutta: Jadavpur University, 1981), p. 196.

of reducing the population to fulfil the unattained target.[78] If the original estimates are correct, less than half the bargas have in fact been recorded. That the government's own deadline had to be extended five times, to four times its original length, to achieve half its target does not speak well of the operation, yet the Government of West Bengal stated "this is an achievement any government could be reasonably proud of."[79] According to the CPM state committee publication this record of *barga* recording "was inconceivable during the previous Congress regimes."[80] This ignores the fact that as far back as 1962–65 in a previous land settlement operation 1.3 million sharecroppers had been recorded, 800,000 with completed records and 500,000 with an initial Khasra record. Thus Operation Barga was merely a repeat performance of an earlier Congress government achievement, which has not been mentioned by the Left Front and its supporters.

The Club of Rome's endorsement of Operation Barga stated the Left Front "has carried out a genuine land reform, by distributing to the share-croppers title deeds for the lands they were working."[81] This view is shared by Atul Kohli:

Less than 60,000 sharecroppers were registered over the last three decades in West Bengal. In about five years, however, the CPM regime has succeeded in registering over 1.2 million *bargadars*. Compared to the past performance of the Congress and other governments in the area, therefore, the CPM's current success is spectacular.[82]

Nossiter is equally effusive describing this as a "truly remarkable accomplishment."[83]

These steps culminated in the celebrated "Operation Barga" in 1978, an effective campaign to register sharecroppers officially. Prior to 1977 only some 275,000 share-croppers had bucked the rural power structure and registered. By December 1984 as many as 1.3 million of the estimated 2 million West Bengal sharecroppers – 96 per cent of all "tenants" – were recorded.[84]

Thus both Kohli and Nossiter present an inaccurate account of the Congress record in sharecropper registration accepting Left Front claims as accurate.

The most important shortcoming of the program, however, is not in the total numbers recorded. A survey by the West Bengal Land Reforms Office in Burdwan district covering 10 percent of the district during 1985 found that:

---

[78] West Bengal, *Economic Review 1984–85* (Alipore: West Bengal Government Press, 1985), p. 16.

[79] Tushar Kanti Ghosh, Directorate of Land Records and Surveys, "Operation Barga in West Bengal's Land Reforms", 1980, pp. 18–20; West Bengal, Board of Revenue, Statistical Cell, Land Reforms in West Bengal, *Statistical Report V* (Calcutta: 1981), p. 1.

[80] West Bengal State Committee, *Significant Six Years*, p. 44.

[81] Bertrand Schneider, *The Barefoot Revolution: A Report to the Club of Rome* (London: IT Publications, 1988), p. 107.

[82] Kohli, *The State*, p. 124.

[83] Nossiter, *Marxist State Governments*, p. 184.

[84] *Ibid.*, p. 139.

11.22 percent of the recorded *bargadars* have been thrown out of possession by one way or the other. When converted into the district figure the number of such unfortunate *bargadars* comes to 12,000 ... We would like to keep the issue open for the Social Reformers, Land Reforms Experts and Legislators to think how better protection can be afforded to these actual tillers who are also the weaker section of Society. There is no reason to believe that the *bargadars* ... have given up their *barga* rights willfully. Rather the only presumption is that they have been forced to surrender their rights out of fear in the face of intimidation and coercion (whether direct or indirect).[85]

Considering that Burdwan is arguably the strongest Communist district in the state, this may be an understatement of the true statewide position. The Communist presence has been largely unsuccessful in stopping evictions. If one assumes this rate of eviction to be general, and there is no reason to assume it is not, then more *bargadars* are now being evicted than are being recorded at the current level of 1 to 2 thousand (see figure 2.1), in which case the program should never be ended. The four-village survey by Kirsten Westergaard indicates that even when registration takes place, the traditional lower crop share was generally practised.[86] An ILO sponsored survey of fourteen West Bengal villages found that among recorded sharecroppers the legally stipulated 3/4 crop share was observed more in the breach. Only one of the eleven villages where share proportions were specifically mentioned applied the legal 3/4 share even though all these villages had some recorded sharecroppers.[87] As the twin objectives of Operation Bargadar were 1) to prevent eviction through recording tenancy, and 2) to ensure 3/4 crop share, it is clear that in both respects the program has failed. The mere fact of recording does not in itself appear to make any difference, either to evictions or to increasing crop shares. Its achievement has been only cosmetic as far as can be determined, though as a public relations exercise with analysts of the West Bengal scene it has been fairly successful. If the program has achieved anything at all it may have consolidated the hold of the big sharecroppers–landowners who leased in land from smaller landholders, who would not now have the resources and influence to prevent their lands being lost to bigger recorded sharecropper–landowners. In an inequitable rural society those with the most land can use their resources to ensure their names are recorded and the legal shares enforced, something the weaker party has much greater difficulty in enforcing. The dichotomy between claims and performance was indicated by a government publication dealing with Operation Barga in the

---

[85] West Bengal, Land Reforms Office, *Bargadars in West Bengal and an Assessment of their position in the Field* (mimeographed, August 1985), pp. 13–14.

[86] Kirsten Westergaard, *People's Participation, Local Government and Rural Development: The Case of West Bengal* (Copenhagen: Centre for Development Research, March 1986), pp. 58, 67, 86.

[87] Nripen Bandyopadhyaya, *Evaluation of Land Reform Measures in West Bengal: A Report* (Calcutta, Cyclostyled by the Centre for Studies in Social Sciences, 1983).

CPM stronghold of Burdwan, which stated "the performance of the officers connected with the programme was considered fair, though the claim achievement was much below the target."[88] This is perhaps understandable since state projects are not usually finished on schedule if they are completed at all. For all the delay it was one of the most important attempts at land reform currently underway in the country, which says little for land reform in India. The Government explained the delay by noting "the enormous difficulties of carrying out any programme aiming at slight realignment of social and economic power structure in a highly stratified agrarian society."[89] Noting the fluctuation in the monthly averages of *barga* recordings from a high of 45,000 in November 1978 to a low of 5,000 in January 1981, the Land Reforms Commissioner stated that "this oscillation indicates that the momentum of the official machinery cannot be kept at a steady pace merely by pressure from above. It perhaps highlights the lack of matching pressure from below to sustain or to accelerate the pace of recording."[90]

The bureaucracy felt frustrated by this lack of cooperation and mobilization from the peasant organizations and Leftist parties in the villages. A workshop of the leading administrators of the program stated that "the participants felt that the expected degree of support from the voluntary organisations was not forthcoming."[91] In what could be taken as a criticism of the Left Front parties, the Land Reform Commissioner noted that "in the absence of a well-spread-out and vibrant organisation of the genuine poor ... meaningful agrarian reforms are not possible." Operation Barga therefore "will fall far short of achieving substantial progress for its supposed beneficiaries."[92] The Scheduled Castes and Tribes Commission took the same position, noting:

that the middle level peasantry are controlling the most powerful rural Organisation named as Kisan Sabha (CPM) as well as the Panchayati Raj institutions in the State. The Commission, therefore, apprehend that on account of political barriers from the middle level peasantry who controls the reins of local bodies at the grass root level it may not be possible to push through the drive for the recording of *bargadars* in the same manner as it was initially envisaged by the State government.[93]

The Commission noted that the government bureaucracy at the grass-roots

[88] West Bengal, Land Reforms Office, *Land Reforms*, p. 11.
[89] West Bengal, Statistical Cell, Board of Revenue, *Land Reforms in West Bengal V*, p. 1.
[90] West Bengal, Statistical Cell, Board of Revenue, *Land Reforms in West Bengal: Statistical Report VI* (Calcutta: West Bengal Government Press, 1981), p. 2.
[91] West Bengal, Board of Revenue, *Workshop on Land Reforms (II) Operational Decisions*, May 4–5, 1979 (Calcutta: West Bengal Government Press, 1979), p. 2.
[92] D. Bandyopadhayay, "Road to Effective Land Reform," 1979 (mimeographed), p. 12.
[93] India, Ministry of Home Affairs, *Second Report of the Commission for Scheduled Castes and Tribes*, April 1979 – March 1980 (Delhi: Government of India, Controller of Publications, 1981), p. 428.

level had a "class-caste affinity" with the vested interests and these field officers "often hobnobbed with the middle level peasantry" which partly accounted for slackness in *barga* recordings.[94] In its tour of West Bengal the Commission found many of the CPM Panchayat leaders, while outwardly paying "lip service to the problem of recording of *bargadars*", in fact had sympathy with the landowners which they themselves were.[95] CPM followers were recorded as *bargadars* to the exclusion of others, while *barga* families who had been working the same land for generations, found CPM followers had been recorded in their place. The identity of the CPM local leadership with the landowners was confirmed by district level officials including the District Magistrate and Additional District Magistrate (Land Reforms) of Burdwan, who indicated this as the reason for non-cooperation with *barga* recordings in some of the CPM Panchayats.[96] Lacking their own independent power the poor sharecroppers and agricultural laborers were at a severe disadvantage without the active support of the Leftist parties in the villages or the local bureaucracy. The Commission felt that when the "*bargadars* are able to stand up on their own the composition of the rural leadership is bound to change for the better. The Commission feel that this may happen but it may be time-consuming."[97]

The control of the middle peasants and vested interests over the Panchayats, the Kisan Sabha, and Leftist parties in the villages often hindered implementation and meant that the bureaucracy had to undertake the program single-handed. The Leftists in the state administration blamed the lack of *barga* recording on poor and inadequate party mobilization of the peasantry, which was often the result of the CPM Kisan Sabha being controlled by middle peasants who would lose if the *barga* laws were enforced. The party made no efforts to remove this obstacle within their own organizations. The bureaucracy and the local party organizations in the villages were therefore often working at cross purposes and with the opposition of the local village party units and the Panchayats. The lack of party backup and complementary political work for Operation Barga and the Panchayat program created frustration among Marxist bureaucrats who felt they were doing all the work but the party was trying to take all the credit for it, even when the party's local units were opposing the program. The failure of *bargas* to come forward to have their names recorded when the land settlement officers visited the villages was in large part the failure of the ruling parties. The conception of the schemes was good but the parties, by failing to give proper local support, hindered the program at the village level. Those that were recorded are probably disproportionately from the more prosperous landowning sharecropper

94  *Ibid.*
95  *Ibid.*, p. 427.
96  *Ibid.*
97  *Ibid.*

class. The program therefore in practice served to perpetuate rural inequalities
and will make equalization through land reform more difficult in future.

Though West Bengal's own Land Reforms Commissioner considered the
tenancy program to have failed, the World Bank's *1990 World Development
Report* claimed West Bengal's tenancy reforms were "successful."[98] The World
Bank's 1990 Report states the West Bengal tenancy rights are inheritable but
only the richer and more influential sharecroppers are likely to be able to inherit
anything, as even many living recorded sharecroppers are unable to retain rights
to their land. If one examines the considerable number of fraudulently recorded
tenants, recorded tenants who lost their land anyway, and the nearly 2/3rds who
were never recorded in the first place, as well as the majority who appear not
to get the legally stipulated crop shares, then the World Bank's claim of program
success is dubious. The World Bank's sources and their criteria for success are
not specified in the report but if the West Bengal program is a model of success,
one has to wonder how many other models of successful development would
stand up to critical scrutiny.

In short, the landed classes have not disappeared, but what has happened is that
elite classes have consolidated their position in the Communist movement and
prevented further Left Front reform moves, as interviews with government program
administrators confirm. Operation Barga was ended not by a lack of deserving
*bargadars*, but because the Left Front's influential sharecropper supporters were
already recorded and further work would threaten those supporters already in
possession of land. Hence it was stalled by Communist politicians in deference to
their elite base interests though less than half the *bargadars* were ever recorded.[99]

For all the praise the Left Front received for Operation Barga, the recording
of *bargadars* was initiated by the British administration and like the Scheduled
Caste affirmative action programs, the British initiators of these programs
should be credited for launching programs the Communists later adopted. Even
a comparison of Congress era *barga* recording methods with those of the Left
Front does not reveal any better quantitative or qualitative performance by the
Communists.[100]

**Rural credit and inputs**

Land Reform without institutionalized support in the form of inputs and credit
could lead to the loss of redistributed land given to the landless, through

---

98 World Bank, *World Development Report 1990* (Oxford: Oxford University Press, 1990),
   pp. 64–5.
99 Theodor Bergmann, *Agrarian Reform in India* (New Delhi: Agricole Publishing Academy,
   1984), p. 152.
100 Todarmal, *Land in West Bengal* (Calcutta: Anima Prakashani, January 1990), pp. 390–1.

mortgaging of land as collateral to secure loans at exorbitant rates of interest from landowners and moneylenders. It was critical to the success of the land-reform program that the required input and particularly credit could be given to *bargadars* and recipients of vested lands. "Merely recording the names of the sharecropper and alloting vested lands to the landless cultivators will not be meaningful and effective unless institutional credit is provided to such farmers to reduce substantially their economic dependence on the landlord-cum-money lenders."[101]

The money lenders charge from 150 to 300 percent interest per annum.[102] Since short-term production and consumption loans in rural West Bengal amount to Rs. 450 crores a year, of which less than Rs. 150 crores is provided by institutions such as banks and cooperatives, this leaves the remaining Rs. 300 crores coming from the private moneylenders often at exorbitant rates of interest.[103] As is usually the case, it is the richer farmers who have access to bank and cooperatives credit at low interest rates and the poorest sections that have to pay the exorbitant rates to moneylenders, who themselves may borrow at lower interest rates from the banks. The effect of moneylenders charging exorbitant rates of interest resulted, according to one survey in West Bengal, in 32 percent of landless casual laborers reporting having lost some of their land for failure to repay loans.[104] A publication of the Directorate of Land Records and Surveys noted the traditional deficiencies of the rural credit system.

Against this backdrop of the usurious moneylenders doing monopoly-style rolling business, the Co-operatives and the Commercial Banks pale into insignificance. Co-operative sector, by and large, continued to be at the beck and call of the big man as it has been rightly pointed out in some responsible quarters. The Co-operative movement seems to be nothing more than a hand-maid of the vested interests with the reluctant acquiescence, if not willing consent, of the authorities concerned. It is a pity that the Co-operative institutions at all levels have degenerated into hot-beds of corruption. That most Co-operatives could not up till now meet the needs of small or marginal farmers is a widely accepted fact. In other words, even now the new allottees in Government lands are looked down upon as untouchables. From knowledgeable sources it is heard that the big farmers and absentee landlords used the money borrowed from Co-operatives at attractive rates of interest for usury. The alibi made for pursuing their selfish ends by the influential members of the Co-operative Societies who are big men, is that the poor farmers cannot offer much security. If we fall back upon our own experience in the field

[101] West Bengal, Board of Revenue, *Guidelines for Bank Financing to Share-Croppers and Patta Holders* (Calcutta: Government of West Bengal, 1981), p. 5.
[102] Government of India, *Second Report of the Commission for Scheduled Caste and Scheduled Tribes*, p. 245.
[103] Roy Choudhury, "Land Reforms."
[104] Pranab Bardhan and Ashok Rudra, "Labour Employment and Wages in Agriculture: Results of a Survey in West Bengal, 1970," *Economic and Political Weekly*, November 8–15, 1980, p. 1945.

we can say that the small farmers are more scrupulous in repaying instalments in due time than the rich landlords as the small men cannot afford the luxury of litigation.[105]

As with the other programs in rural development, the primary avenue for implementation was through the state bureaucracy and public sector enterprises. The Board of Revenue instructed the local administration to ensure that the target of credit recipients was reached within the time schedule in order for the banks to be able to recycle the loans in subsequent crop seasons.[106] The government later readily admitted that this program was less than a resounding success. The Land Reforms Commissioner stated only 5 percent of the target population could be covered in 1979–80 leaving 95 percent still dependent on the traditional moneylenders.[107] "Organisational deficiency" has prevented a breakthrough being achieved. The government claimed that "nowhere else so much effort was made to give institutional financial cover to so many having so little." However, with only 0.16 percent of the 2 million target population receiving bank loans under the Integrated Rural Development Program the Board of Revenue admitted it had "miles to go."[108] A year later after the 1981 Kharif season, under which a target of 1/4 million sharecroppers and assignees of vested land were to be given institutional finance, only 130,655 actually became beneficiaries. The Land Reforms Minister claimed this was "no mean achievement," but admitted that while *bargadar* recording was half completed, institutional finance for them had "only made a beginning."[109] The number of recipients had increased from 59,114 in 1979 to 71,054 in 1980 to 130,655 in 1981. However, the percentage of the yearly target achieved was less impressive in 1980 and 1981 than in 1979.[110]

The state government blamed the deficiencies of the program on reservations found among a section of the bank managerial staff as to the viability and desirability of financing non-bankable entities like sharecroppers and marginal farmers. The government claimed these nationalized banks had a social obligation to develop these target groups. It accused them of acting as an "instrument … syphoning off resources from one area to the other, thereby helping in an unbalanced and lopsided development of regions and groups."[111] It noted the regional disparity between deposits and advances in Bengal compared to other

[105] Sarkar and Prasannan, *What Happened*, p. 12.
[106] West Bengal, Board of Revenue, *Workshop on Land Reforms* II, p. 6.
[107] West Bengal, Statistical Cell, Board of Revenue, *An Evaluation of Land Reforms in West Bengal* (Calcutta: Government of West Bengal, 1981), i.
[108] West Bengal, Statistical Cell, Board of Revenue, *Land Reforms*, V, iv.
[109] West Bengal, Statistical Cell, Board of Revenue, *Land Reforms*, VII, p. 2.
[110] *Ibid.*, p. 13.
[111] West Bengal, Combined Statistical Cell of the Board of Revenue and Land Utilisation and Reforms and Land and Land Revenue Department, *Bank Loan and West Bengal: A Statistical Report* (Calcutta: West Bengal Government Press, 1979), p. 1.

areas of the country. While in Bengal the percentage of advances on deposits is only 63.89, and when Calcutta is excluded, a mere 27.42 percent (Calcutta being 79.58 percent), Chandigarh is 346.65 percent, and Delhi is 117.53 percent. The bias against Bengal and most particularly rural Bengal is undoubted.[112]

However, the banks' reluctance to advance loans in rural West Bengal is not without justification as the proportion of loans recovered is significantly lower in West Bengal than in other major states. In June 1975 it was 31.6 percent in West Bengal and improved to 41 percent in June of 1978 but in both cases remained below the all-India figure of 50.2 percent of agricultural advances. In 1979–80, the major bank with the best recovery rate was the State Bank of India with only 32 percent, followed by the Central Bank 30 percent, United Bank 28 percent, and the United Commercial Bank 26 percent.[113] From the banker's point of view it would be ruinous to throw good money after bad by advancing loans in West Bengal. The Governor of the West Bengal State Level Bankers' Committee noted "that due to poor repayment of Bank loans it might be difficult on the part of the Commercial Banks to go in a bigger way for financing under the scheme during the current year."[114] While a State Government conference on Land Reforms in the CPM stronghold of Burdwan noted that 75 percent of the loan target had been fulfilled in 1979, only 27.9 percent of the loan advanced was recovered. "The role expected to be played by the Panchayats and the officials for processing those cases left much to be desired. The negative approach of the institutions was one of the main reasons for the poor perform- ance so far this year and the *bargadars* were hardly to be blamed."[115] The Director of Land Records and Surveys noted that the loan scheme's "success is not likely to be encouraging due to various constraints including apathy of the Commercial banking system."[116]

The budgetary allocation to the rural credit program by the Communist government indicates a lack of political will required for meeting the demand of the poorer classes for loans. Though resources are necessarily limited, much more could have been done to meet the demands had priority been given to the program. Without an alternative source of credit it would be too much to expect the poor to jeopardize their only source of finance, namely the landlords, by recording themselves as *bargadars*. The Scheduled Castes and Scheduled Tribes Commission suggested to Jyoti Basu and the Minister of Land Reforms that as the performance of the banks in providing financial assistance to the poorest sections was unsatisfactory the state government could step in by

[112] *Ibid.*, p. 1.
[113] West Bengal, Board of Revenue, *Guidelines for Bank Financing*, p. 7.
[114] *Ibid.*, p. 90.
[115] West Bengal, Land Reforms Office, *Land Reforms*, p. 11.
[116] Ghosh, "Operation Barga," p. 24.

providing 50 crores as loans which would meet the input requirements of a million acres of land. With a budget of over 1,000 crores this should not be difficult and could form the base of a revolving fund to provide financial coverage to *bargadars* and the weaker sections.[117] Nothing, however, came of this.

This failure at the Ministerial level was reflected at the local level in apathy to the program of financing the poorer sections by the rural leftist parties. As most activists of the left parties were of "rural middle class origin with vague ideological commitments" they were "chary regarding the prospects of the poor farmers swamping the limited institutional finance through sheer numbers, at the expense of their own segments." This reluctance of the rural Communist cadre to help the poorer classes only added to the traditional obstacles the poorest classes faced in obtaining credit. The vast majority of farmers who utilize bank and co-operatives credit "belong to large, medium and 'bhadralok' segments of the rural society." They have the resources, contacts and procedural knowledge lacking in the lower classes, that enables them to avail themselves of institutional credit.[118] The bias of the institutions against lending to the poor has thus been reflected in the rural left which, as beneficiaries of these loans, are reluctant to have them further distributed to the poor, thereby threatening their share of institutional loans and interest from money lending. The failure of the Left Front to make an effective breakthrough in providing credit, far less removing the power of the moneylenders, was one of its greatest failures.

Ironically, the very reason for which banks were reluctant to further expand rural credit later became a serious problem for the Left Front as well. Their whole program of rural credit was being jeopardized by non-payment of loans. In July 1982, the Left Front decided to launch a campaign to persuade farmers not affected by drought to start repaying agricultural loans so that their base could be further expanded, but "the campaign actually never got going in an appropriate form." In fact when, at the behest of Jyoti Basu, the Minister of Co-operatives, Nirmal Bose of the Forward Bloc attempted to have 100 crores of the state's cooperative bank's agricultural loans recovered it met resistance from the Left. "In some districts, like Birbhum, Midnapore, Burdwan etc., the Left parties, including the local CPM, and the CPI activists, had brought out leaflets exhorting the farmers not to pay up bank's loan."[119] "This non-cooperation by a segment of the Left" led Jyoti Basu to issue a statement printed in hundreds of thousands of copies calling for repayment of loans, as otherwise institutional credit could not expand.[120] It appeared unlikely that the loans could be recovered if penalties were not imposed, as persuasion had proved futile.

---

[117] Government of India, *Second Report of Commission for Scheduled Castes and Tribes*, p. 428.
[118] Barman, "New Challenges," p. 39.
[119] *Ibid.*
[120] *Ibid.*

Due to the problems and delays in obtaining Presidential assent for any legislation passed by the State government, the Left Front has attempted to utilize existing Congress legislation to implement progressive changes. Given the lengthy Congress rhetoric about eradicating poverty and the development of socialism, much of the legislation was considered suitable for use in the Communist government. The Congress being notorious for not implementing its own progressive legislation, it remained only for the Communists to implement the old Congress laws. This applied also to organizations set up by the Congress for social change. One important organization created to introduce the "Green Revolution" in West Bengal was the Comprehensive Area Development Corporation which would select one or two small areas in each district for intensive inputs of fertilizers, high-yielding variety seeds, and irrigation facilities. The introduction of the Green Revolution to these areas would have a demonstration effect and result eventually in the spread of modern farming throughout the State. When introduced in the early 1970s the program was denounced by Hare Krishna Konar.

The whole planning is not only impractical, but is a matter of deep conspiracy. It is a mischievous plan made to expedite the development of capitalism on the base of landlordism. It means the development of a few landlords at the top in the capitalist way with the help of public money and rapid pauperisation of the ordinary and poor peasants, eviction of share-croppers and increase in the number of the landless and jobless agricultural labourers at the base. With the help of this project a few middle peasants may go upwards but most of them will inevitably experience a rapid fall.[121]

When the Communists came to power in 1977, they inherited the project and decided to adopt it as a means of effecting rural change and development. A member of the CPM State Committee was put in charge of the program and its original scope was expanded. New programs for providing loans to the rural poor and village cooperatives, and sale of cheap consumer goods were introduced.[122] While these new programs of the Left Front Government were claimed to be largely successful, the original project of introducing the Green Revolution to Bengal was only partly successful. The introduction of High Yielding Variety crops depended on reliable sources of irrigation which, due to malfunctioning of tubewell pumps and erratic power supply, was not always forthcoming. The original CADP proposal under the Congress ministry that 9,300 villages be supplied with 3,000 MW of electricity for irrigation proved impossible with only 50 MW being provided in 1979.[123] If the electricity and

---

[121] Konar, *Agrarian Problems*, p. 239.
[122] West Bengal Comprehensive Area Development Corporation, "Comprehensive Area Development Project, Ratua-II P.O. Sambalpur-tal, Malda" (mimeographed).
[123] Timir Basu, *Bhumi*, p. 14.

pumps were not functioning at critical periods the crops would be ruined and the losses to the experimental farmers would provide a demonstration effect opposite to that originally intended. The Left Front, by adding new programs to the CADP for the benefit of the rural poor, did not alter the fundamental deficiency in the original programs of introducing the Green Revolution. The results after five years under Left Front direction proved disappointing. V.M. Rao, in reviewing the CADC publication *Rural Development: The CADC Experience* by Biplab Dasgupta, notes that the statistics presented indicated no improvement in cropping intensity or yields as a result of increased irrigation.[124] "The repayment of crop loans disbursed by the Farmers' Service Co-operative Societies appears to be as tardy as elsewhere in the country."[125] Though the program appears to have brought some limited benefits to those areas covered, the demonstration effect for other areas appears to be minimal, if it exists at all.

The program for credits and inputs appears to have been the least successful of the Left Front programs in agrarian transformation. It was, however, at least a program, albeit a grossly inadequate one. The attempt to improve agricultural wages, though advocated by the Left Front, was never even to reach the stage where it could justifiably be called a program.

### Agricultural labor

Of the Left Front's policies for social transformation those relating specifically to agricultural labor have received a secondary priority. Operation Barga's publicity has far outweighed that given to the struggle for agricultural labor, though in a Communist Party it would have been logical to assume the opposite to be the case. Aside from the Food for Work Programme, the major policy designed to benefit the agricultural labor class has been minimum wage legislation passed by Congress governments, with subsequent increments. That this has been observed in the breach is common knowledge. Jyoti Basu admitted this but has argued that even if not fully implemented some increase towards this goal has taken place. It has also been correctly pointed out that implementation of this legislation would hurt the middle peasants who can least afford to pay the legal minimum wage. Implementation of the legislation has therefore been virtually a dead issue with the Left Front government, though it has always made a point of utilizing existing progressive Congress legislation for social change. Though Jyoti Basu and the CPM have made claims for improving wages of agricultural labor, no convincing evidence has been produced from any

---

[124] V.M. Rao, "Promises on Rural Development," *Economic and Political Weekly*, December 18, 1982, p. 2045.
[125] *Ibid.*

quarter to prove this assertion. It is universally accepted, however, that minimum wage legislation was not implemented. A survey by the West Bengal
Labour Department found 90 percent of agricultural laborers were not aware of
the minimum wage rates fixed by the Government.[126] The legislation can
therefore be taken as meaningless. This is proved by the state government's
monthly and district-wise agricultural wage statistics for nine categories of
agricultural labor, where hardly any of the 34,614 rates listed since 1960 met
prevailing minimum wage legislation. A computer analysis of these wage rates
since January 1960 illustrates the plight of agricultural labor in West Bengal.
The wage rates are published by the Central government in *Agricultural Wages
in India* for men and women field labor, defined as ploughmen, sowers, reapers,
harvesters, weeders, and transplanters.[127] The main defect of the statistics is that
when the series was begun in 1951, they were planned to be published within
a few weeks of collecting but now take up to a decade to publish. The raw data
for 1969 to 1972 had therefore to be collected from the Central Government
office in Simla and the data from then till June of 1981 from the West Bengal
Government which tabulates it. This is the only data collected which shows
monthly and district-wise trends over time.[128] As statistics are collected from
more developed *taluka* villages, generally "the most commonly current" wage
rates reported are, if anything, on the high side of the prevailing district
wages.[129] The wage rates for *Agricultural Wages in India* are 30 to 40 percent
higher than the National Sample Survey and also Agricultural Labour Enquiries
of the *Studies in Economics of Farm Management*.[130] While *Agricultural Wages
in India* are collected by local land revenue officials from an average of 1.8
villages per district, NSS average 12 and SEFM 10.[131] As the latter two surveys
do not make for comparisons over time and area with political developments
they are unsuitable for detailed political analysis. *Agricultural Wages in India*
are for casual labor which is more active in labor agitations than attached
labor.[132] Casual labor represents 83.6 percent of Bengal agricultural labor

[126] Kalyan Chaudhuri, "Disturbed Industrial Situation," *Economic and Political Weekly*, May 1,
      1976, p. 657.
[127] Government of India, Directorate of Economics and Statistics, Ministry of Agriculture, "Agri-
      cultural Wages in India." Government of India, Labour Bureau, Ministry of Labour, *Agricul-
      tural Labour in India: A Compendium of Basic Facts*, p. 4.
[128] V.M. Rao, "Agricultural Wages in India – A Reliability Analysis", *Indian Journal of Agricul-
      tural Economics*, vol. 27, no. 3, July–September 1972, p. 38.
[129] *Ibid.*, pp. 39–49; A.V. Jose, "Real Wages, Employment, and Income of Agricultural Labourers,"
      *Economic and Political Weekly*, Review of Agriculture, March 1979, p. A16.
[130] V.M. Rao, "Agricultural Wages in India – A Reliability Analysis," p. 38.
[131] V.M. Rao, "Agricultural Wages in India," p. 43.
[131] *Ibid.*, pp. 49–50.
[132] Pranab Bardhan and Ashok Rudra, "Types of Labour Attachment in Agriculture: Results of a
      Survey in West Bengal, 1979." *Economic and Political Weekly*, August 20, 1980, p. 1483.

compared with 10.9 percent who are attached and 5.5 percent who are semi-attached.[133] As the rates reported tend to be from relatively prosperous and developed villages, connected to urban influences, the laborers surveyed are more exposed to political struggles, and therefore would be among the first to experience improvements introduced by Communist governments. Payment in kind has been converted to their cash equivalents according to the local retail prices for these commodities.[134] As analysis of money wages in themselves has certain limitations due to inflation, a real wage has been determined for male and female agricultural labor by districts and months. The only available deflater collected on a district and monthly basis that corresponds to the *Agricultural Wages in India* series is the minimum price of common rice. This is also the best single deflater for agricultural labor as it constitutes 46.14 percent of their total expenditure. Total food expenditure is 80 percent with non-food items occupying the remaining 20 percent.[135] These 1971–72 figures have remained relatively stable over the years. In the 1956–57 statistics, rice comprised 49.51 percent of agricultural labor expenditure with total food expenditure at 79.11 percent, fuel and light 8.17 percent, and clothing 5.16 percent.[136] All West Bengal wage rates were deflated by the minimum price of rice and the General Consumer Price Index for Agricultural Labour. The period since 1960 was divided into the six periods of Congress and Communist government for purposes of comparison. Also the districts were divided into the three categories of strong, medium, and weak Communist influence to determine correlations between levels of Communist organization and improvements in real and money wage rates. The strong Communist districts were Burdwan, Hooghly, Howrah, and Twenty-Four Parganas, the districts of medium Communist strength were Nadia, Bankura, Midnapore, and West Dinajpur, and the weak Communist districts were Darjeeling, Jalpaiguri, Murshidabad, Malda, Cooch Behar, Purulia, and Birbhum. As the districts of greatest Communist strength were also the most economically developed industrially and agriculturally it was not possible to isolate economic variables from political factors. There were no strong Communist districts that were relatively under-developed or economically developed districts that were weak Communist bases. For this reason the strong Communist districts had the highest wages followed by medium and weak districts, but what influence Communism or economic development had on this pattern cannot be definitely determined. However, the lack of significant fluctuation between regimes indicates that the higher wages

[133] *Ibid.*, p. 1480.
[134] A.V. Jose, "Real Wages," p. 16.
[135] *National Sample Survey*, July 1971–June 1972, 26th round, report no. 239, "Consumer Expenditure for Cultivator Households, Rural," p. 65.
[136] *National Sample Survey*, August 1956–August 1957, 11th and 12th rounds, p. 96.

in strong Communist districts are due to greater economic development and urban influence.

The Communists claim they are in a sufficiently strong position in rural Bengal to lead agricultural labor in struggles for wage increases. This would certainly appear to be the case. According to the CPM, its West Bengal Kisan Sabha has increased from 1,284,892 in February 1978 to 3,860,992 in 1981 and 7,037,456 in 1987.[137] As 70 to 80 percent of them are said to be from the agricultural labor and poor cultivator class, this is a sizeable force considering that the 1981 census figures for West Bengal are 3,848,852 agricultural laborers and 4,751,647 cultivators.[138] The CPM states that "the driving force of peasant struggle are the agricultural labour and poor cultivators" who "even from the point of view of numbers form 70 percent of the cultivator class."[139]

From 1973 in our state, on the basis of wages and other demands there has been sincere effort to organise the peasant movement and struggle. The participation of agricultural labour and poor cultivators in different political matters has considerably increased.[140]

The CPM claims to have made significant improvements in the lot of agricultural labor. "Last year during sowing and harvesting seasons, the struggle was spread over the whole state and it covered nearly 12,000 villages. About 1/3rd of the agricultural labourers have been able to get 8 Rupees 10 paise minimum wages. In the remaining 2/3rd section of agricultural labour there has been an increase in wages by at least 2 to 3 Rupees."[141] The General Secretary's Report to the CPM's All India Kisan Sabha made even greater claims of success, claiming full implementation of the 9.58 Rupees minimum rate had been achieved, with some places even having wages higher than this minimum wage.[142] Jyoti Basu has said that, eschewing the confrontational strategy of the Second United Front, the Left Front is now attempting to improve the lot of agricultural labor gradually. While admitting minimum wage legislation has not been fully implemented, he has claimed that conditions have improved.[143] The State government's 1980–81 *Economic Review* claims a 20 percent increase in

---

[137] West Bengal State Conference, CPM, *Rajnaitik-Sangathanik Report* ("Political Organisational Report"), 14th Plenary Session, December 27, 1981–January 1, 1982 (Calcutta: West Bengal State Committee, CPM, March 1982), pp. 55–6; Sampad Pal, "West Bengal Thirteen-Point Programme to Streamline Party Organisation," *People's Democracy*, March 27, 1983, p. 5.

[138] "Government of India, Registrar General and Census Commissioner, *Census of India 1981, Provisional Population Totals: Workers and Non-workers*, Series-1, Paper 3, 1981, p. 46.

[139] West Bengal State Conference, *Rajnaitik-Sangathanik*, p. 69.

[140] *Ibid.*, pp. 69–70.

[141] *Ibid.*, p. 69.

[142] All India Kisan Sabha, Twenty-Fourth Conference of the 8th–11th November, 1982, Midnapore, West Bengal, *General Secretary's Report* (New Delhi: 1982), p. 32.

[143] Jyoti Basu meeting with the Commission for Scheduled Castes and Scheduled Tribes, October 24, 1979.

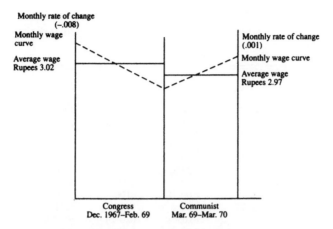

Fig 2.2. Explanatory note on agricultural wages

Average wages during a regime (3.02 and 2.97) show the average of all the monthly wages in that period of rule. However it does not show if, during the regime, wages were increasing or decreasing. Rate of change does this. It shows if wages were improving or not during the life of a regime. Thus if wages are improving the rate of change numbers will be positive (.001) and if wages are decreasing over that regime (-.008) the numbers will be negative. Both real and money wages and rates of change are required to give an accurate picture of the level and changes in wages over time. Since regimes do not change with calendar years an annual index would be a less accurate fit when comparing political regimes, than the present one which marks regimes changes down to the month rather than the whole year. For the above example, wages were on average higher during the Congress government (3.02) than under the Communists (2.97). This shows the laborers were on average better off under the Congress. This average, without rate of change figures, would be misleading, however. In fact monthly rate of change shows the workers were becoming worse off under Congress (-.008) while under the Communists their lot was improving (.001).

the agricultural labor wages rate from 1976–77 when the Left Front came to power and 1979–80.[144] "This improvement in wage rate has been as much a result of additional production programmes undertaken in agriculture as of an increase in the bargaining power of the agricultural labourers."[145]

The computer analysis of the West Bengal Governments' agricultural wage statistics does not bear this out however (see tables 2.10–13). This can be seen

[144] West Bengal, *Economic Review 1980–81* (Calcutta: West Bengal Government Press, 1981), p. 41.
[145] *Ibid.*

Table 2.10. *Average daily wages (Rupees) of male agricultural field labor and monthly rate of change (shown in brackets) over political regimes in districts of varying Communist strength*

| Regime | | Bengal | Weak | Medium | Strong |
|---|---|---|---|---|---|
| Congress | Jan. 60 – Mar. 67 | 2.08 | 2.00 | 1.98 | 2.30 |
| | | (0.013) | (0.008) | (0.015) | (0.017) |
| Communist | Apr. 67 – Nov. 67 | 3.11 | 2.94 | 3.02 | 3.51 |
| | | (0.085) | (0.085) | (0.108) | (0.060) |
| Congress | Dec. 67 – Feb. 69 | 3.02 | 2.73 | 3.22 | 3.33 |
| | | (-0.008) | (-0.003) | (-0.020) | (-0.010) |
| Communist | Mar. 69 – Mar. 70 | 2.97 | 2.78 | 3.09 | 3.18 |
| | | (0.001) | (0.003) | (0.000) | (0.000) |
| Congress | Apr. 70 – June 77 | 3.99 | 3.70 | 4.22 | 4.28 |
| | | (0.030) | (0.030) | (0.030) | (0.040) |
| Communist | July 77 – June 81 | 6.42 | 6.11 | 6.30 | 7.07 |
| | | (0.025) | (0.024) | (0.001) | (0.049) |

Table 2.11. *Average daily wages (Rupees) of female agricultural field labor and monthly rate of change (shown in brackets) over political regimes in districts of varying Communist strength*

| Regime | | Bengal | Weak | Medium | Strong |
|---|---|---|---|---|---|
| Congress | Jan. 60 – Mar. 67 | 1.63 | 1.57 | 1.54 | 1.84 |
| | | (0.009) | (0.006) | (0.010) | (0.128) |
| Communist | Apr. 67 – Nov. 67 | 2.40 | 2.09 | 2.41 | 2.92 |
| | | (0.067) | (0.051) | (0.073) | (0.087) |
| Congress | Dec. 67 – Feb. 69 | 2.38 | 2.06 | 2.54 | 2.78 |
| | | (-0.008) | (0.003) | (-0.023) | (-0.013) |
| Communist | Mar. 69 – Mar. 70 | 2.23 | 1.96 | 2.31 | 2.63 |
| | | (0.004) | (0.008) | (0.010) | (-0.007) |
| Congress | Apr. 70 – June 77 | 3.24 | 2.95 | 3.38 | 3.59 |
| | | (0.030) | (0.027) | (0.030) | 0.034) |
| Communist | July 77 – June 81 | 5.47 | 5.10 | 5.45 | 6.13 |
| | | (0.026) | (0.027) | (0.007) | (0.044) |

*Source:* Compiled by computer from Government of India periodical *Agricultural Wages in India.*

by calculating the average daily wages and real wages (measured in kilos of rice) over three Communist and three Congress regimes, as well as the rate of change during these regimes. The rate of change is the slope coefficient of the linear time trend obtained for a particular regime, whereas the average daily wage is the arithmetic mean.

The sharpest pattern is the fall in real wages as a result of the 1966–68 period

Table 2.12. *Average daily real wages (kilos of rice) of male agricultural field labor and monthly rate of change (shown in brackets) over political regimes in districts of varying Communist strength*

| Regime | | Bengal | Weak | Medium | Strong |
|---|---|---|---|---|---|
| Congress | Jan. 60 – Mar. 67 | 2.71 (-0.009) | 2.65 (-0.012) | 2.71 (-0.003) | 2.85 (-0.010) |
| Communist | Apr. 67 – Nov. 67 | 1.68 (-0.122) | 1.67 (-0.079) | 1.74 (-0.089) | 1.66 (-0.170) |
| Congress | Dec. 67 – Feb. 69 | 1.95 (0.055) | 1.90 (0.046) | 2.16 (0.048) | 1.95 (0.071) |
| Communist | Mar. 69 – Mar. 70 | 2.30 (0.005) | 2.20 (-0.001) | 2.47 (0.003) | 2.34 (0.004) |
| Congress | Apr. 70 – June 77 | 2.16 (0.003) | 2.11 (0.002) | 2.40 (0.001) | 2.11 (0.006) |
| Communist | July 77 – June 81 | 3.15 (-0.004) | 3.02 (-0.006) | 3.15 (-0.016) | 3.43 (0.007) |

Table 2.13. *Average daily real wages (kilos of rice) of female agricultural field labor and monthly rate of change (shown in brackets) over political regimes in districts of varying Communist strength*

| Regime | | Bengal | Weak | Medium | Strong |
|---|---|---|---|---|---|
| Congress | Jan. 60 – Mar. 67 | 2.14 (-0.008) | 2.08 (-0.010) | 2.11 (-0.003) | 2.30 (-0.009) |
| Communist | Apr. 67 – Nov. 67 | 1.29 (-0.091) | 1.19 (-0.061) | 1.38 (-0.076) | 1.37 (-0.120) |
| Congress | Dec. 67 – Feb. 69 | 1.53 (0.041) | 1.43 (0.038) | 1.70 (0.030) | 1.64 (0.056) |
| Communist | Mar. 69 – Mar. 70 | 1.73 (0.007) | 1.55 (0.006) | 1.84 (0.009) | 1.93 (-0.002) |
| Congress | Apr. 70 – June 77 | 1.73 (0.005) | 1.66 (0.005) | 1.91 (0.005) | 1.77 (0.006) |
| Communist | July 77 – June 81 | 2.67 (-0.001) | 2.52 (-0.002) | 2.72 (-0.011) | 2.97 (0.007) |

*Source:* Compiled by computer from Government of India, Directorate of Economics and Statistics, Ministry of Agriculture, periodical *Agricultural Wages in India*, and Government of West Bengal, Department of Food and Supplies, monthly rice prices.

of food scarcity, which was alleviated with the Central Government supply of grain and improved crops after Presidential Rule was imposed from December 1967. It is only recently that the losses incurred during this period were made up in terms of real wages. The Bengal average male real daily wage for field labor over six regimes was 2.71, 1.68, 1.95, 2.30, 2.16, and 3.15 kilos of rice.

There does not appear to be any significant difference in rate of change between Congress and Communist regimes in terms of money or real wages. This would seem to indicate that economic factors such as food shortages and crop failures have the greatest impact. In comparing the Left Front government with the previous Congress regime there are no statistically significant differences in rates of change. The Congress regime in fact had a slight increase in the rate of change for money and real wages, followed by a decline in real wages under the Communists and a decline in the increase of money wages. The average real and money wages were higher under the Left Front government than the preceding Congress regime due to the gains made under the Congress not being completely eroded under the Communist regime. The lack of any statistically significant difference between the two regimes in rate of change indicates that the Communists have not made any noticeable impact in terms of agricultural wages since coming to power, despite claims to the contrary. As real wages have decreased from a base of 100 in 1950–51 to 87 in 1956–57 and to 72 in 1965–65, the long term trend may be to a decline.[146]

The strong, medium, and weak Communist districts were defined according to the traditional bases of Communist support in the early 1960s. Over the years the Communists increased their support to the point where they were in a dominant position in all the districts. This expansion of influence into weak Communist areas has not been reflected in an improvement in agricultural wages relative to strong Communist areas. The disparity between strong and weak districts has remained relatively constant despite the Communists' achieving a dominant influence in formerly weak Communist districts. Money wages in weak Communist districts as a percentage of strong districts over the six political regimes was 86.9, 83.76, 81.98, 87.42, 86.4, and 86.4 percent for male field labor. In real daily wages the disparity was less, with weak districts as a percentage of strong being 92.9, 100.6, 97.4, 94, 100, and 88 percent over political regimes. The same relatively constant disparity is also apparent with female field labor where real daily wages in weak Communist areas are 90.4, 86.86, 87.1, 80.31, 93.78, and 84.84 percent of strong Communist districts. This also holds true for money wages with weak as a percentage of strong being 85.32, 71.57, 74.10, 74.52, 82.17, and 83.19 percent.

Female money wages have converged with male agricultural field labor wages over the years being 80, 78, and 78 percent of male wages in strong, medium and weak Communist districts under the first Congress regime, gradually improving to 87, 87, and 83 percent of male wages under the present Communist government. This improvement appears not to be related to changes in political regimes.

---

[146] N. Krishnaji, "Wages of Agricultural Labour," *Economic and Political Weekly*, Review of Agriculture, September 1971.

It seems that Communist presence and organizational expansion as reflected in electoral results and party membership have not been reflected in improvements in the lot of agricultural labor. The avoidance of class struggle by the Left Front does not appear to have delivered any tangible benefit to agricultural labor. Though there is provision for penalties for non-implementation of minimum agricultural wages, enforcement is inadequate at best and often non-existent in many areas.[147] Enforcement would alienate middle peasants, who often lack the means to pay the minimum wage, thereby alienating the party from its own rural cadre and party base. As agricultural labor's participation in the party is limited, it would require their mobilization by party cadre from the middle peasantry who have nothing to gain from it and often something to lose. Kirsten Westergaard's four-village study provides an example of CPM policy in Burdwan district which must have been repeated numerous times during the Left Front government.

There has been considerable agitation among agricultural labourers in the area. This has caused a conflict within the CPI(M), as the agitation was led by the previous pradhan – also CPI(M). It was contrary to the party line which is against movements likely to alienate the middle peasants. As a result of a strike amongst agricultural labourers the daily wage rate was increased to Rs. 10 (including cash and kind payment). There was much resentment among many of the landowning peasants who are dependent on hired labour, and the pradhan was dismissed by the party leadership.[148]

The poor performance in the agricultural labor field might be understandable had a similar situation existed elsewhere in India. However, West Bengal has the worst record of any Indian state from 1982–85, with Assam and occasionally Karnataka having worse real wage rates prior to this period (table 2.14). Had West Bengal agricultural productivity been less than other states this might have been justifiable, but Bengal had the fourth highest productivity per agricultural worker among Indian states during 1984–85 indicating the economic potential for higher real wages.[149] Between 1984–85 and 1986–87 West Bengal per capita rural income from agriculture lagged behind only Punjab and Haryana, indicating the exploitation of agricultural labor appears to be the worst in India.[150]

The Left Front suggested that by its decentralizing of the political process, and placing more power in the hands of village councils, reform implementation would be more effective. However, the experience has been that decentralization without prior displacement of local elites only enhances the local elites'

---

[147] West Bengal, Department of Labour, *Labour in West Bengal 1980* (Calcutta: Government of West Bengal, 1981), pp. 54–5.
[148] Westergaard, *People's Participation*, pp. 73–4.
[149] A.V. Jose, "Agricultural Wages in India," *Economic and Political Weekly*, Review of Agriculture, June 25, 1988, p. A50.
[150] Government of West Bengal, *Economic Review 1989–90* (Calcutta: State Planning Board, 1990), p. 14.

Table 2.14. Index numbers of real wage rates of male agricultural laborers

| Year | Andhra | Assam | Bihar | Gujarat | Kar-nataka | Kerala | Madhya Pradesh | Maha-rashtra | Orissa | Punjab | Tamil Nadu | Uttar Pradesh | West Bengal |
|---|---|---|---|---|---|---|---|---|---|---|---|---|---|
| 1956–57 | 100.00 | 100.00 | 100.00 | 100.00 | 100.00 | 100.00 | 100.00 | 100.00 | 100.00 | 100.00 | 100.00 | 100.00 | 100.00 |
| 1957–58 | — | — | — | — | — | — | — | — | — | — | — | — | — |
| 1958–59 | 119.20 | 88.70 | 98.33 | 109.52 | 111.51 | 102.60 | 103.70 | 99.25 | 98.10 | 101.31 | 97.04 | 113.92 | 92.02 |
| 1959–60 | 111.20 | 96.23 | 97.50 | 136.73 | 113.67 | 106.49 | 125.40 | 87.31 | 91.43 | 106.11 | 95.56 | 121.52 | 96.32 |
| 1960–61 | — | — | — | — | — | — | — | — | — | — | — | — | — |
| 1961–62 | 124.00 | 94.98 | 100.00 | 117.01 | 114.39 | 118.18 | 118.80 | 114.18 | 119.05 | 120.52 | 94.07 | 143.04 | 108.59 |
| 1962–63 | 121.60 | 86.61 | 94.17 | 115.65 | 110.79 | 136.36 | 113.20 | 106.72 | 115.24 | 121.40 | 105.19 | 144.30 | 89.57 |
| 1963–64 | — | — | — | — | — | — | — | — | — | — | — | — | — |
| 1964–65 | 116.00 | 73.64 | 89.17 | 102.04 | 97.84 | 120.78 | 93.40 | 93.28 | 127.62 | 103.06 | 99.26 | 110.13 | 94.48 |
| 1965–66 | 112.00 | 77.82 | 88.33 | 103.40 | 74.10 | 122.73 | 91.50 | 89.55 | 109.52 | 131.00 | 97.04 | 135.44 | 90.80 |
| 1966–67 | 109.60 | 66.53 | — | 101.36 | 72.66 | 134.42 | 81.10 | 97.76 | 104.76 | 102.18 | 88.89 | 120.25 | 89.57 |
| 1967–68 | 120.80 | — | — | 108.84 | 74.10 | 154.55 | — | 100.75 | 80.00 | 117.47 | 97.04 | 121.52 | 79.14 |
| 1968–69 | 118.40 | 71.97 | 104.17 | 110.88 | 76.26 | 145.45 | 92.40 | 107.46 | — | 141.48 | 100.74 | 164.56 | 87.73 |
| 1969–70 | 120.80 | 82.85 | — | 106.80 | — | 143.51 | 92.45 | 115.67 | — | 153.28 | 96.30 | 155.70 | 93.25 |
| 1970–71 | 139.20 | 80.75 | 106.67 | 120.41 | 89.21 | 148.70 | 99.00 | 108.21 | 95.24 | 155.02 | 108.89 | 174.68 | 88.96 |
| 1971–72 | 132.47 | 74.45 | 103.55 | 126.37 | 92.30 | 165.18 | 98.30 | 104.42 | 94.76 | 152.37 | 107.48 | 175.35 | 92.58 |
| 1972–73 | — | — | — | — | — | — | — | — | — | — | — | — | — |
| 1973–74 | 115.38 | 72.75 | 96.91 | 95.89 | 81.01 | 147.77 | 87.20 | 83.62 | 85.48 | 128.81 | 101.04 | 147.74 | 80.40 |
| 1974–75 | 102.36 | 63.69 | 87.81 | 79.55 | 67.95 | 123.01 | 74.30 | 69.59 | 70.16 | 122.19 | 81.10 | 130.76 | 70.64 |
| 1975–76 | 121.89 | 72.39 | 122.10 | 110.42 | 84.31 | 140.44 | 99.80 | 71.55 | 83.50 | 140.05 | 101.19 | 209.60 | 87.61 |
| 1976–77 | 135.43 | 76.82 | 148.21 | 149.46 | 103.32 | 161.17 | 115.10 | 80.38 | 115.58 | 154.57 | 99.66 | 221.33 | 90.79 |
| 1977–78 | 140.97 | 79.21 | 127.54 | 137.54 | 114.07 | 165.87 | 108.80 | 84.13 | 110.08 | 147.19 | 97.91 | 175.08 | 98.64 |
| 1978–79 | 157.00 | 77.09 | 127.52 | 145.58 | 116.00 | 169.12 | 114.30 | 95.43 | 113.93 | 150.40 | 109.64 | 191.73 | 99.68 |
| 1979–80 | 155.65 | 72.99 | 119.06 | 135.05 | 108.64 | 178.06 | 102.90 | 93.18 | 103.43 | 143.59 | 116.32 | 181.64 | 95.53 |
| 1980–81 | 150.76 | 74.68 | 113.97 | 128.77 | 96.97 | 195.24 | 98.30 | 84.48 | 100.11 | 131.74 | 113.73 | 159.91 | 91.76 |
| 1981–82 | — | — | — | — | — | — | — | — | — | — | — | — | — |
| 1982–83 | 170.17 | 83.26 | 125.36 | 144.20 | 96.32 | 201.77 | 124.20 | 99.04 | 91.48 | 133.55 | 109.77 | 189.04 | 81.86 |
| 1983–84 | 187.89 | 88.31 | 131.77 | 155.38 | 93.46 | 179.79 | 136.40 | 117.30 | 114.80 | 143.44 | 107.25 | 215.43 | 87.36 |
| 1984–85 | 201.97 | 96.95 | 155.63 | 182.53 | 92.38 | 195.65 | 143.30 | 132.71 | 133.92 | 151.04 | 128.99 | 229.63 | 92.37 |

Source: A.V. Jose, "Agricultural Wages in India," Economic and Political Weekly, June 25, 1988, p. A55.

power.[151] West Bengal decentralization, as reflected in revitalization of village councils, did not enhance the power of the old elite, but created a new one, a class less wealthy than the old pro-Congress elite, but nevertheless better off than the majority of the rural population. It is this middle class that has delivered to the Communists repeated electoral victories with the support of the lower classes. However, political control by the middle class has been consolidated in their hands with no evidence of power displacement to the lower class. The old pro-Congress elite is unlikely to regain political control in the rural areas in the foreseeable future, as their class and vote base is too narrow to displace the middle classes that have seized the political initiative. While this has given electoral stability to the Communist government, it has not brought appreciable benefits to the lower classes. Agricultural laborer wage demands have not been pressed, since the wealthiest landed elite might be able to meet their demands, but the middle classes would be unlikely to be able to compete with them.[152] Hence avoidance of class struggle becomes imperative. The CPM policy of a rural middle- and lower-class alliance, though it may have validity elsewhere in India, has become outdated in West Bengal where it has served to enhance middle-class dominance. The party by default has given priority to middle-class control, by attempting to control lower-class aspirations within demands acceptable to the middle landed classes in the middle–lower class alliance. To turn around and promote lower-class demands however, would threaten violent confrontation, possible Central government removal of the Communist government, not to mention alienating the middle-class elite and narrowing the Communist electoral base to the lower-class majority. The disruption of food production is also a possibility though difficult to predict in advance. The Left Front has good political reasons for not pressing for radical reform; however, its compatibility with lower-class politicization and socio-economic emancipation is dubious. The lower class can best be described as giving critical support to the Left Front, perceiving it as having done more than the Congress, but providing little in terms of real life improvement. One survey found the lower-class perception to be that of deterioration in living standards due to drought, crop failure, and rising prices.[153] An updated National Sample Survey of three districts found food consumption to have stagnated and housing conditions to have deteriorated, but social consumption to be improved by 1985–86 over the 1972–73 survey.[154] Without organized action and a viable

[151] Ronald J. Herring, *Land to the Tiller: The Political Economy of Agrarian Reform in South Asia* (New Haven: Yale University Press, 1983), p. 53.

[152] Westergaard, *People's Participation*, p. 75.

[153] *Ibid.*, pp. 46, 86.

[154] Nikhilesh Bhattacharya, Manabendu Chattopadhyay, Ashok Rudra, "Changes in Level of Living in Rural West Bengal: Social Consumption," *Economic and Political Weekly*, August 15, 1987, p. 1410.

alternative, the lower class views do not translate into changing vote patterns or influencing Left Front government policy.

The West Bengal experience adds little to the debate on whether agrarian reform must precede a power redistribution in favor of the lower classes. The lower classes never seized the dominant political position in rural Bengal, and agrarian reform was never implemented to a degree sufficient to change economic relations and create lower-class economic self-sufficiency. The threat of lower-class *embourgeoisement* through land reform thus never arose. With 3,000 million Rupees of annual rural short-term loans still provided by private moneylenders out of 4,500 million, both land and independent credit sources are largely beyond the reach of the poor.[155] The lower classes remain both politically and economically subordinate. Though the Left Front did succeed in lowering the dominant power base from the old Congress elite to a new and frequently opportunist pro-Communist middle-class elite, thereby depriving the old elite of access to some state patronage, the subordinate classes have been left politically and economically marginal in the village policy formation process. While a more militant lower-class base might have prodded the Left Front into more radical action, the CPM has strived to prevent such radical actions from threatening the lower–middle peasant alliance.[156] As long as dependency relations have every prospect of being maintained with tacit government acceptance, such militancy is unlikely to lead to a successful outcome for the lower classes, hence it is logical for them to maintain conflict within limits acceptable to the dominant elite. One agricultural laborer according to Kirsten Westergaard expressed "the general view" of the CPM: "We joined the CPI(M) with many hopes. But it seems we only tagged along fruitlessly to their processions and meetings. We did not get any benefit. We have no hopes of getting any benefit from anyone. Even the panchayat could not do anything."[157]

It was not that the top CPM leadership was inherently more sympathetic to the class interests of the middle class than the poorer classes, rather the political dynamics of the rural economy made their pursuing agricultural labor interests problematic.

Because in irrigated paddy cultivation all but the very smallest holdings require hired labor at peak periods, and labor costs are the single largest component of cultivation costs, small owners and tenants are likely to oppose one of the major demands of a radical labor movement, higher wages. This makes an alliance between the "semilandless" and landless difficult to achieve. It also means that where small owners and

[155] P. Roy Choudhury, "Land Reforms: Promise and Fulfilment," *Economic and Political Weekly*, December 27, 1980, p. 2172.
[156] Westergaard, *People's Participation*, p. 74.
[157] *Ibid.*, p. 76.

tenants are numerous relative to labor, resistance to the organization of labor will be greater.[158]

Such class differences, while making the Left Front's avoidance of class struggle understandable, do not preclude a more radical strategy. "It is almost certainly true that landless agricultural labor is too economically dependent for sustained independent political action, but as others have noted, labor's economic dependence may be offset by political organization."[159] The Left Front failed to use its considerable state power to support political organization for lower-class demands, thereby maintaining worker dependency by default. While the West Bengal Communists have achieved unprecedented success for an Indian opposition party in their state re-election record, through avoiding divisive class demands, the emancipation of the lowest classes on which their ideology is based has been put on the backburner. It remains to be seen if this situation will ever be transformed into a more radical strategy in favor of the lower classes.

[158] Marshall M. Bouton, *Agrarian Radicalism in South India* (Princeton: Princeton University Press, 1985), p. 145.
[159] *Ibid.*, p. 146.

# 3    Poverty alleviation and redistribution programs

Socio-economic change in rural West Bengal required implementation of social welfare programs as well as the redistribution of income from the surplus-producing farmers. The intent and effectiveness of these policies was at the outset determined by the class orientation of the policies concerned. Given the difficulty of categorizing the rural poor, Scheduled Caste and Tribe statistics can be used as a fair approximation of the poorer classes and for this reason they have been singled out for particular analysis. The property redistribution programs were conceived to redistribute a surplus but ultimately provided the primary benefits to those with the surplus production capacity.

While these policies were conceived to assist the poor, in their actual implementation propertied classes were to obtain disproportionately greater benefits. The ability of influential groups to obtain preferential access to government goods and services was hardly unique to West Bengal. However, some observers have assumed that, having a Communist government, West Bengal would circumvent these rural elites, thereby providing a unique experiment in Indian development policies. Ultimately, however, traditional values, dependency relationships, and lack of Left Front mobilization were to prevent the changes that had been initially expected.

## Untouchable desegregation

With South African desegregation, the Indian untouchables will be the only segregated population left in the world. As 2.4 percent of humanity and 1/7th of India's population, they have been by far the largest segregated population. Though Bengal has the third highest percentage of untouchables in India, I have been told by Bengali professors that Bengali untouchables are not segregated, unlike in some other parts of India. Dr. Arun Ghosh, Member of the Indian Planning Commission and former Vice-Chairman of the West Bengal State Planning Board claims, that in West Bengal "no prejudice exists in relation to caste or creed."[1] Atul Kohli states that as far back as the twelfth century

---

[1] Arun Ghosh, *West Bengal Landscapes* (Calcutta: K.P. Bagchi & Co., 1989), p. 208.

"untouchables would eat with members of cleaner castes."[2] On a tour of rural Bengal with a Calcutta-based CPM cadre, I enquired if the Brahmin-owned restaurant we were in admitted untouchables. Without needing to ask, the CPM member replied they would not be allowed. According to Rabindra Ray "The Bengali Hindu population ... takes its religion, including caste (particularly in matters of marriage) as seriously as the rest of India. Ideas about pollution and untouchability are the same as elsewhere in India."[3] In fact, under the Left Front even rural government school feasts continue to be segregated, and this continuity of segregation has been definitively confirmed by village-level anthropological studies.[4]

With the existence of segregation confirmed by scholars of rural Bengal, it is surprising that academics who have devoted part of their careers to development policy in West Bengal should be unaware of its existence. As this segregation represents a daily humiliation for millions of rural untouchables, it seems extraordinary that so many in the Bengali elite are unaware of its continuance. My impression from visiting South Africa was that the psychological effects of Apartheid were less than those of untouchability, due to the common culture and shared values of Hindu philosophy creating greater personal internalizing of ascribed lower social rank. Such was the strength of caste feeling that Bengali untouchable CPM members complained that only a "minuscule" minority of CPM members were free of caste prejudice. This in part explains the failure of the Left Front to desegregate rural Bengal even though this untouchability has been legally abolished. As only 22 percent of the West Bengal population are Scheduled Caste this is not sufficient to create a majority constituency in favor of actual (as opposed to formal) desegregation. While in South Africa a segregated majority provides the Communists with a useful political issue, in India integration is divisive. In this sense, untouchability is closer to the Black American situation, though the lack of an Indian constituency analogous to the dominant American non-southern majority, makes desegregation difficult for the Indian left to support in practice. According to one advocate of untouchable human rights, "The high caste Hindu Left leadership ignored the problem of Untouchables because it found the issue inconvenient. The very fact that in the Marathwada massacre and Gujarat caste

---

[2] Atul Kohli, "From Elite Activism to Democratic Consolidation: The Rise of Reform Communism in West Bengal" in *Dominance and State Power in Modern India: Decline of a Social Order, Volume* II, edited by Francine Frankel and M.S.A. Rao (Delhi: Oxford University Press, 1990), p. 395.

[3] Rabindra Ray, *The Naxalites and Their Ideology* (Delhi: Oxford University Press, 1988), p. 58.

[4] Marvin Davis, *Rank and Rivalry: The Politics of Inequality in Rural West Bengal* (Cambridge: Cambridge University Press, 1983), p. 76; Ronald P. Rohner and Manjusri Chaki-Sircar, *Women and Children in a Bengali Village* (Hanover: University Press of New England, 1988), p. 40.

war, no left party has sided with the Untouchables, verifies the total disenchantment of the Untouchables with the Indian Marxists."[5] Significantly the Left
Front does not include desegregation in its election manifestos; there are
probably more votes to be lost than gained on the integration issue. Though
hardly a principled position, it is politically expedient.

This exclusion of untouchables from decision-making power within the
Communist Parties is typical of other parts of India as well. The CPI and CPM
in the Punjab "are dominated not by the proletariat but by the landowning and
ruling castes ... Once incorporated, they effectively became the Communist
movement in the Punjab, stamping it with an identity radically different from
anything that seemed sympathetic to the Untouchables."[6] In essence the Communist

strategy is to give something to everybody, not to subtract resources and power from the
rich and dominant classes and add them to the poor and oppressed classes. Otherwise
the CPM, for example, would have used the powers it already has to heavily tax rural
kulaks and transfer substantial benefits to the poor. It prefers, however, to demand a
rising share of centrally collected revenue with which to disburse patronage.[7]

Such comments on the nature of Indian Communism are relatively rare, however, as the dominant academic view assumes rather than questions Communist
determination to emancipate the lowest classes. The law banning the practice
of untouchability is constitutionally within the Left Front's power to enforce. It
did not implement the law because of the reactionary nature of its party and
class base. Despite the radical rhetoric of the Communists, their rural base is
arguably more reactionary than the South African white community, which has
resulted in untouchability outlasting South African Apartheid even in a Communist state and in a country where it is legally abolished.

The Left Front government has taken a class view of the problems affecting
the rural poor. The Chief Minister has indicated that with this perspective of
helping the rural poor the "Untouchable" Scheduled Castes will also be
helped, not on a caste basis but as members of the poorest and most exploited
classes. Therefore as a large portion of the rural poor are Scheduled Castes and
Tribes they will be major beneficiaries of the Left Front rural development
programs.[8]

As the Untouchable Castes have been listed or Scheduled in the Indian
constitution as eligible for reserved jobs and various subsidies designed to

---

[5] V.T. Rajshekar, *Dalit: The Black Untouchables of India* (Atlanta: Clarity Press, 1987), p. 76.

[6] Mark Juergensmeyer, *Religion as Social Vision: The Movement against Untouchability in
20th-Century Punjab* (Berkeley: University of California Press, 1982), pp. 198, 201.

[7] Achin Vanaik, *The Painful Transition: Bourgeois Democracy in India* (London: Verso, 1990),
p. 132.

[8] Jyoti Basu interview with the Scheduled Castes and Tribes Commission, October 24, 1979.

remove their social disabilities, statistics are more extensively gathered on their socio-economic progress than on the poor in general.

There has been a certain ambiguity in West Bengal regarding the practice of untouchability. On the one hand it has the second largest number of untouchables in India comprising 11.46 percent of India's untouchables. These 12,000,768 represent 21.99 percent of Bengal's population, the third highest proportion in the country.[9] However, as there is little intercaste violence aimed specifically at untouchables the problem has never been taken very seriously. Compared with the thousands of murders and rapes in other parts of India, the intercaste harmony of Bengal has appeared to confirm the impression of Bengalis being tolerant of intercaste differences. However the violence against the Scheduled Castes in other parts of the country is also a reflection of the increasing awareness and resistance of the untouchables to upper caste oppression which had hitherto been accepted as legitimate. The violence is indicative of the inability of the upper castes to legitimize their rule among the lowest castes, violence being the last resort of the upper castes determined to perpetuate their control in the face of their loss of moral authority.

The lack of atrocities in West Bengal is therefore not in itself indicative of the absence of prejudice and discrimination or of its general practice. The contemporary anthropological studies of rural West Bengal make it clear that untouchability is very much an accepted practice with enforcement of residential segregation, endogamous marriages, ritual ranking, and proscribed behavior on the basis of caste.[10] There has been no serious or concerted attempt by the Left Front to remove any of these prohibitions. Their elimination has never been an issue in the Left Front and the continued existence of casteism is just one of the givens of the situation. Though there are no legal constraints, the Left Front has left the issue of increasing social consciousness in abeyance. Their Marxist class analysis seems to have left this form of social discrimination that is peculiar to India beyond the scope of immediate government concerns. The central government has an administration specifically dealing with discrimination, and this is replicated at the state government level where each state has its own administration to deal with untouchability. As with the rest of the country however, this administration in West Bengal has little influence or power. It often takes the form of an academic and statistical monitoring service with more of a cosmetic function than a real one.

Among political parties there is a general tendency not to appoint the best Scheduled Caste candidates for party tickets to constituencies reserved for the

---

[9] Government of India, Ministry of Home Affairs, *Selected Statistics on Scheduled Castes*, Occasional Papers on Development of Scheduled Castes (2) (New Delhi: Government of India Press, June 1984), pp. 3, 9.

[10] Davis, *Rank and Rivalry*, pp. 134–41.

Scheduled Castes. This could be because the better candidates might establish local bases of their own and pose a threat to the party leadership. As a result, with a few exceptions, the party candidates chosen tend to be those most subservient to the party leadership and most likely not to press their own community interests. This reservation policy had its historical basis in the Poona Pact of 1932. The colonial government was willing to grant separate constituencies for the untouchables which would have given them independent control of parliamentary and assembly seats, thereby providing them with a potential balance of power and greater political influence. To prevent the political emancipation of the untouchables which could have threatened Congress interests, Gandhi went on a fast forcing the untouchable leader Dr. Ambedkar to capitulate and agree to untouchable candidates being nominated by political parties in general constituencies which the higher castes would numerically dominate and politically control. As a result of Gandhi's efforts the untouchables have remained politically subservient, without the independent power base they would otherwise have acquired.

Ironically the Bengal Scheduled Castes were more influential during the last years of the colonial period when they were communally better organized and the colonial government promoted them as a counterfoil to the Congress landowners. As long as the Scheduled Castes formed a coalition with the Muslims it was impossible for the Congress to form a government in Bengal from which they were effectively excluded from 1927 till independence and partition. With partition the Scheduled Castes' political importance as a possible coalition partner holding the balance of power was permanently lost, both in West and East Bengal which came under complete caste Hindu and Muslim dominance respectively.

### Education

Next to agrarian reform, the most important avenue for improving the economic and social conditions of the poorer classes is probably education. Providing education should not be an exceptionally difficult problem for Bengal as the state has a long literary tradition and a highly developed cultural output in literature and fine arts. As a concurrent subject under the Indian constitution giving joint jurisdiction to state and central governments, the state has in practice a wide measure of educational autonomy. Bengali intellectuals had achieved a status both nationally and internationally out of proportion to the size of their state, and this cultural output was a continuing source of pride to a state so often depicted by outsiders as a byword in poverty.

The education system the Communists inherited on coming to power in 1977, however, had been deteriorating over many years. Referring to the Congress period the *New York Times* correspondent, Joseph Lelyveld, noted:

when exams are held, the invigilators or proctors who are supposed to prevent cheating are threatened with physical violence if they dare to try. Routinely, most of them collect five rupees, about 70 cents, from each student as a fee for looking away. New questions are rarely posed for then it would be impossible to locate the answers in the "bazaar notes."[11]

The Communists attempted to prevent this mass copying with some limited success.[12] Nevertheless the invigilators continue to collect their rupees from students during exams regardless of whether the student cheats, and they keep a lookout for the Vice-Chancellor's flying squad to warn the cheating students. Once when the law students were caught by the flying squad they went on a rampage in protest.

With such a pervasive decline in educational standards it would have been difficult for the Communists to improve conditions. Rather than reform the system they had inherited they attempted to strengthen their influence within it.

The Communists had for some time a strong and even dominant position in the teachers' unions at various levels, so when the Communists came to power it was only to be expected that they would move to consolidate their position.[13] In doing so they were carrying on the traditions of their Congress predecessors who had continually interfered in academic affairs. The Vice-Chancellor of Calcutta University was traditionally the nominee of the ruling Congress Party and prone to implement their directives, though the new Communist-appointed Vice-Chancellors were said to have been more subservient to the ruling party. Without directives from party headquarters or the Secretariat no significant initiatives were undertaken. To get a post-secondary teaching post in Calcutta required connections and string-pulling with the Communists. Such blatant interference created resentment in the academic community. One college teacher noted

with shock that academic institutions are being turned into a happy hunting ground for politicians. Previously the practice was largely to appoint non-political and administrative heads as presidents of academic institutions. But now those belonging to the ruling parties, regardless of their competence and suitability, have been inducted into such posts to the obvious detriment of education and culture.[14]

From the Communist point of view such interference was considered legitimate as they felt they had previously been discriminated against in appointments and promotions and this realignment only served to redress the balance. There

---

[11]  Joseph Lelyveld, *Calcutta* (Hong Kong: The Perennial Press, 1975), p. 31.

[12]  Ashis Chakrabarti, "Muddle in Academic Field," *The Statesman*, August 25, 1982, p. 10.

[13]  West Bengal State Conference, CPM *Rajnaitik-Sangathanik Report* ("Political-Organizational Report"), 14th Plenary Session, December 27, 1981–January 1, 1982 (Calcutta: West Bengal State Committee, CPM, 1982), p. 74.

[14]  Chakrabarti, "Muddle," p. 10.

were criticisms that academic standards were suffering as a result of less academically qualified candidates being chosen, but from the Communist viewpoint it was necessary to stack the institutions with its own nominees so the educational system could be reoriented to a progressive outlook that served the people. In reality the educational system in India was deteriorating and Bengal was no exception, so a few transfers and appointments would hardly make much difference. The biggest controversy raised at the post-secondary level was over transfers of Presidency College professors from this premier college of Calcutta University to district colleges, where it was alleged their talents would be wasted on less meritorious students. Fundamentally it was a question of whether a top college dominated by Bengal's elite should be maintained as a privileged institution or the limited resources spread to enhance less prestigious colleges attracting less meritorious students of generally lower socio-economic status. The controversy, however, in due course died down with the leaders of the CPM-controlled teachers' union receiving the prize postings to Presidency College, where they would be in a position to consolidate their own and their party's position.

At the elementary school level a controversy was raised when the Left Front decided to abolish English teaching up to Class V.[15] Since the elite and upper middle class all went to private schools, they were unaffected and could continue to perpetuate their position. For the middle and lower classes however, such a move would effectively hinder their prospects of significant upward mobility through competing for good jobs which required a fluency in English. Abolishing English would ease the study load at the primary level and assist the lower classes. While the Left Front's policy was well-meaning in reflecting a desire for mass education, it provided a marginal benefit to the great majority and a major hindrance to a small minority who might hope for significant upward mobility. The most popular criticism of the policy was that it encouraged a dualism in education, with children of affluent families blessed with an opportunity of English medium schools and the large underprivileged majority denied the scope.[16] Due to parental pressure for English study, many government schools continued teaching the subject in defiance of government instructions. In the Communists' second term of office the new Left Front Chairman Saroj Mukherjee indicated no action would be taken against these schools, which effectively meant the policy would be implemented at local discretion.[17]

Though Bengal's literary and intellectual output undoubtedly exists, it tends to create a false impression that the Bengali people as a whole are that way

[15] *Ibid.*
[16] *Ibid.*
[17] Editorial, "Less Fear to Learn?," *The Statesman*, January 23, 1983.

inclined. In fact this literary output was a product of the Bhadralok tricaste elite which continues to dominate Bengal's political and intellectual life. It does not extend very far down the caste class pyramid. Despite Bengal's literary output, the Government of India's Ministry of Education and Culture accurately named West Bengal as one of the nine states "educationally backward in elementary education" which together comprise 3/4 of the non-enrolled children.[18] Between the 1971 and 1981 Census West Bengal fell from sixth to ninth place in literacy among Indian states. The literacy rate increased from 33.20 percent to 40.94 percent, but this increase is deceptive. Among Scheduled Castes who are mostly from the poorest classes only 24.37 percent are literate, which is the tenth place among Scheduled Caste state populations. Among the non-Scheduled Caste groups the literacy rate is 48.12 percent, ranking sixth among Indian non-Scheduled Caste groups. This indicates that the Scheduled Castes and the lower classes in general are relatively worse educated in West Bengal than in many other parts of the country and are particularly badly educated when compared to their fellow Bengalis of high caste. Furthermore, the enrolment gap between the Scheduled Castes and Tribes and other groups has increased, as shown in table 3.1.[19] Nor is the situation likely to improve. The proportion of Scheduled Caste children attending primary school from classes I–V as a percentage of the Scheduled Caste population is the third worst of twenty Indian states. For boys it is the second worst and for girls the seventh worst. The growing gap between general and Scheduled Caste and Tribe enrolment is shown in figures 3.1–3. This indicates that the Scheduled Castes are not only relatively badly placed educationally but will in future fall further behind the general population of West Bengal. Other states appear to have achieved more in education of the lower classes. In this respect the Left Front has been negligent in spreading education to the lower classes, as any expansion in formal education would first be noticed by increased enrolment amongst Scheduled Caste children. Though the salaries of school teachers have been significantly increased, this has not improved their performance or served to spread education further afield. While school teachers, particularly in rural areas, are an influential group which it is useful for the Left Front to control, the influence of the lower classes, including the Scheduled Castes, is less directly felt except at election time. Nor has the Left Front been more forthcoming with non-formal and adult education. According to the Union Education

[18] India, Planning Commission, *Report of the Working Group on the Development of Scheduled Castes during the Sevenih Five Year Plan 1985–90* (New Delhi: mimeographed, February 1985), p. 92; India, Ministry of Home Affairs, *Second Report of the Commission for Scheduled Castes and Tribes*, April 1979–March 1980 (Delhi: Government of India, Controller of Publications, 1981), p. 146.
[19] *Selected Statistics on Scheduled Castes*, pp. 2, 27, 30.

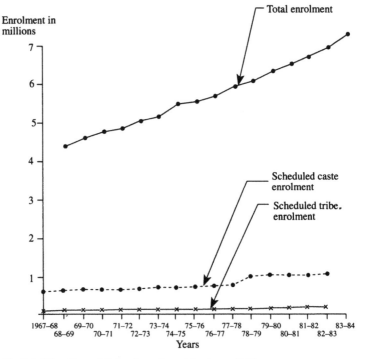

Fig 3.1. West Bengal School enrolment in classes I–V

*Source:* India, Ministry of Education & Culture, *Trends of Educational Development of Scheduled Castes and Scheduled Tribes* (New Delhi, 1983) West
Bengal, *School Education in West Bengal 1984*

Ministry, 53 percent of the funds allocated to the Bengal government for adult
literacy remained unutilized.[20] According to the Maoists:

There have been occasional references to the possibility for the Panchayats to take up
adult education schemes, but the general level of Left Front thinking on education as a
factor for social change (the less said about revolution the better) lags far behind the ideas
even of bourgeois liberals as regards off-time education, adult education, non-formal
education, general equalisation of education opportunities, eradication of illiteracy and
general alternatives to the present system of schooling.[21]

Compared to the issue of the transfer of professors from Presidency College or

[20] Editorial, "Neglecting Adults," *The Statesman*, February 23, 1983.
[21] CPI, "The Left Front Government in West Bengal: From Class Collaboration to Class Capitulation," *For A New Democracy*, vol. 1, no. 10–12, December 1978–February 1979 (Calcutta:
Provisional Central Committee of the Communist Party of India – Marxist–Leninist), p. 109.

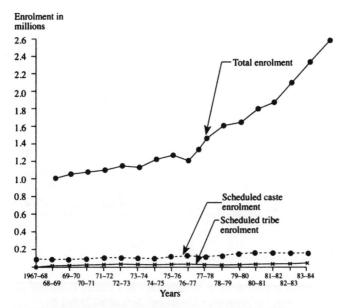

Fig 3.2. West Bengal School enrolment in classes VI–VIII

*Source:* India, Ministry of Education & Culture, *Trends of Educational De-velopment of Scheduled Castes and Scheduled Tribes* (New Delhi, 1983) West Bengal, Director of Information, Department of Information & Cultural Af-fairs, *School Education in West Bengal 1984*

appointment of a Vice-Chancellor for Calcutta University, the question of adult literacy hardly received Left Front attention or mention in the press, indicating the concerns of the politically and socially relevant section of Bengal society and the Communists' own lack of concern for a mass education program. The CPM state *Political-Organisational Report* dismissed the issue in one sentence saying "adult education has not gained ground because of the obstruction of the Secretariat,"[22] a surprising statement considering the Left Front effectively controls the Secretariat, the days of an independent bureaucracy having been effectively eroded by the politicians over the years. In fact it was part of the general Communist tendency in government of failing to develop new or original programs and merely continuing or expanding old programs where vested interests were already established. While in other countries the Communists reaped political dividends through mass literacy programs, the

[22] Communist Party of India, *Rajnaitik-Sangathanik Report*, p. 37.

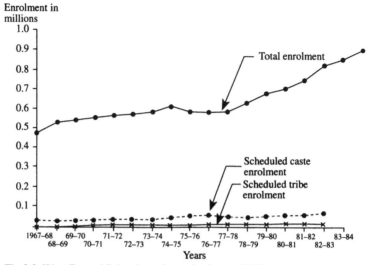

Fig 3.3. West Bengal School enrolment in classes IX–X

Sources: India, Ministry of Education & Culture, *Trends of Educational Development of Scheduled Castes and Scheduled Tribes* (New Delhi, 1983) West Bengal, Director of Information, Department of Information & Cultural Affairs, *School Education in West Bengal 1984*

CPM showed no significant interest in this, though in the long run only land reforms could have been considered of greater importance than mass adult literacy for consolidating the Communist ideology and political base in the State. The absence of an adult mass literacy program was symptomatic of a lack of originality, dynamism, and interest in the lowest strata of society which Communist parties of equivalent strength and resources have shown elsewhere, but the CPM has been slow to demonstrate.

Under the Left Front, expenditure on secondary education came to exceed primary level education with both elementary and post-secondary education reducing their share of the education budget. According to a World Bank study:

This change in allocation is difficult to comprehend in view of the high primary school dropout rate in West Bengal. An explanation may lie in the ability of private secondary school owners to lobby for and obtain state support. West Bengal government grants to private "aided" secondary schools increased six-fold in the years 1976/77–1986/87 and now exceed primary level outlays.[23]

---

[23] World Bank, *India: Poverty, Employment, and Social Services* (Washington, D.C.: The World Bank, 1989), p. 128.

Table 3.1. *West Bengal school enrolment*

| Years | General | Scheduled Caste | Scheduled Tribe | Co-efficient of Equality* Sch. Caste | Sch. Tribe |
|---|---|---|---|---|---|
| **Age 6–11** | | | | | |
| 1979–80 | 63.99 | 11.39 | 2.60 | 80.94 | 72.29 |
| 1980–81 | 65.95 | 11.68 | 2.66 | 80.53 | 71.76 |
| 1981–82 | 67.99 | 11.70 | 2.68 | 78.25 | 70.13 |
| 1982–83 | 70.13 | 11.75 | 2.70 | 76.19 | 68.50 |
| 1983–84 | 73.75 | 11.90 | 2.75 | 73.37 | 66.34 |
| **Age 11–14** | | | | | |
| 1979–80 | 16.84 | 1.70 | 0.35 | 47.05 | 36.98 |
| 1980–81 | 18.43 | 1.72 | 0.40 | 42.44 | 38.61 |
| 1981–82 | 19.10 | 1.76 | 0.42 | 41.90 | 39.12 |
| 1982–83 | 21.50 | 1.77 | 0.43 | 37.42 | 35.58 |
| 1983–84 | 23.85 | 1.78 | 0.45 | 33.93 | 33.57 |

* Government of India Educational Co-efficient of Equality:

$$\frac{\text{Percentage Enrolment of Scheduled Castes/Scheduled Tribes to Total Enrolment of All Communities}}{\text{Percentage Population of Scheduled Castes/ Scheduled Tribes to Total Population}} \times 100$$

*Source:* School Education in West Bengal 1984, Department of Information and Cultural Affairs, Government of West Bengal, 1985.
Enrolment figures are in lakhs (hundreds of thousands).

Table 3.2. *Composition of education expenditures (percentage)*

| | India 1976–77 | 1986–87 | West Bengal 1976–77 | 1986–87 |
|---|---|---|---|---|
| Elementary level | 47.5 | 46.8 | 42.7 | 39.6 |
| Secondary level | 32.3 | 32.6 | 37.6 | 44.1 |
| Technical and higher level | 20.2 | 20.6 | 19.7 | 16.3 |
| Total | 100.0 | 100.0 | 100.0 | 100.0 |

*Source:* World Bank, *India: Poverty, Employment, and Social Services*, 1989, p. 128.

The World Bank study concludes these calculations indicate "large leakages" which warrant greater "accountability and control over how money is spent."[24] The change in West Bengal government orientation is indicated in table 3.2. Though corruption is only implied in these allocations, the elitist orientation of the Left Front government's education policies is perceptible.

## Employment

For education to improve the economic condition of the Scheduled Castes it must be translated into increased employment in non-traditional occupations. To ensure that this happens it is a constitutional requirement that around 15 percent of government jobs be filled by Scheduled Castes. This varies between states roughly corresponding to the proportion of Scheduled Caste population. For central government employees in West Bengal it is 20 percent for direct recruitment and 15 percent for promotion. For Scheduled Tribes it is 6 and 7.5 percent respectively.[25] For West Bengal state government employment the reservation for both employment and promotion is identical, being 15 percent for Scheduled Castes and 5 percent for Scheduled Tribes. In actual practice only 1.85 percent of first class jobs, 2.62 percent of class 2 jobs and 6.60 percent of class 3 jobs are filled by Scheduled Castes in the West Bengal government. Out of eleven states listed, West Bengal is second worst in both first and second class jobs and second worst out of twelve states for third class jobs.[26] Of complaints to the Scheduled Castes and Tribes Commission regarding service matters Bengal had the third most out of nineteen states.[27] Of the teaching staff at West Bengal universities only 1.15 percent are Scheduled Caste, ranking twelfth out of eighteen states.[28]

## Central government financed Scheduled Caste programs

The Central government ministries sponsor a number of programs for the benefit of the Scheduled Castes which, though wholly or partly funded by the center, are administered by the state governments. The West Bengal government has consistently complained about the unfair distribution of revenues to West Bengal. In regard to Scheduled Caste programs at least, the Central government has maintained one of the highest levels of assistance to West

[24] *Ibid.*, p. 129.
[25] India, Ministry of Home Affairs, *Third Report of the Commission for Scheduled Castes and Scheduled Tribes* (Delhi: Government of India, Controller of Publications, 1983), p. 99.
[26] *Second Report of the Commission for Scheduled Castes and Scheduled Tribes*, p. 275.
[27] *Ibid.*, p. 276.
[28] *Third Report of the Commission for Scheduled Castes and Scheduled Tribes*, p. 111.

Bengal, ranking second or third among the Indian states. The Left Front government, despite having the second highest number and third highest proportion of Scheduled Caste population in their state, has not shown a corresponding interest. The West Bengal government's outlay for the Scheduled Castes under the Special Component Plan, which "involves earmarking of outlays by all divisible sectors" under annual state plans to benefit the Scheduled Castes, is among the worst in the country. For the financial years 1980–81 through 1983–84 it ranked fifteenth, thirteenth, thirteenth, and eleventh out of twenty states as a percentage of state annual plan outlays. On a per capita basis even in its year of highest outlay it is the worst in the country as seen from the following plan.

Special Component Plan outlay in 1981–82 per Scheduled Caste person

| Rupees | State | Rupees | State |
| --- | --- | --- | --- |
| 36.55 | West Bengal | 92.21 | Maharashtra |
| 65.11 | Andhra Pradesh | 501.32 | Manipur |
| 49.64 | Bihar | 74.04 | Orissa |
| 102.78 | Gujarat | 47.61 | Punjab |
| 140.87 | Haryana | 54.92 | Rajasthan |
| 111.01 | Himachal Pradesh | 147.69 | Sikkim |
| 93.74 | Karnataka | 91.10 | Tamil Nadu |
| 82.69 | Kerala | 3081.66 | Tripura |
| 59.48 | Madhya Pradesh | 44.05 | Uttar Pradesh |

The above comparison is inaccurate as the administrators of the Special Component Plan claim the plan is "non-existent" at the district level, its only existence being confined to the planning documents put out by the West Bengal government Secretariat. District level expenditures included under the Plan are actually expenditures of other subsidies that are not entitled to be counted in the plan. The plan is therefore misleading as it creates the impression of implementation which is in fact not there. Significantly, according to the plan administrators, the Special Component Plan Co- ordination Committee headed by the Chief Minister has never met and neither has the Secretariat Committee for the Special Component Plan headed by the Chief Secretary. This low priority would be justified if the poor in Bengal were relatively better off economically than in other parts of the country. In fact the opposite is the case. West Bengal has 52.54 percent of its population below the poverty line, the fifth highest in the country. The rural population has 58.94 percent below the poverty line ranking the fourth worst in the country. However, its urban population has only 34.71 percent below the poverty line ranking eleventh highest out of twenty one. The rural–urban disparity is therefore greater than average in West Bengal, and the poverty for which Calcutta is known affects a smaller part of its population than in the rural areas of the state.[29]

While the Central government assistance for the Special Component Plan from 1980–81 to 1984–85 to West Bengal ranks third highest for the first three years and second highest for the last three years among Indian states, this program ranked only fifteenth to eleventh in the percentage of the Bengal plan devoted to it compared to the other states. By contrast, the Bengal state government's contribution towards the share capital required in setting up the Scheduled Castes Development Corporation ranked third and second highest in 1981–82 and 1982–83 respectively. This high contribution was due to the stipulation that the Corporations be financed by both the State and Central governments in the ratio of 51:49.[30] In order to receive funding from the center for the program the state government was obliged to contribute its share of a potentially recoverable expenditure. Thus aid has only been forthcoming in appropriate levels when preceded by the Central government's conditional offers of assistance. When no such obligation is stipulated the state government feels free to reduce the levels of assistance to the Scheduled Castes.

The most important centrally financed scheme is the Integrated Rural Development Programme (IRDP) administered by the state governments and designed to help the rural poor cross the poverty line. The eligible groups are defined as Scheduled Castes, Tribes, Agricultural Laborers, Artisans, and Marginal workers with an annual household income of under 3,500 Rupees.[31] The Scheduled Castes and Tribes comprise 33.55 percent of the total West Bengal rural population. In West Bengal the IRDP beneficiaries were chosen by the largely Communist-controlled Panchayats as follows:

|  | 1980–81 | 1981–82 | 1982–83 |
|---|---|---|---|
| Total beneficiaries | 37,415 | 67,338 | 95,607 |
| Number of Scheduled Caste and Tribe beneficiaries | 10,522 | 29,920 | 29,637 |
| Percentage of Scheduled Caste and Tribe beneficiaries | 28.1 | 44.4 | 30.9 |

---

[29] Government of India, Planning Commission, *Sixth Five Year Plan 1980–85* (New Delhi: Government of India Press), p. 16.

[30] *Selected Statistics on Scheduled Castes*, p. v.

[31] Government of India, Planning Commission, Programme Evaluation Organisation, *Evaluation Report on the Integrated Rural Development Programme* (New Delhi: mimeographed, May 1985), p. iv; Government of India, Planning Commission, *Report of the Expert Group on Programme for Alleviation of Poverty* (New Delhi: Government of India Press, February 1982), p. 6; *Report of the Working Group on the Development of Scheduled Castes*, p. 52.

In two of the three years the Scheduled Castes and Tribes were below their proportion of the total population. The Expert Group on Programmes for Alleviation of Poverty of the Planning Commission recommended 40 percent as the minimum that should go to the Scheduled Castes and Tribes from these programs.[32] The Working Group on the Development of Scheduled Castes recommended a minimum of 50 percent of IRDP funds go to the Scheduled Castes and Tribes and noted that as a result of government efforts during the sixth five year plan 41.71 percent of IRDP funds went to the Scheduled Castes and Tribes in 1983–84.[33] West Bengal's shortfall in this regard indicates a misallocation of IRDP funds by the Communist Panchayats, possibly to more prosperous high castes not entitled to it. A sample survey of the IRDP in Darjeeling District of West Bengal by the Programme Evaluation Organisation of the Planning Commission reveals a similar underrepresentation of Scheduled Castes and Tribes.[34] Considering that 109.254 million Rupees has been spent during the financial years 1980–81 to 1982–83 on the IRDP in West Bengal, any diversion of funds from the most eligible potential beneficiaries is significant. As the Communist Panchayats chose the beneficiaries, unlike in other states where it is left to the administration, this indicates that Panchayats may not be the most appropriate channel for allocating development aid to the lower classes. The administration appears therefore to have more autonomy from the rural propertied interests than the Panchayats in India. Distribution through the Panchayats amounts to giving development aid to the dominant political parties controlled at the village level by landed interests. It is probably for this reason that the Left Front has been so insistent on distributing aid through the Panchayats rather than the bureaucracy, as this amounts to a form of patronage for and by its own rural supporters controlling the Panchayats. This is why Congress-controlled Panchayats have often had difficulty collecting funds through the CPM-controlled district and block-level Panchayats. This political patronage has important national implications as there have been persistent demands that development aid be distributed through the Panchayats which "must be given the stature of being *units of self-government*."[35]

The redistribution of land above the ceiling limits in accordance with national guidelines is more difficult to analyze as much of the land donated or appropriated to the state is unfit for cultivation. Of 67,580 cases in West Bengal as of February 21, 1984, 48,039 were voluntary donations and only 19,541 were on official initiative. This indicates that much of the land was not worth the

[32] *Report of the Expert Group on Programmes for Alleviation of Poverty*, p. 68.
[33] *Report of the Working Group on the Development of Scheduled Castes*, p. 53.
[34] *Evaluation Report on the Integrated Rural Development Programme*, p. 183.
[35] L.C. Jain *et al.*, *Grass Without Roots: Rural Development Under Government Auspices* (New Delhi: Sage, 1985).

landowners fighting for in court. Of the officially initiated cases West Bengal ranked ninth in the country. However, it was the highest in the number of cases still pending due to bureaucratic lethargy and court injunctions. In terms of area taken possession of and distributed it ranked eleventh and in terms of the number of beneficiaries it was fourth. In terms of area given to Scheduled Castes it was eighth and in numbers of Scheduled Caste beneficiaries fourth. The program therefore appears relatively better than the others though the voluntary nature of most of the land cases indicates much of the land may be of marginal value, so a definitive statement would require a breakdown of land quality and the relative proportions of Scheduled Caste and other poor beneficiaries.

The nationwide scheme for rural house sites and construction assistance for landless laborers was not well implemented. Bengal ranked eleventh in number of house sites allotted and thirteenth as a percentage of those eligible. It was seventh in the number of houses constructed and sixth as a percentage of houses constructed on allocated sites.[36]

Under the Congress government's 20-Point Program the elimination of bonded labor was given priority. This was to be done by the state governments through their identification, release, and rehabilitation. As of 1984 161,075 bonded laborers were identified and released and of these 119,219 were rehabilitated.[37] Neither the Gandhi Peace Foundation survey nor the Bengal government filed returns for the state, indicating it was not a problem in West Bengal. The more statistically rigorous National Sample Survey Organisation, however, estimated 21,600 bonded laborers in West Bengal making it the fourth highest number in the country, and also the fourth largest as a percentage of state populations.[38] The Gandhi Peace Foundation national estimate was 2,617,000, the National Sample Survey Organisation 345,000, and the various state governments 120,561. This last lowest figure was officially adopted, pending further identification. The Gandhi Peace Foundation failed to identify any bonded labor in several states such as West Bengal, indicating a less than scientific survey, even though it came up with by far the highest estimate. The Bengal government's official view that it is not a local problem and therefore not in need of special attention ignores the most statistically rigorous survey of the NSS indicating that West Bengal has one of the most serious problems in this regard.[39]

In terms of outlays and actual expenditure on the welfare of Scheduled Castes, Tribes, and other Backward Classes West Bengal ranks tenth in Indian states,

---

[36] *Selected Statistics on Scheduled Castes*, p. 71.

[37] *Ibid.*, p. 73.

[38] *Report of the Working Group on the Development of Scheduled Castes*, p. 74.

[39] National Sample Survey Organisation, "Survey of 32nd Round on Employment and Unemployment started July 1977 and completed June 1978," *Sarvekshana*, April 1979, p. S590.

an allocation seriously short of what might have been expected from the Left Front government.[40]

## Public health

The public health system in Bengal had an inadequacy typical of underdeveloped economies. The most that could be expected of the Left Front was to eliminate corrupt practices in the allocation of supplies, and improve staff efficiency. Neither was effectively undertaken. Several years after the Left Front took power a social worker observed: "There are hospitals, but sincerely speaking, their doors are closed for the poor, despite being free. Poor people do not get a chance of admission without negotiating, without manipulating and paying black money."[41] While support staff misappropriated supplies, some doctors were caught in a false billing racket with pharmaceutical company employees. Health financing has not been a priority with the Left Front government when expenditures are compared with the national average (table 3.3). As with other programs, however, it offered scope for job patronage. "The Bengali Marxists ... felt it was not opportune to organize popular mobilization in the health sector. In Bengal, as elsewhere, the CHV (Community Health Volunteer) programme was used first as a means of reinforcing the dominant political apparatus by distributing pseudo-jobs to the young unemployed."[42]

One supporter of the Left Front who was attempting to raise foreign donations for a new public hospital in Calcutta observed that hospital management was the key to successful operation and this required effective control of the union demands. Even if the Left Front could control its own unions, rivals would soon subvert the efficient functioning of any hospital that was built.

## Refugee rehabilitation

One of the biggest problems West Bengal had faced was the influx of millions of East Bengal refugees. Those from the middle and upper classes had the resources and connections to start a new life in West Bengal without being primarily dependent on government assistance. For the poorest refugees government assistance was necessary for their rehabilitation. When in January 1964 communal violence in East Pakistan resulted in a fresh influx of refugees, the Central Government in consultation with the West Bengal Government

---

[40] Third Report of the Commission for Scheduled Castes and Scheduled Tribes, p. 34.

[41] Dennison Berwick, "Sacred and Profane," The Sunday Times Magazine (July 1, 1990), p. 30.

[42] Bruno Jobert, "Populism and Health Policy: The Case of Community Health Volunteers in India," Social Science and Medicine, vol. 20, no. 1 (1985), p. 15.

Table 3.3. *Inter-state comparison of health expenditure*

| | Share of total revenue expenditure (percentage) | | Real per-capita revenue expenditure (80–81 Rs.) | |
|---|---|---|---|---|
| | 1976–77 | 1986–87 | 1976–77 | 1986–87 |
| Andhra Pradesh | 10.8 | 8.7 | 18.1 | 30.4 |
| Bihar | 10.1 | 8.7 | 8.7 | 15.0 |
| Gujarat | 9.8 | 10.1 | 20.2 | 39.6 |
| Haryana | 8.6 | 9.7 | 20.4 | 37.5 |
| Himachal Pradesh | 9.8 | 10.8 | 31.4 | 63.7 |
| Karnataka | 10.5 | 7.4 | 20.0 | 23.2 |
| Kerala | 11.4 | 8.6 | 24.8 | 29.3 |
| Madhya Pradesh | 12.6 | 7.0 | 17.6 | 18.3 |
| Maharashtra | 8.9 | 11.1 | 20.3 | 44.7 |
| Orissa | 9.4 | 11.0 | 15.7 | 32.2 |
| Punjab | 8.9 | 8.3 | 24.1 | 32.8 |
| Rajasthan | 11.9 | 11.4 | 21.4 | 32.8 |
| Tamil Nadu | 12.7 | 11.4 | 22.9 | 33.3 |
| Uttar Pradesh | 8.3 | 9.3 | 10.0 | 19.1 |
| West Bengal | 14.1 | 9.3 | 22.0 | 25.4 |
| India | 11.1 | 10.6 | 17.6 | 29.5 |

*Source:* The World Bank, *India: Poverty, Employment, and Social Services*, 1989, p. 130.

decided that all those needing relief assistance would be settled outside Bengal under the care of the Central Government, while those who remained in West Bengal would be responsible for their own rehabilitation.[43] Inevitably it was the poorest classes who were forced to resettle outside the state in the Dandakaryana area bordering Orissa and Madhya Pradesh. Here they were subject to corrupt and capricious government and local officials. The Communists demanded that these refugees be settled in the uninhabited Sundarbans Ganges Delta of West Bengal. This helped the Communists to obtain a political following among these refugees as they had been badly treated by the Congress government. This Communist commitment presented no difficulty as long as they were in opposition. On assuming power the CPM had to live with its past commitments and the expectations it had raised while in opposition.

Nowhere was the CPM's switch of its role and policy on assuming power as sharp as on the issue of accepting the refugees from East Bengal. The refugees had been such strong supporters of the Communist Party that the Communists found it necessary to explain to the local West Bengalis that the CPI was not just a party of East Bengal refugees, so dominant was the refugee influence in the Communist organization.[44] Even in the first Left Front government most of the top-ranking CPM cabinet members were from East Bengal, including Jyoti Basu, Ashok Mitra, Prasanta Sur, and Khrishnapada Ghosh. The State Secretary Promode Das Gupta was also from East Bengal. The CPM had built up its base in part through taking up the cause of the refugees and demanding that they be settled in West Bengal rather than dispersed throughout the country as was the Congress government policy.[45] Jyoti Basu had presented their case in the legislative assembly in the 1950s and early 1960s during the B.C. Roy government. As late as December 1974 Jyoti Basu had demanded in a public meeting that the Dandakaranya refugees be allowed to settle in the Sundarbans.[46] In 1974–75 leading members of the subsequent Left Front government, including Ram Chatterjee the Minister of State Home (Civil Defence) Department, had assured the refugees that if the Left Front came to power they would arrange their resettlement in West Bengal.[47] At a meeting of the Eight Left Front Parties in 1975 it was resolved that the refugees be settled in the Sundarbans and a memorandum to that effect was proposed to be submitted to

[43] Saroj Chakrabarty, *With West Bengal Chief Ministers: Memoirs 1962 to 1977* (Calcutta: Orient Longman, 1978), p. 136.
[44] K.N. Vaid, *Gheraos and Labour Unrest in West Bengal* (New Delhi: Shri Ram Centre for Industrial Relations and Human Resources, 1972), p. 140.
[45] *Economic and Political Weekly*, April 1, 1967, p. 633.
[46] *Onlooker*, March 16–31, 1979, pp. 22–3.
[47] Mangaldev Visharat MP, Laxmi Narayan Pandey MP, and Prasannbhai Mehta MP, "Report on Marichjhapi Affairs," (MPs nominated by Prime Minister Desai to visit and investigate Marichjhapi), April 18, 1979, p. 7 (mimeographed).

the Governor.[48] At that point the Left's fortunes were at a very low ebb and the CPM had defined West Bengal as being in a state of "semi-fascist terror." Three years later the Communists came to power and found their refugee supporters had taken them at their own word and sold their belongings and land in Dandakaranya to return to West Bengal. As the *Economic and Political Weekly* noted: "now that the Congress is out of power, would the refugees be far wrong in expecting the CP(M) to practice what they preached?"[49] The last thing, however, the Left Front wanted was a refugee influx which might damage the prospects of an economic recovery in the state and divert scarce resources from other development projects. The state government attempted to involve the Central Government in a large financial commitment to rehabilitating the refugees in West Bengal but this was turned down. At this point the CPM could have made an issue of central discrimination against Bengali refugees, but the Janata Government was an ally of the CPM government, which in turn was financially dependent on the center for much of its development programs and on Presidential assent for its legislation.

In all nearly 150,000 refugees arrived in West Bengal from Dandakaranya.[50] Most were detained in camps set up by the Communist government and forcibly deported back to Dandakaranya. However, from May 1978 about 30,000 Scheduled Caste refugees under the leadership of Satish Mandal, President of the "Udbastu Unmayansit Samity," a former close associate of the Communist Party's refugee program, managed to cross the riverine delta area and set up a settlement at Marichjhapi.[51] By their own efforts they established a viable fishing industry, salt pans, health center, and schools. The state government was not disposed to tolerate such settlement, stating that the refugees were "in unauthorised occupation of Marichjhapi which is a part of the Sundarbans Government Reserve Forest violating thereby the Forest Acts." The refugees had come "with the intention of settling there permanently thereby disturbing the existing and the potential forest wealth and also creating ecological imbalance ... They forcibly went to Marichjhapi defying Government instructions and directions."[52] Whether the CPM placed primacy on ecology or merely

---

[48] Letter from All India Scheduled Castes/Tribes and Backward Classes Employees Co-ordination Council to Bhola Paswan Shastri MP, Chairman of the Commission for Scheduled Castes and Scheduled Tribes, "... Refugees of Marichjhapi Island."

[49] Kalyan Chaudhuri, "Victims of Their Leaders Making," *Economic and Political Weekly*, July 8, 1978, pp. 1098–9.

[50] Visharat *et al.*, p. 8.

[51] *Ibid.*, Ranjit Kumar Sikar, "Marichjhapi Massacre," *The Oppressed Indian*, July 1982, p. 21.

[52] Letter from Deputy Secretary, Refugee Relief and Rehabilitation Department, Government of West Bengal, to Zonal Director, Ministry of Home Affairs, Office of the Zonal Director, Backward Classes and ex-officio Deputy Commissioner for Scheduled Caste and Scheduled Tribes, Eastern Zone, Subject – "Problems of Refugees from Dandakaranya to West Bengal," no. 3223-Rehab/DNK-6/79.

feared this might be a precedent for an unmanageable refugee influx from Bangladesh and loss of political support in the area is debatable. By then all the other recent refugees had been forcefully driven out of the state so the Marich-jhapi refugees were at most a potential rather than an actual threat and their remaining was not a financial liability for the state government. Despite this, when persuasion failed to make the refugees abandon their settlement, the West Bengal Government started an economic blockade of the settlement on January 26, 1979 with thirty police launches. The community was teargassed, huts razed, and fisheries and tube wells destroyed, thereby depriving them of food and water. When the refugees tried to cross the river for food and drinking water on January 30th their boats were sunk and some of them were drowned. On the 31st of January police opened fire killing thirty-six persons. With their food and water supplies cut off or destroyed, the refugees were forced to eat wild grass and drink from improvised wells. The Calcutta High Court ordered a two week lifting of the state government blockade but this was never properly imple-mented. In all thirty-six refugees were killed by police firing, forty-three died of starvation as a result of the blockade, twenty-nine by disease and 128 from drowning when their boats were scuttled by the police. All of these victims were listed by name and age in an appeal for redress from the Central Government.[53] When these police actions failed to persuade the refugees to leave, the State Government ordered the forcible evacuation of the refugees which took place from the 14th to 16th of May 1979. One senior IAS officer reported that Muslim gangs were hired by the government to assist the police, as it was thought Muslims would be less sympathetic to the refugees. Several hundred men, women, and children were believed to have been killed by the police in the operation and their bodies dumped in the river to be washed out by the tide. Photographs were published in the Ananda Bazaar Patrika and the Opposition members in the State Assembly staged a walkout in protest.[54] However, no criminal charges were laid against any of the officials or politicians involved. Prime Minister Desai, wishing to maintain the support of the Communists for his government, decided not to pursue the matter. Of the refugees who attempted the migration "4,128 families perished in transit, died of hunger, starvation, exhaustion, and many were killed in Kashipur, Kumirmari, and Marichjhapi by police firings."[55]

[53] Letter from All India Scheduled Castes/Tribes and Backward Classes Employees Co-ordination Council to Bhola Paswan Shastri MP, Chairman of the Commission for Scheduled Castes and Scheduled Tribes, Subject – "Genocide committed on the Scheduled Caste Refugees of Marichjhapi Island."

[54] Amrita Bazaar Patrika, February 8, 1979.

[55] Sikar, "Marichjhapi Massacre," p. 22; Atharobaki Biswas, "Why Dandakaranya a Failure, Why Mass Exodus, Where Solution?," The Oppressed Indian, July, 1982, p. 19.

Within the CPM which had taken the decision there was some dissatisfaction with the way the party leadership had handled the matter. The CPM cadre felt the leadership had handled the question in a "bureaucratic way" when it could have used the issue to develop a mass movement on behalf of the refugees and against Central government discrimination and neglect. The Communists had big refugee organizations which could have organized the refugees and brought them to Bengal. Instead of utilizing the situation to rehabilitate the refugees and in the process develop a solid Communist base among them, only force was resorted to by the CPM. The CPM cadre who were unhappy with the policy, however, could do nothing; no one on the CPM State Committee opposed Promode Das Gupta on this issue. The CPM State Committee *Political-Organisational Report*, in reviewing Marichjhapi, reversed previous Communist policy, stating that now "there was no possibility of giving shelter to these large number of refugees under any circumstances in the State."[56] The Land Revenue Minister Benoy Chowdhury made the unsubstantiated accusation that some foreign agencies were behind Marichjhapi.[57] The CPM blamed vested interests, reactionary forces, Congress (I), and P.C. Sen for using the issue for political gain and claimed the CPM had met the challenge at a political level for over a year, ultimately achieving success with the return of the refugees in May 1979.[58]

Others, however, took a different lesson from the Marichjhapi massacre and questioned the bonafides of the Communists to represent the poorest strata of Bengali society. A journalist in the Bengali daily *Jugantar* noted:

the refugees of Dandakaranya are men of the lowest stratum of the society ... They are mainly cultivators, fishermen, day-labourers, artisans, the exploited mass of the society. I am sorry to mention that they have no relation with [the] elite of society. If it is a matter of any body of the family of a *Zamindar*, doctor, lawyer or engineer, the stir is felt from Calcutta to Delhi, but in this classified and exploited society, we do not feel anything for the landless poor cultivators and fishermen. So long as the state machinery will remain in the hands of the upper class elite, the poor, the helpless, the beggar, the refugees will continue to be victimised.[59]

It was an ironic statement to make about what was a supposedly Communist government representing the poor and exploited. As a final twist to the episode, the CPM settled its own supporters in Marichjhapi, as Promode Das Gupta had earlier advocated, occupying and utilizing the facilities left by

---

[56] Communist Party of India (Marxist), West Bengal State Conference, *Rajnaitik-Sangathanik Report* ("Political-Organisational Report") adopted 14th Plenary Session December 27, 1981 – January 1, 1982 (Calcutta: West Bengal State Committee, Communist Party of India – Marxist, 1982), p. 14.

[57] *The Statesman*, February 19, 1979.

[58] Communist Party of India – Marxist, *Rajnaitik-Sangathanik Report*, p. 14.

[59] Sikar, "Marichjhapi Massacre," p. 23, quoting *Jugantar* May 29, 1979.

the deported refugees.[60] The issues of ecology and the Forest Act were conveniently forgotten.

A Professor of Community Medicine from the All India Institute of Medical Sciences, who later visited the refugees in Dandakaranya, reported that those returning were now dispossessed, having sold their land and belongings to make the trip to West Bengal, while those who had remained behind were now better off. An air of gloom hung over the refugee colonies and the people went about their lives in a mechanical way without enthusiasm. The refugees did not mix with the local population and clung to their Bengali culture though prospects for return to Bengal were remote. Ironically by 1985 the Left Front was again taking up the issue of refugee rehabilitation but with little likelihood or expectation of success, indicating the program was more for public consumption and potential political capital.

### Agricultural taxation

There has been an often acrimonious debate about how successful the Left Front has been in its reform program. Much of the academic discussion has relied on evidence from a few village sample surveys. This analysis of village level policy implementation has dominated the academic debate, to the neglect of state level policy formulation analysis. By examining how the state government formulated an innovative agricultural taxation bill, and then changed the bill after presentation to the Legislative Assembly, it will be shown that political pressures from the surplus producing farmers could abrogate the policies of even India's most radical national Communist Party. This indicates that the farmers' lobby has found an influence across the party spectrum and agrarian taxation reform has reached its limits. With significant taxation augmentation from the surplus-producing farmers now politically impossible in India, other revenue enhancing measures must be sought for development expenditures. As Indian state governments have no other constitutionally mandated taxation sources, not already heavily taxed, state government development revenues cannot be significantly increased without overriding the surplus producing farmers' lobby. As the West Bengal case shows that confronting these farmers is not politically possible even when ruling party elites would like to do so, other revenue sources will have to continue to be utilized exclusively. State governments in India which are constitutionally empowered to deal with agrarian issues, will not be able to use the agricultural sector as a significant revenue source, but will continue expenditures on agricultural development at the expense of the urban sector. Though the West Bengal Left Front government

---

[60] *Amrita Bazaar Patrika*, June 27, 1978.

was inclined to tax the surplus-producing farmers, and presented legislation to that effect, the amendment to the legislation indicates an end to enhanced agricultural taxation in India for the foreseeable future.

Agricultural taxation has been seen as a politically safe and viable alternative to land redistribution where landlords are too influential to be expropriated. Incremental taxation avoids the confrontational and often violent effects of land reform, while achieving much the same goal by redistributing wealth in society. As landlords produce most of the marketable food needed to feed the non-agricultural population, progressive taxation is less likely to cause the short-term disruption of food production that might result from land confiscation.

In India, however, it is land redistribution which has been undertaken since independence, while agricultural taxation has been virtually abolished. That a seemingly revolutionary redistribution should have been undertaken while reformist taxation measures were abandoned seems paradoxical. This is due to the class pyramid of colonial Indian rural society having least electoral influence at the top among the biggest landlords, while the middle landed classes have greatest political power to deliver the vote at election time. The abolition of the zamindari system and the gradual elimination of the largest estates have transformed the former elite into a new middle class, while enabling some peasant proprietors to expand their holdings and wealth. Land reform allowed this middle class to consolidate income and political influence through land redistribution and the green revolution. It is a class large and influential enough not only to prevent further land redistribution, but to ensure a gradual lowering of taxation, and its replacement with government subsidies. Land reform thus promoted a middle landed class that produced a marketable surplus, but left the poorest third of the population suffering from malnutrition. All attempts by government and aid agencies have failed to alter this inequitable characteristic of rural India today. Only further land reform or redistribution through agricultural taxation can be expected to change this situation.

When the Communist Left Front coalition took power in West Bengal after the ending of the Emergency in 1977, it was expected that in West Bengal at least this intractable pattern would change. Not only was the ruling Communist Party of India – Marxist the most radical of the two major Communist parties, but it had an overwhelming popular mandate. Furthermore, both land redistribution and agricultural taxation were within its state jurisdiction, making agrarian reform a logical first step in the program of the Left Front government. Though state legislation had to be signed by the central government-controlled President of India, and was subject to Supreme Court challenge, this would not preclude many agrarian reform measures from becoming law. Progressive agricultural taxation as a fairly modest reform measure would almost certainly have been accepted by the central government after passage through the state legislative assembly.

As most other revenue sources are under central government jurisdiction, the need for agricultural taxation would seem compelling for a state government intent on economic development. As the main sources of West Bengal government revenue are sales taxes (55.85 percent in 1982) which have already been increased as far as practicable, agricultural taxation is potentially the largest virtually untapped revenue earner.[61]

Table 3.4. *Receipts of land revenue as percentage of total revenue*[62]

| | |
|---|---|
| 1793–94 | 69 % |
| 1808–09 | 61.1% |
| 1818–19 | 73.1% |
| 1839–40 | 70.6% |
| 1850–51 | 66.5% |
| 1871–72 | 42.8% |
| 1881–82 | 35.5% |
| 1891–92 | 36.5% |
| 1901–02 | 33.9% |
| 1911–12 | 31.4% |
| 1938–39 | 16.1% |
| 1953–54 | 8.6% |

Historically, agricultural taxation was the main source of government revenue. During the Mughul period land revenues varied from 1/3rd to 1/2 of total produce.[63] In the colonial period there was a gradual decline in the proportion of land revenues to total government revenues and this continued after independence (table 3.4). By the late 1950s Indian land taxes were only about 1 percent of total agricultural income compared to 5 percent before the Second World War.[64] In colonial Bengal the tax in 1874 was 16.6% percent of net farm income and in

---

[61] Government of India, Ministry of Finance, Department of Economic Affairs, *Report of the Taxation Enquiry Commission 1953–54* (New Delhi: Government of India Press), vol. III, p. 216.

[62] The central government contributed 41.6 percent of total state disbursements in 1979–84, representing 32.6 percent of the center's aggregate resources. The states raised 38.9 percent of total taxation from 1974–79 so their revenue raising powers were therefore significant, especially considering that their agricultural taxation was virtually non-existent. Government of West Bengal, Information and Cultural Affairs Department, *Reply to Questionnaire: Commission on Centre–State Relations* (Calcutta: WBG, July 1984), pp. 20, 23; Government of India, Planning Commission, *Draft Five Year Plan, 1978–83*, vol. II, p. 89.

[63] Bikram Sarkar, "Legal Aspects of Land Reform Measures in West Bengal" (Calcutta University Ph.D. thesis, 1982), p. 21

[64] Richard M. Bird, *Taxing Agricultural Land in Developing Countries* (Cambridge, MA: Harvard University Press, 1974), p. 133.

1911–17 7.1 percent. By 1978 this had fallen to .25 percent or one part in 400.[65] The Left Front therefore had precedents for a greatly enhanced land revenue levy, with only the political influence of the rural landowners to oppose it.

The possibility of increasing land taxes had been the subject of considerable controversy in post-independence India, as Bengal's low tax assessment was typical of Indian states which had jurisdiction in this matter but chose not to enforce higher land taxes. The central government Taxation Enquiry Commission of 1953–54 had recommended higher agricultural income tax, seeing no justification for exempting agricultural income or treating it separately from non-agricultural income earnings.[66] The 1971 Final Report of the Direct Taxes Enquiry Committee stated:

There is urgent need for agricultural income being subjected to a uniform tax more or less on par with the tax on other incomes so as to eliminate the scope for evasion of direct taxes imposed by the Union government. Agriculture should also contribute to the national exchequer in much the same way as other sectors are doing. It is also necessary on grounds of equity and distributive justice.[67]

The central government appointed a Committee on Taxation of Agricultural Wealth and Income under the Chairmanship of a leading economist, K.N. Raj. The report submitted in 1973 recommended a progressive agricultural holding tax based on crop yield. The large virtually tax-free accumulation of agricultural income among the landlords was to be removed by tying taxes to rising agricultural income on a level comparable with the non-agricultural sector. Like all other recommendations in this matter, nothing was implemented. The Madhya Pradesh government which actually introduced legislation to this effect had it watered down by the landlord lobby and its implementation was indefinitely postponed.[68] Agricultural taxation has therefore been a non-starter in India and the trend has been in the opposite direction of subsidizing agriculture at the expense of the urban and industrial sector. As a result of increased productivity through High-Yielding Variety cereals and higher food prices subsidized by the government, land values and agricultural income have increased several fold while tax has remained at pre-independence levels, dating as far back as 1935. Considering that agricultural tax has been the major source for revenue historically and a major potential source for development funding, the non-taxation of this sector is an important cause of India's slow industrialization. The advent of democracy and the need of political parties to obtain landlord support to deliver the votes at election time has been detrimental to

[65] Sarkar, "Legal Aspects," p. 273.
[66] Government of India, *Report of the Taxation Enquiry Commission 1953–54*, vol. III, pp. 221–3.
[67] Government of India, Ministry of Finance, *Direct Taxes Enquiry Committee Final Report* (New Delhi: Government of India, 1971), p. 175.
[68] Sarkar, "Legal Aspects," p. 275.

development by preventing increased agricultural taxation.[69]

With the Communists coming to power in West Bengal, this landlord opposition could be expected to be overruled as the Communist vote bloc was composed of the poor and landless who would gain from enhanced land taxes. As the richest landlords backed the Congress party rather than the Communists, the traditional obstacle to land taxation should not threaten the Communists' rural base. Ashok Mitra, the Left Front CPM Finance Minister, confirmed that the Communists would do all they could to tax the rich peasants as this "was the only class which could be submitted to a 'stiff agenda of taxation' by a State government."[70] This expectation appeared to be fulfilled when the Governor in his Left Front prepared speech to the Bengal Legislative Assembly stated that the new *West Bengal Land (Farm-Holding) Bill*

aims at introducing an element of progression in the land revenue system by exempting the smaller owners of land with lower productive potential from the revenue burden and by imposing an increasing graduated scale of revenue on holdings with rateable value exceeding the exemption limits. This bill, which is the first of its kind in this country, is currently under the scrutiny of a Select Committee of this House (i.e. the West Bengal Legislative Assembly).[71]

The bill was the product of an ongoing debate in the state government resulting from the Raj Committee Report. The Congress West Bengal Cabinet in its meeting of June 19, 1974 decided to have a field study conducted to determine the feasibility of implementing the Raj Committee Report. The West Bengal Board of Revenue constituted a state-level committee on June 4, 1975 to give guidance to this study team regarding possible implementation of the Agricultural Holding Tax in West Bengal. The State Level Committee submitted its report on November 4, 1977 after the Left Front had taken office. The Committee found that lack of experienced staff made unfeasible the collection of such a large quantity of data as would be required for implementing the Raj Committee recommendations. The idea of an Agricultural Holding Tax was therefore dropped. Preliminary calculations also indicated that if implemented at the recommended level, the Holding Tax would raise significantly less revenue than was already being collected.[72] After the State Level Committee recommended that the Raj Committee recommendations were unworkable in West Bengal, a Task Force was set up to look into alternatives.[73] The economist Amaresh Bagchi and Professor I.S. Gulati composed the first draft of the *West*

---

[69] T.V. Sathyamurthy, *India Since Independence – Centre–State Relations: The Case of Kerala*, vol. I (Delhi: Ajanta Publications, 1985), p. 75.

[70] *Ibid.*, p. 83.

[71] Sarkar, "Legal Aspects," p. 264.

[72] *Ibid.*, pp. 271–2.

[73] The members were Finance Secretary M.G. Kutty, Special Secretary Land and Land Reforms S.P. Mallik, Director of Land Records and Surveys B.K. Sarkar.

*Bengal Land (Farm -Holding) Revenue Bill 1978* at the Centre for Development
Studies at Trivandram, Kerala in April 1978. The draft was processed by the
Legislative Department as Bill #75 of 1978 and discussed on August 23, 1978
with Benoy Chowdhury (CPM), the Minister of Land and Land Reforms, the
Land Reforms Commissioner, and the Secretaries of the Panchayats and Community Development Department, the Legislative Department, and the Director
of Land Records amd Surveys. The bill was introduced to the Assembly by
Benoy Chowdhury and published on November 23, 1978.[74] The bill gave tax
rates:

a) On first 1000 Rupees of total rateable value          1 percent
b) On next 4000 Rupees of total rateable value          3 percent
c) On next 5000 Rupees of total rateable value          4 percent
d) On next 5000 Rupees of total rateable value          6 percent
e) On the balance of total rateable value          8 percent

The bill was then referred to a Select Committee of the Assembly under the
Chairmanship of Benoy Chowdhury. The Select Committee met six times
between January 24, 1979 and April 25, 1979 before finalizing its recommendations. The *West Bengal Land Holding Revenue Bill 1979* was passed by the
Assembly on August 30 and received Presidential assent on April 16, 1980. The
bill, however, as modified by the Select Committee of MLAs and passed by the
Assembly, was significantly different from what the Task Force and the Minister had presented to the Assembly as the draft bill. The new law stipulated the
following rates on land holdings:

a) On first 5000 Rupees of total rateable value          Nil
b) On next 1000 Rupees of total rateable value          2 percent
c) On next 1000 Rupees of total rateable value          3 percent
d) On next 3000 Rupees of total rateable value          4 percent
e) On next 3000 Rupees of total rateable value          5 percent
f) On next 3000 Rupees of total rateable value          6 percent
g) On the balance of total rateable value          8 percent

The new law now eliminated taxation of the first 5,000 Rupees of total
rateable value. More significantly the method of valuing total rateable value
had been changed from the original bill presented to the Assembly. Previously
it had been defined as the "cash value per hectare of the gross output of the main
crops or any other major produce grown in that area."[75] The Select Committee

---

[74] Sarkar, "Legal Aspects," pp. 277–8.
[75] *Ibid.*, p. 280.

had however added a proviso that "where adequate relevant data ... are not available, an amount of *10 per cent of the market value of land* in the areas *may* be considered as the rateable value of the area." The landholdings could be aggregated on the family farm basis for tax purposes or on an individual ownership basis. As anything under Rs. 5,000 rateable value was now exempt from taxation an individual method of rating would increase the landholders exempted area, by dividing ownership among individual family members for tax purposes. The original bill as presented to the Assembly was designed to change the inequitable land revenue system where rates had been on the decline since the days of the permanent settlement, to a new system which would apply a progressive tax tied to agricultural productivity and income. The bill was an effective compromise between the need to tax according to holding size and income and the administrative problems that would have arisen in trying to collect the large amount of data required by the Raj Committee recommendations. As finally passed, however, the bill changed tax on yield to tax on market value of land. According to the Director of Land Records and Surveys:

the shift from the value of the yield to the market value of the land remains rather unexplained unless we conclude that the State elects to adopt a soft line with the landed propertied class particularly in the upper and middle groups of peasants. Two relevant questions that have already been posed are: (1) What compelled the Select Committee to depart from the original scheme of calculation of the rateable value of land and (2) Did the Left Front Government develop cold feet when it came to realise that such a scheme would be adversely affecting (or going against the interest of) rich peasants and upper stratum of the middle peasants?[76]

With a 10 percent of market value rate giving an exemption limit of 50,000 Rupees market value or 5,000 Rupees rated value, the land holding tax would only "apply to a small fraction of the landowning households."[77] The *West Bengal Land Reforms (Amendment) Bill* already passed by the Left Front on September 29, 1977 had exempted from taxation non-irrigated land below 6 acres (2.428 hectares) and below 4 acres (1.619 hectares) for irrigated land.[78] As seen from the following chart this excluded 91.6 percent of households and 58 percent of the land from taxation.[79]

[76] *Ibid.*, p. 284.
[77] *Ibid.*, p. 285.
[78] Government of West Bengal, Board of Revenue, *Compendium of Instructions on Land Reforms*, vol. II (Up to December 31, 1980) (Kadapara: West Bengal Government Press, 1980), p. 16.
[79] National Sample Survey Seventeenth Round of 1961–62. Later surveys do not give a 6-acre breakdown of landholdings. The National Sample Survey Twenty-Sixth Round of July 1971 – September 1972 gives land between 2.50 and 4.99 acres or less comprising 77.62 percent of landowning households and 27.8 percent of the land. The cumulative percentage between 5 and 7.49 acres or less is 90.26 percent of households and 52.97 percent of the land. (N.S.S. Twenty-Sixth Round, Tables on Land Holdings West Bengal, vol. I, p. 66.)

| Size class of holding | Percentage number of households | Percentage area owned by households |
|---|---|---|
| Below 6 acres | 91.6 percent | 58.0 percent |
| 6 to 10 acres | 4.3 percent | 14.0 percent |
| 10 to 14 acres | 2.4 percent | 12.3 percent |
| 14 to 18 acres | 0.8 percent | 7.0 percent |
| 18 acres and above | 0.9 percent | 8.7 percent |
| Total | 100.0 percent | 100.0 percent |

In placing the *West Bengal Land Reforms Bill 1977* before the house, Benoy Chowdhury, the Minister of Land and Land Reforms, had admitted that:

As a result of the enlargement of exemption limit and reduction in the rate of Land Revenue contemplated in the clause 6 of the Bill which are to be given effect to from the 1st Baisakh, 1385 B.S., the demand of land revenue may, on a very rough estimate, come down from Rupees 702 lakhs to Rupees 161 lakhs. This is, however, a purely ad hoc measure pending replacement of land revenue by a graded land tax, working out details of which will naturally take some time.[80]

In comparison with earlier land revenue legislation, however, even the largest holdings would have to pay significantly less tax as indicated by table 3.5. Not only would the smallest farmers be exempted from tax but the largest landlords would obtain a significant decrease in taxes at the expense of reduced state revenues available to the Left Front government. As envisaged in the draft *Land (Farm Holdings) Revenue Bill* introduced to the Legislative Assembly on November 23, 1978, this temporary anomaly would have been removed by a progressive tax on the bigger landlords which would have increased revenues to 12.43 crores, from the 4.13 crores under the existing *Land Reforms (Amendment) Act* given assent by the President on February 3, 1978. However, after the Select Committee of MLAs had revised the bill and it had become law, it had been significantly changed. Whereas before the 1977 Left Front Land Reforms amendment a farmer owning 6 acres paid 60 Rupees tax on non-irrigated land and 90 Rupees on irrigated land, after the Amendment this was reduced to 30 and 45 Rupees respectively. For 16 acres it was 160 Rupees on non-irrigated and 240 on irrigated land before the 1977 amendment after which it decreased to 80 and 120 respectively.[81] Under the new *Land Revenue Bill* passed by the Assembly the latter landlord would have to pay 476 Rupees on

[80] Sarkar, "Legal Aspects," pp. 286–7.
[81] *Ibid.*, pp. 293–4.

Table 3.5. *Land revenue rates under different legislation*

| Mean area with rate per acre | Revenue in non-irrigated area | | | Revenue in irrigated area | | |
|---|---|---|---|---|---|---|
| | Up to April 14, 1972 | From mid April 1972 | From mid April 1978 | Up to April 14, 1972 | From mid April 1972 | From mid April 1978 |
| 8 acres @Rs. 6.00 | Rs. 48.00 | Rs. 96.00 | Rs. 48.00 | Rs. 48.00 | Rs. 144.00 | Rs. 72.00 |
| 12 acres @Rs. 12.50 | Rs. 150.00 | Rs. 300.00 | Rs. 150.00 | Rs. 150.00 | Rs. 450.00 | Rs. 225.00 |
| 16 acres @Rs. 4.00 | Rs. 64.00 | Rs. 128.00 | Rs. 64.00 | Rs. 64.00 | Rs. 192.00 | Rs. 96.00 |
| 20 acres @Rs. 6.00 | Rs. 120.00 | Rs. 240.00 | Rs. 120.00 | Rs. 120.00 | Rs. 360.00 | Rs. 180.00 |

*Source:* Bikram Kesari Sarkar, "Legal Aspects of Land Reforms Measures in West Bengal" (Calcutta University Ph.D. thesis November 1982), p. 288.

his 16 acres of land when calculated on a family basis, which represented a significant increase. "This will lead to endless and time consuming litigations. Such *raiyats* will prefer 'person-wise' assessment. Then the 'area-wise' averaging becomes a meaningless exercise."[82] By use of a person-wise assessment, only about 1 percent of total landowners or about 70,000 landlords would be required to pay any tax, which would average about 500 Rupees. All but the very biggest landlords engaged in personal cultivation would therefore be exempt and only 3.5 crores revenue would be raised as against 12.43 crores originally envisaged in the bill presented to the Assembly. With the ongoing fragmentation of land through inheritance even this revenue would decrease over time, as increased land market value would be unlikely to keep pace with a declining land–person ratio. The transformation of the bill at the Select Committee stage was an indication "of the pressure of the landed class particularly the middle peasantry who are deriving all the benefits of improved agricultural techniques and of the higher prices for agricultural produce."[83] The Director of Land Records and Surveys as one of the bills original formulators noted:

one can reasonably question the effectiveness of the Bill to bring in a fundamental restructuring of the land revenue system. It is criticised in certain quarters that the Bill has been robbed of its teeth by the Select Committee. The impression is that the Left Front Government in West Bengal succumbed to the same compulsions which had successfully stalled all attempts to bring reason into the direct system of land taxation, with all its inequities and failures.[84]

The fact that the Minister was able to place the bill before the assembly only to have it watered down by the MLAs, shows that while the Minister and his cabinet colleagues were willing to implement innovative legislation, their party's landed class base, as represented through their MLAs, were sufficiently influential to have the key clauses changed. By the final meeting of the Select Committee all parties from right to left were in agreement with the bill, an unusual unanimity indicative of the powerful landlord lobby found in all the parties. The IAS administrators who had formulated the original legislation were not entitled to participate in the Select Committee of MLAs and could only look on as the bill was modified from a progressive piece of legislation to something even more favorable to the landed interests than the existing laws. The Minister, though realizing the implications of the modifications nevertheless acquiesced in these revisions under the pressure of the MLAs. The official CPM policy, which remained unchanged, served only to show the difference

[82] *Ibid.*, p. 294.
[83] *Ibid.*, p. 296.
[84] *Ibid.*, pp. 291–2.

between theory and practice under the Left Front government. Nothing illustrates better the limitations on reform imposed by the Communists' own landlord base and the inability or unwillingness of the Party leadership to stand up to them. While the urban middle class IAS administrators could formulate radical agrarian legislation at no cost to their own careers and property, the CPM leadership, being dependent on their landlord base to get elected to power, had no such freedom of action. Thus their own radicalism was thwarted not by their own change in ideology, or even by the constitutional limitations imposed by the central government, but by their own landlord base. Clearly this base was too important to be challenged even to the extent of significantly raising their taxes. This did not augur well for the Communists' being able to jettison the landlords at a future date when confronted with conflicting demands from their own lower class base. Significantly the CPM did not attempt to justify its volte-face, but claimed the new legislation freed 80 percent of landholdings from any levy. "The Left Front government can rightly claim to be a pioneer in this matter in the whole of India."[85]

The failure to implement a progressive agricultural tax indicates not only the influence of landed interests on the elective process but the lack of lower class articulation and pressure within the political system. This could be attributed to the fact that the taxation issue did not directly affect the rural poor and landless, who therefore did not push for its implementation. Had the failure to implement agricultural taxation been the only sign that the government favored the landowners this might not have been conclusive. However, every single major piece of Communist reform legislation and implementation in favor of the lower classes was ultimately to fail. These failures, when acknowledged, have been attributed to constitutional constraints, financial restrictions, and above all to a hostile central government. The taxation issue is therefore particularly relevant to the debate on Left Front performance as it shows these constraints were not always present. Even when the state had the constitutional authority and power to pass progressive legislation, it failed to do so. The Left Front failed to utilize the power it had at its disposal due not in this case to external constraints, but to lack of political will in the face of landowner opposition within its own constituency. Problems of bureaucratic inertia, corruption, and inefficiency often blamed for failures in Third World policy implementation, cannot be the cause of the Left Front's not passing the original legislation. The reason was exclusively the need of the Communist elite to serve the interests of their landowner class base.

The elected Communist representatives at the lowest levels can safely be

[85] Subrata Paul, "Radical Change in Land Revenue System," *People's Democracy*, September 30, 1979, p. 5; "Land Reforms in West Bengal," *People's Democracy*, May 3, 1981, p. 12.

assumed to be from the landed interests or related to them. It is these village councillors and those at higher levels in elected office who are the channels through which landed interests are represented to the MLAs. Given the extent of their political control at the village level, it is understandable why the Left Front backed away from progressive agricultural taxation. They did not have the organization and lower-class leadership capable of supplanting the rural elite in the event that the Communists antagonized them with progressive taxation. The Left Front leadership, whatever their personal inclinations, have become hostage to the interests of their elite rural class base.

This has profound implications for Indian politics. If the most radical national Communist party in India would not pass even relatively innocuous reforms because of the influence of its landed support base, then the lower classes could expect no significant reform in their own interest. In effect there was no major political party to represent them, despite over a half-century of slowly evolving electoral democracy. The failure must lie primarily in a lack of lower-class political articulation, as a more militant following would have been reflected in a more radical leadership. Though existing Communist leadership failures are also responsible, both factors played a part in the current impasse.

The failure of both reform and revolution in West Bengal indicates a period, if not of Communist eclipse, then at least of stagnation in terms of radical socio-political development. Without more grassroots political articulation this pattern will not change. In *The Political Economy of Agrarian Change* published in 1974, Keith Griffin noted, "In India the urban areas have become increasingly resentful of subsidizing agricultural prices while exempting landlords from taxation, and it may not be possible for the landed interests to resist the demands for agricultural income taxes much longer."[86] Nearly a generation later it was clear the landlords did successfully resist the demands of even India's Communists, and in fact enhanced their tax position in West Bengal. In agricultural taxation the Left Front did worse than nothing, even though the legal and financial constraints operative in other policy spheres were absent. The imposition of significant agricultural taxes can no longer be seriously contemplated in any foreseeable political conjuncture in India. The limits of substantial agrarian reform in favor of the lowest classes have been reached, and only a major change in the political equation can alter this.

Significantly both the civil service and the Left Front cabinet were prepared to propose a progressive agricultural taxation bill. It was the Communist MLAs most in touch with the "grassroots" electoral base that effectively vetoed the

---

[86] Keith Griffin, *The Political Economy of Agrarian Change* (London: Macmillan Press, 1974), p. 218.

proposal. This does not augur well for radical change in party policy from grassroots pressure as the local elected party officials are opposed to the progressive agrarian taxation measures that the party leadership had supported. Increasing rural politicization has brought new vested interests to bear on the party leadership, without equivalent pressure from the most destitute segment of rural society. A "radical" party leadership has thus found its legislative program blocked by its own newly acquired landed class base, and is unwilling to incur the negative political consequences of using the state apparatus to confront these class interests. A class that was useful to the Communists in gaining entry into the village community and developing their electoral base became an obstacle to more radical reform in favor of the lower classes. This class base in the end proved powerful enough to have an effective veto over Communist agricultural taxation policy. While the Communists initially saw this class as a secondary and disposable ally of the rural landless, it has now come to dominate Communist agrarian taxation policy. The Communist leadership, despite a preference for more radical measures, has accepted this influence as legitimate, and in the case of agricultural taxation as the determinant of government policy.

The agricultural taxation issue in West Bengal shows the limits to revenue enhancement for economic development. However, the importance of the issue is greater than merely exploring another potential state revenue source. It illuminates a rural class whose political influence transcends the ideological divisions of right and left in India. Its influence can determine the policy of even Communist parties ideologically inclined to oppose its interests. Challenging this lobby would threaten the Left Front electoral base and potentially the marketable surplus food production on which consumers depend. Given potential electoral losses and cuts in food production, the surplus- producing farmers are not a lobby that can be ignored by even a revolutionary ruling party. While ruling parties have had to oppose food price increases demanded by these farmers in order to prevent consumer starvation, opposition parties including Communists in other states have supported these surplus-producing farmer demands. As failure of the West Bengal government to increase agricultural taxation has no immediate impact on consumers, the policy could be quietly changed without serious opposition. In the longer term, however, it limits the ability of state governments to promote economic development through imposing financial constraints on development programs. This has contributed to the limitations of state-sponsored economic development in West Bengal. In the end the Left Front had to depend on traditional revenue sources and retreat from innovative taxation measures. This retreat may have served to increase the longevity of the Left Front government, but eroded the reason it has for being in office in the first place. With reforms no longer contemplated, longevity in office has meant increasingly little. Having taken this course the Left Front has attempted to manage within these constraints, seeing no more promising alternative strategy. Only a favorable change in the central government is likely to enhance the possibilities for radical state government intervention. The eventual outcome of such a conjuncture is difficult to predict. It is unlikely, however, to be able to challenge the surplus-producing farmer lobby, and more likely will increase its importance.

### Food prices

Even at the theoretical level the rich and middle peasant orientation of the CPI and CPM became evident in the controversial policy of demanding increases in agricultural prices.[87] Any increase in government agricultural procurement prices will primarily help market producers and hurt consumers, including the agricultural laborers and poor peasants who have to purchase foodgrain. Just how small a proportion of the rural population would be the primary beneficiaries of produce price increases is indicated by the fact that aside from the 40 percent who are landless, 76 percent of the landowners are "small and marginal farmers operating only 24 percent of land the overwhelming majority of whom hardly ever retain marketable surplus and more often than not have to go in for consumption purchase for longer or shorter periods,"[88] leaving only the top 15 percent of rural society to benefit from the price increases the Communists advocate and well over half to be detrimentally affected. According to Hanumantha Rao, Member of the Planning Commission:

Payment of greater price over and above the remunerative prices will not help the small farmers. On the other hand it directly enriches the capitalist and larger farmers whose produce forms 80 percent of the marketed surpluses. Hence exclusive emphasis on raising prices beyond cost of production would strengthen the capitalist sector and would most adversely affect the rural poor where wages lag behind prices.[89]

Though this is the consensus among economists, the CPI leader Indradeep Sinha is reported to have stated in countering Hanumantha Rao's argument against price increases that "when the correlation of forces change in favour of socialism, we will take the advice of Mr. Hanumantha Rao and till such time let Mr. Rao revise his views on this issue" implying the primacy of the rich peasants in determining policy as long as they remain hegemonic in the rural areas or at

[87] Dev Nathan, "On Agricultural Prices," *For a New Democracy*, special issue, October–February 1981–82 (Calcutta: Provisional Central Committee, Communist Party of India – Marxist–Leninist, 1982), pp. 88–95, also published in *Economic and Political Weekly*, Review of Agriculture, December 1982.

[88] Ashis Barman, "New Challenges for Left," *Link*, January 26, 1983, p. 38.

[89] C.H. Hanumantha Rao, "Small Farmer can be viable and more Productive," *Link*, January 26, 1983, p. 48.

least are the most readily mobilizable within the party.[90] A correspondent of the *Economic and Political Weekly* noted that for the CPI to campaign for increasing prices along with "the Lok Dal champions of rich farmers does not appear to be a sound move in these circumstances. But obviously the rich farmers lobby inside the party has clout enough to push the CPI in that direction."[91]

The CPM readily admitted its middle and rich peasant base.

Whatever Kisan movement was organised and led was mainly oriented to the middle and well-to-do peasant sector, instead of the growing members of agricultural labour and poor peasant sections. The relative new opportunities for well-being that presented themselves to the middle and rich peasant sections in no small way influenced the CP in the rural areas, and in particular, a good chunk of the cadre of middle and rich peasant origin occupying leading positions in the rural party committees ...

The class composition of the once-united CP as well as of our party after its breaking away from the revisionists is predominantly petit-bourgeois in character. Ninety percent of the leading bodies and cadres comprise of middle and rich peasant sections. The fact that both in the general membership of the party and its committees from the village level to every higher committee up to the CC, elements of proletarian and semi-proletarian origin do not constitute a considerable force, let alone the majority, even after four decades in our country speaks volumes for the failure of the communist movement in our country. True, this state of affairs continues not because the leadership is either unaware of it or has not adopted some good resolutions from time to time stressing the need for increasing proletarianisation of the party, but it is mainly and solely due to the serious defects in building the mass workers' and peasants' revolutionary movements.[92]

Despite this middle and rich peasant base, the party at a policy and theoretical level originally adhered to a poor peasant and landless laborer orientation. The switch in the CPM's orientation towards the middle peasantry took place within a few years. Sundarayya's *Explanatory note on Certain Agrarian Issues* represented the original party position based on a dual price for landlords and smaller peasants. Landlords would be forced to relinquish their produce at low prices to compensate for higher prices paid to smaller peasants. Consumers would pay a reasonable price fixed between the high and low prices set by the government.

If the landlords who possess and control a preponderant portion of the marketable agricultural produce are forced to hand it over to the state at low prices, it will be economically feasible to assure a fair price for the toiling peasants and essential supplies to the consumers at prices within their reach.[93]

---

[90] B.M., "Agricultural Prices and the Left," *Economic and Political Weekly*, October 23, 1982, p. 1722.

[91] *Ibid.*, p. 1721.

[92] P. Sundarayya, *An Explanatory Note on the Central Committee Resolution on Certain Agrarian Issues* (Calcutta: Communist Party of India – Marxist, 1973), p. 46.

[93] *Ibid.*, p. 46.

By October 1976 this dual price policy was dropped and condemned as "lopsided and wrong."[94] The middle and rich peasant orientation of the CPM was finally confirmed in theory by the Central Committee's document *"The Peasant Upsurge and Remunerative Price Issue"* which criticised Sundarayya's radical position.

No doubt, while fighting against the reformist deviation in the peasant movement, we landed ourselves into some sectarian mistakes in 1973–76 and tried to work out the slogan of two prices and came out against the increase in the prices of foodgrains on the plea that it benefits the landlords and hits the consumer. This partly was the result of our failure to take note of ... the necessity of struggling to win over the rich peasants.[95]

As a result of this error the party lost ground to the Akali Movement in the Punjab, and the landlords were able to lead the movement initially on this issue.[96] By belatedly participating in this movement the CPM claimed "the movement went much beyond the narrow aims of these landlord elements" who had started it, namely to the middle and rich peasants who also stood to make smaller gains from the issue.[97] B.T. Ranadive at the CPM Eleventh Congress in 1982 refuted criticisms that this was a policy for the rich peasants at the expense of the poor.

Whether it is the rich peasant or anybody, the small producer is bound to be attracted. Is this so difficult for statisticians to understand? This is where the lack of class outlook comes ... It is asked, are we likely to lose our bearings when we support this mass struggle for remunerative price? What happens to the agricultural workers? What happens to the poor peasants? And that question is justified, because there is very little assurance of a poor peasant getting the remunerative price, unless he is well-organised. That is his education.[98]

The difficulty with this was that the poor peasant wouldn't be getting the higher remunerative price; he would be paying it, along with the agricultural laborer who would have to starve a little more as a result. Only middle peasants had any surplus to market and while they would not make as much as rich peasants and landlords from the price increase, the CPM correctly pointed out that this little extra would enable them to remain viable and keep their land thus avoiding the proletarianization of the middle peasantry. On the negative side only about

---

[94] Communist Party of India – Marxist, *Report and Resolution on Organisation* adopted by the Salkia Plenum, December 27–31, 1978 (New Delhi: May 1979), p. 51.

[95] Communist Party of India – Marxist, Central Committee, *The Peasant Upsurge and Remunerative Price Issue* (New Delhi: April 1981), p. 7.

[96] *Ibid.*, pp. 4, 13.

[97] All India Kisan Sabha, Twenty-Fourth Conference of the 8th–11th November 1982, Midnapore, West Bengal, *General Secretary's Report* (New Delhi: 1982), p. 12.

[98] B.T. Ranadive, "Speech Introducing Draft Political Resolution," in *Main Speeches at the Eleventh Congress*, Vijayawada, January 26–31, 1982 (New Delhi: Communist Party of India – Marxist, July 1982), pp. 42, 44.

15 percent of the rural population would gain and most of the rest would suffer, including particularly the poorest classes who could least afford to pay the higher prices. While Ranadive was right in pointing out this would help educate the poor peasants, it would hardly be in the direction of the Communist parties who had caused them to starve in the first place through having to pay the higher prices. That only 1 percent of agricultural laborers were organized at all was admitted by the CPM and these were largely in middle and rich peasant dominated organizations.[99] How they were therefore to struggle to make up for the price increases with wage increases was never explained. Even if they eventually could be organized, in the interim they would starve. When the *New York Times* correspondent Joseph Lelyveld stated "Indian politics never had much to do with the lives of the very poor, except verbally" it could also be applied to the CPI and CPM.[100] In their attempts to gain a quick base in the countryside, the Communist parties have ignored such realities in taking up, in conjunction with the right, an issue popular with the rural rich. That the Communist parties could support the policy of price increases indicates their real class orientation. They justify this by arguing that at the stage of democratic revolution the rich peasant "kulak" class remain allies of the revolution.[101] That the mainstream Communist Parties could advocate such a policy appears inconsistent. However, being in opposition, they did not have to live with the results of their policies, while the ruling Congress had to take the more responsible position of opposing it.

During the Janata regime the Minister of Agriculture asked one of his advisors to make a case for a substantial increase in the procurement price. The advisor responded that there wasn't a case for it, as the result would be starvation for millions of people who couldn't afford to pay the increase, and at the next election he would be out of power. Interestingly enough, the Janata Minister of Agriculture, Bhannu Pratap Singh, who had not implemented the higher prices he demanded when he was in power as it was untenable, later took the lead in demanding it when he returned to the opposition after Indira Gandhi's come-back in 1980. He set up the Central Kisan Coordination Committee along with the CPM's peasant organization and others to fight for price increases.[102] The West Bengal CPM, since they were in power, had to live with their policies, unlike the central CPM, and therefore opposed the price increase, resulting in the party center having to impose its position on the state unit.

---

[99] Communist Party of India – Marxist, *Political-Organisational Report*, adopted at Eleventh Congress, Vijayawada, January 26–31, 1982 (New Delhi: October 1982), p. 168.

[100] Lelyveld, *Calcutta*, p. 28.

[101] Nathan, "On Agricultural Prices," p. 2101; Indradeep Sinha, *The Changing Agrarian Scene: Problems and Tasks* (New Delhi: People's Publishing House, 1980), p. 149.

[102] All India Kisan Sabha, p. 12.

When in Parliament, the Agriculture Minister made a statement that the West Bengal Government had opposed the increase in prices of paddy, it created a bad impression among the members who expect us to be in the lead in fighting against the anti-peasant policy of the Government. Subsequently, the West Bengal Government took a correct position in entering the market and protecting the peasants from distress sales by paying them the price of Rs. 105 to Rs. 113 per *quintal* of paddy. It may be mentioned here that five PBMs (Politburo members) had met the West Bengal State Committee, and after discussions in the State Committee, we came to a common understanding leaving no room for confusion.[103]

In fact opposition to the higher prices came from a wide range of sources, from periodicals like *Link* and *Economic and Political Weekly* to sections of the party itself. An article in the *Economic and Political Weekly* commenting on this switch in policy questioned how "the landlords, within a short span of less than a decade, become innocuous and how were they silently allowed to reap the benefits of higher procurement prices."[104] Aside from the West Bengal unit of the CPM, the Tamil Nadu State Committee also expressed "certain differences and reservations" on the issue.[105] At the CPM peasant organization's Twenty-Fourth Conference in 1982 H.S. Surjeet admitted that "many, including some who are known as Marxist economists, have been arguing for a lower price for paddy and other foodgrains in the name of the interest of the consumers."[106] "This blanket stress placed on the reported question of remunerative price for agricultural produce, a demand of both the CPI and the CPI(M), did not seem to win the enthusiastic approval of some important Marxist Kisan Sabha leaders."[107] Though they kept their differences private, this appears to be based on the fact that higher prices would benefit only about 10–15 percent of farmers with marketable surplus, to the detriment of most of the rest.

One leading delegate from West Bengal, for instance has challenged the whole line of the AIKS in the name of West Bengal experience. There may be other delegates from West Bengal who, perhaps, are in agreement with him ... He emphasised that only when they were able to take up the question of land and wages, were they able to build a strong base among the agricultural workers and poor peasants. He then posed the question whether the policy which the AIKS was pursuing was not within the frame-work of the bourgeois path.... He also raised the question of peasant unity whether it is the unity with the rich and middle peasants or poor peasants? He narrated the experience of the

[103] Communist Party of India – Marxist, *Political-Organisational Report*, Eleventh Congress, p. 51.
[104] M.S.S. Pandian, "From Muzzaffarpur to Midnapur: Story of Missing Landlords," *Economic and Political Weekly*, January 22, 1983, p. 98.
[105] Communist Party of India – Marxist, *Political-Organisational Report*, Eleventh Congress, p. 51.
[106] All India Kisan Sabha, p. 33.
[107] Barman, "New Challenges," p. 40.

West Bengal land struggles – how they had occupied *benami* and surplus land and made a big advance. He then came to the conclusion that instead of waiting for legal assent to the comprehensive land legislation, occupation of land would have to be resorted to.[108]

This strategy was rejected by the delegates, only 127 of whom were agricultural laborers, being outnumbered by the middle peasants with 259 delegates and other occupations including middle classes and traders with 322 delegates.[109] The CPM All India Kisan Sabha advocates that these higher prices be offset by government provision of foodgrains to consumers at fair prices, though the public distribution system's record is poor and in any case the financial burden on the government would be heavy. This contradiction, however, has been exposed by the CPM's assumption of power in West Bengal where policies have to be implemented which cannot benefit both rich and poor, producer and consumer, at the same time. Opposition parties often support issues that give a certain political mileage but become liabilities when they are brought to power. The issue of increasing remunerative prices is tenable for an opposition party but cannot be implemented by those in power without alienating the rest of society.

The CPM decided in 1978 to form a separate all-India agricultural workers organization.[110] It was not till October, 1981 that the All-India Agricultural Workers Union was formed and not till November of 1982 that it had its first conference.[111] Interestingly enough the new organization made no mention of demanding price increases, even though the CPM Politburo members Harkishan Singh Surjeet and M. Basavapunniah were ranked first and second on the organization's council.[112] They were also members of the Kisan Sabha Central Committee which did advocate increased prices.[113] Clearly, if both organizations were to represent the interests of their constituency, these CPM leaders and the party in general would be placed in a conflicting position. If the Agricultural Workers' organization ever got off the ground it would be in conflict with its sister peasant organization and the CPM. Perhaps for this reason there was "resistance to the formation of a separate agricultural workers' organization" in the Kisan Sabha.[114] The new organization, unless completely emasculated, would not serve for unity in the party or among the party's rural constituency, as higher prices were a divisive issue on which a compromise

---

[108] All India Kisan Sabha, pp. 27–8.
[109] *Ibid.*, p. 93.
[110] Communist Party of India – Marxist, *Political-Organisational Report*, Eleventh Congress, p. 53.
[111] All India Agricultural Workers' Union, *Statement of Policy and Constitution*, adopted by the First Conference, Midnapore, West Bengal, November 11, 1982 (New Delhi: 1982).
[112] *Ibid.*, p. 14.
[113] All India Kisan Sabha, p. 98.
[114] *Ibid.*, p. 27.

between consumers and producers was not possible without prohibitive government food subsidies.

Though the demand for higher prices could hardly be termed Marxist or even progressive, it was advocated by the CPM for practical political reasons. Agricultural laborers and poor peasants were the most difficult to organize. They had no independent means of livelihood to enable them to resist the landlords who controlled the government apparatus at the village level. For the Communists to make an entry with this class, given their debt bondage and oppression, would be extremely difficult and require years of patient work. On the other hand the landlords, middle, and rich peasants were more politically conscious and had their own means of livelihood. As the landlords would gain the most from any price increase, the Communists could get their support and the cooperation of the village-level state police and administration. It was the quickest way for the Communists to gain a rural base, without the resistance of the "feudal" classes with whom they would now be allied. The difficulty was that once they gained a rural base by this method it would be very difficult to switch roles and support the exploited classes, having been already identified by the poorest classes as the party of the landlords and rich peasants. In West Bengal, where they have been in a position to change their orientation in favor of the poorest classes, they never did so and show no signs of doing so in the future. The CPM Political-Organizational Report criticized the Naxalites for orientating exclusively to the exploited classes, to the detriment of all peasant unity.

We have also to take note of the disruption caused by the activities of the Naxalites in various parts of the country. The most pernicious part of their activities is their attempt to pit agricultural workers and landless tribals against the rest of the peasantry ... The Naxalites, from their end, are ... disrupting the unity of the peasantry and sabotaging the struggle of both the agricultural workers and tribals and the peasantry. The organised kisan movement has to expose and isolate these Naxalite elements and relentlessly pursue the path of building peasant unity.[115]

The CPM on the issue of advocating price increases were doing the same disruptive activity but on behalf of the landlords and rich peasants. The fact was there was no objective basis for unity of the peasantry, as they represented conflicting interests. Only by subterfuges or non-class issues could the Communists hope to achieve this unity. In Communist countries this had been achieved through nationalist appeals and leading anti-colonial struggles, after which the landed classes were expropriated and replaced by communes. Such an approach was much more difficult in Indian conditions. The propertied

---

[115] Communist Party of India – Marxist, *Political-Organisational Report*, Eleventh Congress, pp. 168–9.

classes already had plenty of non-Communist parties to represent them effectively. The interests of all classes in India were represented by numerous parties at local, state, and national levels. The only major political vacuum left was among the poorest classes, whom the Communists were largely ignoring. With the Scheduled Castes and Tribes already being murdered by the landlords, it was difficult to find any issue on which all peasant unity was possible. Even if caste divisions could be overcome the most that could be expected was unity of agricultural labor with the poor peasantry and possibly some middle peasants. Approaching mobilization from the top down was likely to be counter-productive in the long term, as it identified the Communists with the propertied classes, as has already happened in a number of areas. The reasons for their top-down mobilization were perfectly understandable, given the oppressive conditions under which the lowest classes in India lived, but this short-term politically and organizationally expedient strategy could be counter-productive in the long term, as the lowest classes started asserting themselves and found the Communists on the side of their landlords. It is too early to say whether the CPM can make the switch to the lowest classes, but the trend has been in the opposite direction of promoting new vested interests. In fact the demand for all-peasant unity appears to be just a theoretical justification for the politically expedient policy of organizing the most readily mobilizable class of middle and rich peasants.

# 4    Panchayat Raj

A considerable literature has analyzed the nature of Indian rural elite control over village government institutions. It has shown how this rural elite is able to influence government policy and its implementation at the state and national level. The central theme of the literature has been that control by the landed high caste–class elite has effectively prevented the democratization of rural politics and the delivery of development aid to the lower classes. The literature is divided, however, on the extent to which universal franchise will enable the shift of political control to the more numerous lower-class voters. In this respect the Communist experiment with the Panchayats in West Bengal is important for showing the possibilities and constraints on attempting rural change in favor of the lower classes through the Panchayats. As the most radical state government in India, its Panchayat experiment indicates the extent to which change is possible in Indian democracy, and the problems in attempting devolution of power to the villages and the lower classes.

Since the publication of the Indian government's first five year plan in 1953, the Planning Commission's recommendation for devolution of power to village councils or Panchayats for the purpose of rural development implementation has been a matter of controversy.[1] The various attempts of the central and state governments in this direction proved unsuccessful in distributing the benefits of development aid to the lowest classes in the rural areas. In a system of acute inequality, the dominant landed classes used the Panchayats they controlled to corner development aid for themselves thereby helping to enhance their own positions. The Government of India Report of the Committee on Panchayati Raj Institutions admitted:

PRI are dominated by economically or socially privileged sections of society and have as such facilitated the emergence of oligarchic forces yielding no benefits to weaker sections. The performance of PRIs has also been vitiated by political factionalism, rendering developmental trusts either warped or diluted. Corruption, inefficiency, scant

---

[1] India, Planning Commission, *First Five Year Plan* (New Delhi: Planning Commission, 1953), p. 148.

124

regard for procedures, political interference in day-to-day administration, parochial loyalties, motivated actions, power concentration instead of service consciousness – all these have seriously limited the utility of Panchayati Raj for the average villager ... However, PRIs alone could not be picked up for blame in regard to the neglect of the interests of the weaker sections, as even the Government of India did not seem to have followed the lead in favour of weaker sections.[2]

Thus despite the best intentions of the Planning Commission the program produced results opposite to what was intended. It could hardly have been expected otherwise, given the nature of inequality and control exercized in rural India by the higher caste landed elite who have imposed their particular class interests on government policy, at the expense of the general public interest.

Despite the government's socialist rhetoric, and the extension of secret universal franchise, control continues to be in the hands of a rural landed elite. In some areas this landed elite are the traditional highest castes whose power has been retained despite the extension of the franchise. In other areas the highest castes were not the ones with the most land, and in these areas political control by the highest castes has given way to control by more numerous middle castes with the greatest economic resources. In either case, the dominant landed castes have retained control over the economic and political life of India's villages and prevented democratization of Panchayat politics. "Everywhere the peasant proprietor castes have gained at the expense of both the erstwhile zamindari and money lending families and the landless mass."[3] In many areas village politics is in a state of transition from control by the highest castes to that of the landed middle castes, resulting in some of the sharpest factional disputes.

Factional disputes are seen in the literature as being at the heart of traditional village politics. The most powerful landed families inevitably had disagreements among themselves which often originated several generations before, but were never finally resolved. Usually these rival lineages came from the same castes, and often had common ancestors. When necessary the rival family leaders used the patronage relationships with their employees to gather a local following, the size of which was closely related to landholdings. These vertical patron–client alliances extended from the factional leaders of the dominant landed castes downwards to include their lower caste laborers. These vertical alliances did not preclude horizontal alliances between factional leaders, and indeed these alliances were often necessary for weaker factions to overcome the strongest village faction. However, horizontal alliances were rarely formed

---

[2] India, Ministry of Agriculture and Irrigation, *Report of the Committee on Panchayati Raj Institutions* (New Delhi: 1978), pp. 6–7.

[3] Rajni Kothari, "Party Politics and Political Development," *Economic and Political Weekly*, annual number 1967, p. 171.

on a class basis between the lower castes in opposition to the higher castes. Horizontal alliances were therefore the preserve of the dominant faction leaders. The objective of these faction leaders was to become the village "big man," and as such these struggles hardly concerned the interests of the lower classes.

Since landed property was not the exclusive right of the dominant caste, many less-powerful middle and upper castes also strove to increase their landholdings, resulting in some rural competition and economic mobility. Middle castes could often expand their holdings through the clearing of forests and irrigation of previously uncultivated land, and, with increasing land scarcity, by acquiring land mortgaged to them by the poor. In time their lower ritual status in the caste hierarchy could be raised by using their economic resources to emulate upper-caste practices, such as the avoidance of agricultural labor by the hiring of lower-caste laborers. With the introduction of the universal franchise, these upwardly mobile middle landed castes tried to enhance their ritual and political status through the mobilization of new factions to challenge the traditionally dominant rival factions. These new landed middle-caste factions would often ally with opposition parties on the state and national level against the traditionally dominant elite factions which had already allied with the ruling Congress. In Uttar Pradesh the Lok Dal for instance represented the landed middle castes in opposition to the traditional elite affiliated with the Congress Party.[4] Neither party was much concerned with advancing the interests of the lowest classes; however, the electoral nature of the Panchayat system required rival elite factions to mobilize voter support among their respective clients in order to win elections. The group with the largest economic resources and therefore the largest client following would win unless other factions could unite to form an even larger following to defeat it in elections. Whether factional politics was between lineages of the same elite caste or between different elite castes, the class relations remained the same, and even the relative changes of caste ritual and political status were largely irrelevant to the majority of the rural population on the lower end of the class–caste hierarchy. In what is seen as the accepted view of conflict in the Panchayats, Marcus Franda states:

Factions in Indian Panchayats have seldom been led by members of the lowest castes ... In most Panchayats there has been a turnover of factions in power from one election to the next, but, with some notable exceptions, this has either involved transfer of power from a village's highest elite castes and aristocrats to a larger group of land-owning or "dominant caste" or a shift from control by one faction of a dominant caste to control by another. Studies have shown how village elders often accept the unwritten rule that

---

[4] Paul R. Brass, *Caste, Faction and Party in Indian Politics*, vol. I (Delhi: Chanakya Publications, 1983), p. 330.

village leadership is appropriate for members of the so-called clean castes, but that members of the Untouchable or Scheduled Castes should either be brought in as token supporters of particular factions or excluded entirely.[5]

Beyond this common ground the literature is divided on the degree of flexibility within the Panchayat system to democratic change and the articulation of lower-class demands. At one extreme the literature argues that the Panchayats have merely consolidated the interests and control of the dominant landed elite at the expense of the lower classes, making rural change for their own benefit even more difficult. Development aid channeled through the Panchayats has thus been counter-productive in that it puts more resources in the hands of the rural elite. The other extreme sees the Panchayat system as more dynamic, with the present elite-dominated system being merely a transitional phase to a more democratic Panchayat system that will arise as the lower classes become more politically aware. This debate between scholars, politicians, and government officials has continued for a number of years without being conclusively resolved. The trend has been for scholars to be increasingly critical of the Panchayats, while politicians and, to a lesser extent, government administrators have been more supportive.

This difference between the optimists and pessimists is revealed in Uttar Pradesh and Maharashtra which have been studied by several authors who agree on the existing elitism of the Panchayat system but differ in their views of the possibilities for change. In studying Uttar Pradesh, Harold Gould has developed a model describing the present Panchayat system as "transitional" in the direction of a "democratic" Panchayat system where the lower classes will act as classes for themselves under their own leadership.[6] The impetus for this is the secret universal franchise which enables voters to cast ballots according to their own preferences rather than for their patrons as occurs in a public vote. Where each person is equal electorally, the economic inequalities are insufficient to hold the lower classes in political dependence indefinitely. Brass's most recent analysis of Uttar Pradesh, however, provides far less grounds for optimism.[7] He shows that not only are district and village level politics controlled by the same old landed elite, but that their influence extends out of the district directly to the Prime Minister's office. In Gonda district the descendant of the old dominant raja owns at least 1,500 acres, still lives in a palace, chooses the local Congress MLAs and MPs, and intercedes with Indira

---

[5] Marcus Franda, *India's Rural Development* (Bloomington: Indiana University Press, 1979), pp. 126–7.

[6] Harold A. Gould, "Changing Political Behaviour in Rural Indian Society," *Economic and Political Weekly*, special number, August 1967, pp. 1515–22.

[7] Paul Brass, "National Power and Local Politics in India," *Modern Asian Studies*, vol. 18, no. 1, 1984, pp. 89–118.

Gandhi to have a 300-crore factory inappropriately located 2 kilometres from his palace. This is control by the traditional elite of the most personalized kind. However, in the other district of Deoria where there were several landed elite families, no individual, even with the backing, as in this case, of Sanjay Gandhi, could deliver the district vote single-handed. In this district political control, though not the personal prerogative of one man, was nevertheless the monopoly of a very small landed elite. There was no indication that the existing system was in a state of transition to the democratic model suggested earlier by Gould.

In studies of Maharashtra which has a particularly strong Panchayat system, the differences in analysis are more subtle. Traditionally Congress has encompassed all the most important factional divisions, preventing the formation of a factional wing opposed to the Congress Party. All authors agree that the system is dominated by a landed *vetendar* Maratha caste, however the degree of openness of the political system to other non-elite groups is a matter of controversy.[8] Carras gives factional differences an economic base, attributing these political disputes to conflicts of economic interests.[9] Carter and Lele though less causal in their explanations see little competition from outside this traditional elite.[10] Rosenthal, however, describes the elite as "expansive" and able to integrate dissident and upwardly mobile groups into the elite patronage distribution network.[11] This "expansive elite" is by nature co-optive rather than progressive, and only makes concessions that integrate potentially oppositional elites into the system, thereby undermining lower-class mobilization. In what could be a summary of the pessimistic view of Panchayat experience, Rosenthal states "institutionalization is a double-edged political weapon, which can stunt political change at a certain level of development rather than foster it."[12] The creation of Panchayats and the distribution of development aid through them by consolidating elite patronage networks have made rural change by the lower class that much more difficult. While strengthening links between the rural elite and the state and national elite, it has not brought the lower-class electorate any closer to a share of real political power.

These widely recognized failures of the Panchayat system to redistribute wealth and power to the lower classes are attributed by the scholars to the

[8] Anthony T. Carter, *Elite Politics in Rural India* (Cambridge: Cambridge University Press, 1974), p. 4.
[9] Mary C. Carras, *The Dynamics of Indian Political Factions* (Cambridge: Cambridge University Press, 1972), p. 185.
[10] Carter, *Elite Politics*; Jayant Lele, *Elite Pluralism and Class Rule* (Toronto: Toronto University Press, 1981).
[11] Donald B. Rosenthal, *The Expansive Elite* (Berkeley: University of California Press, 1977), p. 313.
[12] *Ibid.*

inability or unwillingness of politicians at the state and national levels to overcome the resistance of the local elites to redistributive measures – either because the politicians are themselves representatives of these rural elites or because the elites are too powerful for government institutions to supplant. In the initial years of the program the view was that at a national level the politicians took a progressive view, and only local elite resistance prevented implementation. With the increasing conservatism of national Indian politics, the academic view has shifted to seeing politicians at all levels as intrinsically linked and mutually dependent on the rural elites. Brass noted in his study of Gonda and Deoria districts in Uttar Pradesh that the "Congress leadership in Delhi sought allies from the most powerful local families with the greatest economic and/or political resources. The Congress operates more than ever before through existing structures of local power, which its economic policies are supposedly designed to eliminate."[13] Electoral politics has made the national leadership more rather than less dependent on the rural vote, which effectively means dependence on the rural elite.

### The West Bengal Panchayats

Though Article 40 of the Indian constitution directed Indian states to establish village councils with developmental responsibilities, the law was observed as much in the breach as in the implementation. West Bengal was typical in holding irregular elections to the Panchayats, when they were held at all. Though elections were only for four-year terms, those inaugurated in the late 1950s and early 1960s were not dissolved until the Communist government called for new elections in 1978. Thus these councils, despite the regulations, held office from thirteen to nineteen years without re-election. Marvin Davis's village-level study shows that this election was not always democratic as the dominant village leadership merely nominated members without a vote being taken. Though this was against the law, the local government Block Development Officer acquiesced in these non-elections. Where members had to come specifically from tribal or lower-caste wards, the high-caste village elite nominated their own clients as representatives of these groups.[14] Over time these councils met less frequently and proved to be just another institution of local elite control.

The study of the West Bengal Panchayat reforms and their effectiveness as a means of rural change is particularly problematic, given the dearth of suitable political studies at local and district levels in West Bengal. Unlike in Uttar Pradesh and Maharashtra, political studies have been almost entirely confined

---

[13] Paul Brass, "National Power," pp. 104–5.
[14] Marvin Davis, *Rank and Rivalry* (Cambridge: Cambridge University Press, 1983), pp. 184–5.

to the state level, with little attention to the dynamics of change in village level politics. The economic studies by scholars such as Ashok Rudra and Pranab Bardhan, make little mention of political affiliations in the samples surveyed.[15] Even the study by Swasti Mitter on the Communist movement in rural Sonarpur is unsuitable because of the location's atypical characteristics. The area is located on the outskirts of Calcutta which residents can commute to by road and rail. Over two-thirds of the population are Scheduled Caste compared with 22 percent in the state as a whole. All eight "branded" landlords were "outright capitalist" Scheduled Caste farmers. "Tension among the Jotedars and peasants was therefore entirely of an economic nature, while extra-economic factors such as religion or caste played a negligible role."[16] The area was involved in the nineteenth century indigo planters' revolt and the Communist-led Tebhaga movement of the 1930s and 1940s. It had elected a Communist MLA in all three elections since 1952, and the Communist following was found to be divided between middle peasants supporting the CPI and the landless supporting the CPM. In every respect it was atypical of rural Bengal, and often the opposite of the norm. It would be difficult to find another area in the state with a similar socio-political make-up.

With the inadequacy of existing micro-level economic and political studies for understanding the nature of Communist entry into village politics, it has been necessary to turn to the anthropological literature. Though analysis of party politics was never an important part of these studies, from this literature it is possible to gain some insights into the nature of Communist rural mobilization and its influence on Panchayat government. It is clear from the anthropological literature that the introduction of Communist ideology into village life was the result of upper caste-class Communist members or sympathizers in the villages mobilizing the lower classes against the predominant landed village elite which had already allied with Congress.

Gouranga Chattopadhyay's study of the Bengali village of Ranjana describes a typical example of an ambitious member of the elite mobilizing the lower classes.

Taking advantage of dissatisfaction in the village against this headman, a local well-to-do Brahmin who was so far not recognized in the village as a man of importance is now trying to become the headman with the support of the poor peasants, who are not pleased with the existing headman. This has brought in another situation. The poor peasants, who have so long been disorganized, had started uniting of late, and had consolidated to a

---

[15] Ashok Rudra, "Extraeconomic Constraints on Agricultural Labour," *Asian Employment Programme Working Papers*, ILO, Bangkok, August 1982; Pranab K. Bardhan, *Land, Labour and Rural Poverty* (Delhi: Oxford University Press, 1984).

[16] Swasti Mitter, *Peasant Movements in West Bengal* (Cambridge: Department of Land Economy, 1977), p. 55.

large extent ... Now this Brahmin is trying to fan their dissatisfaction and become the headman.[17]

In Basudha village studied by the National Institute of Community Development, the traditional Panchayat leadership of the Zamindar family that had controlled the village for decades was challenged by a new upper landed caste leadership influenced by the Communists.[18] The leadership in this struggle against the former Zamindar was led by the Sadgope landed caste members who, though not an urban elite caste, were definitely considered an elite caste in rural Bengal, where they were often the dominant landed caste. In Marvin Davis's study this caste is the dominant elite caste of Torkotala village. During the Communist-led United Front government in the late 1960s this caste was the privileged elite trying to defend themselves in the face of labor disputes, rather than the rival faction leaders challenging the Zamindars as in the previous case.[19]

These anthropological accounts of Communist mobilization in three villages reveal as much as they omit about the process. Only in the case of Basudha is a Communist party membership identified, and then only as a Kayastha of unspecified class. As arguably the most influential elite caste in Bengal it is a fair assumption he comes from the village elite group, even if personal property may be minimal. The other village leaders of the peasant movement in Basudha are from an elite Sadgope caste, who very likely are primarily interested in taking over village leadership from the old Zamindar family, rather than in lower-class emancipation. Indeed, in the other village of Torkotala, the Sadgope caste is already the dominant landed village elite. Here the only village laborer leadership is identified as a Hindu landholder, whose motivation is unclear but sufficiently strong for him to be willing to pay well above the going wage rate. The landholders' suspicions about his motivations may not be without foundation. With a Communist-dominated government in power the best route to village leadership would be in supporting the lower classes, rather than in contesting village leadership as one of several candidates trying for leadership in the traditional factions. The dividends in terms of power and financial returns would far outweigh any losses from being the first to meet labor demands. Unfortunately the leadership's personal motivations are not mentioned, except in the case of one Sadgope member in Basudha who was impressed by the speeches of a Communist state leader. These motivations are more important than class origins in determining the nature of Communist mobilization,

[17] Gouranga Chattopadhyay, *Ranjana: A Village in West Bengal* (Calcutta: Bookland Private Ltd., 1964), p. 44.
[18] Ajit K. Danda and Dipali G. Danda, *Development and Change in Basudha* (Hyderabad: National Institute of Community Development, 1971), pp. 54–8.
[19] Davis, *Rank and Rivalry*, pp. 205–9.

because it is on these local leaders that the direction and limitations of the movement will rest. This does not mean that personally ambitious peasant leaders will not pursue the struggle, but if it rests in merely using the peasant following to replace the old factional leadership with their own personal leadership, then the movement will result in a circulation of elites rather than a significant change in political and class relations. Rosenthal in his study of Maharashtra notes among social scientists "a certain unwillingness to recognize the possibility that ambition may assume an independent character of its own."[20] While a peasant leader only interested in personal advancement may of necessity have to make concessions to his following, he has a fair measure of discretion in the direction and extent of that mobilization, most particularly in those cases when he has been the initiator and instigator of the challenge. Where the peasant leadership are from the village elite, though not members of the dominant faction, there can be a strong temptation to take over village leadership as a faction head rather than as the representative of the lower classes with whom they have no common class interests beyond replacing the currently dominant faction. According to Gould's model whatever the personal motivations of the new peasant leaders, the very fact that the lower classes are mobilized for the first time against their landlords, will politicize the lower classes and eventually enable the creation of their own leadership from among their own class. They will thus become a class for itself, and reject any temporizing which leaders from elite groups might attempt. The movement of the lower classes will thus have a momentum and dynamic of its own which even peasant leaders from the elite groups who began it will be unable to control. Thus the personal motivations or elite background of the peasant leadership will prove irrelevant as the struggle escalates and politicization of the lower classes takes place.

The three Bengali village studies, if seen in the framework of the literature from the rest of India, would not lead to such a radical conclusion. In this perspective the Basudha class disputes would appear as the factional struggle of the landed elite caste to take over village leadership and "big man" status from the old Zamindar family. In Torkotala it is an even more ambitious attempt by a single landlord to take advantage of the Communist-dominated state government's neutralization of the police to seize village leadership from the dominant Sadgope faction with the help of the agricultural laborers. In Basudha the landed Sadgope struggle to remove the traditionally dominant Zamindar family, while in Torkotala where the same Sadgope are already the dominant elite, they are challenged in turn by their former laborers. In a sense Basudha and Torkotala are representative of the progression from Zamindar dominance in the case of Basudha to landowner dominance in the case of Torkotala. The

---

[20] Rosenthal, *The Expansive Elite*, p. 314.

leadership of one family is being replaced by the leadership of a landed caste, which provides a more effective and durable base for elite control of the village. The factional class compositions of the leadership are not different from the elite factions that exist elsewhere in India which aim only at improving elite ritual status and political control. Nevertheless the Bengali elite landed class-castes have organized the lower classes in Communist-influenced struggles against the dominant elite factions. It is clear that the Bengali village leadership is prepared to go further in mobilizing the lower classes against the dominant landed elite than elsewhere in India, where class and inter-elite conflict have not reached such levels of polarization and politicization. In the absence of more extensive and detailed data, it is impossible to give a definitive judgment as to the motivations and ambitions of the Communist-influenced rural peasant leadership; and all that can be said about them is that they come from an elite class-caste rather than from the lower classes themselves.

This elite class–caste composition of the rural Communist leadership is confirmed by the Communists' own admissions and analysis of their leader-ships' backgrounds. About half of the CPI Bengal state peasant organization executive were high-caste Hindus, 31 percent of cultivator castes, 7 percent Muslim, and 4 percent tribal. In the CPM Kisan Sabha Bengal state executive 56 percent were high-caste Hindus, 24 percent cultivator castes, 11 percent Muslims, and 7 percent tribal.[21] Of delegates to the CPM All India Kisan Sabha conference in 1982, 127 were agricultural laborers, 179 poor peasants, 259 middle peasants, 49 rich peasants, 39 landlords, and 322 from other occupa-tions.[22] The CPM Central Committee's resolution on the "Tasks on the Kisan Front" states that "the bulk of our leading Kisan activists come from rich and middle peasant origin, rather than from agricultural laborers and poor peasants. Their class origin, social links and long training given to them give a reformist ideological-political orientation which is alien to the proletarian class point of view and prevent them from actively working among the agricultural laborers, poor and middle peasants with the zeal and crusading spirit demanded of Communists."[23]

The Communists admit that much of their peasant leadership comes from non-dominant middle-class groups challenging the control of the traditional leadership. This is justified as part of their multi-class alliance aimed at breaking the hegemony of the traditional elites, to enable the middle and lower classes to form a dominant alliance at the local level. To achieve this, what is required

---

[21] Ranjit Kumar Gupta, *Essays in Economic Anthropology* (Calcutta: Institute of Social Research and Applied Anthropology, 1979), p. 89.

[22] All India Kisan Sabha, Twenty-fourth conference, 8th–11th November, 1982, *Proceedings and Resolutions*, Midnapore, West Bengal (New Delhi: 1980), p. 93.

[23] P. Sundarayya, *An Explanatory Note on the Central Committee Resolution on Certain Agrarian Issues* (Calcutta: Communist Party of India – Marxist, April 1973), p. 2.

is "a certain amount of mutual understanding and accommodation of interests. This is the only way struggles are won, by isolating the main enemy, by splitting the main enemy, by splitting the ranks of the opposing vested interests, and dealing with them one at a time, and by always trying to keep the majority in the rural society on the side of those struggling through these 'united fronts'."[24] That these struggles have resulted in other parts of India in only inter-elite circulation of leadership is understandable, according to the Communists, given the conservative parties under which these struggles were led. The leadership of the Communist parties will, however, enable these struggles to be extended to involve the lower classes with the eventual creation of their own leadership. The study of Basudha indicated, however, that the lower classes were forced to abandon the struggle because of their economic dependence on the former Zamindar family. It was left to middle and elite interests to fight on against the dominant Zamindar. It was therefore unrealistic for the Communists to expect the lower classes to initially project their own leadership, which in the beginning would have to be provided by the middle and rich peasants who were not dependent on the landlords.[25] The Communists therefore had to utilize a class whose interests were not in the final analysis compatible with lower-class emancipation. The class forces the Communists had to rely on for peasant leadership were therefore not those they would have preferred, but were nevertheless necessary if they were to proceed with village-level mobilization of the lower classes in the initial period. It would be up to the Party leadership to maintain overall direction and control of the movement to ensure the interests of the lower classes were not sacrificed for those of its elite leadership.

West Bengal is no different from the rest of India in having inter-elite rivalries that lead to the mobilization of the lower classes in faction fights for control of the Panchayats. These factional struggles lead to polarization of the villages around rival factions, but in no case does it lead to the dominance of the lower classes over village life, though it appears to have increased their political awareness. The lack of party identification for most of the village peasant leadership would seem to indicate personal leadership ambitions rather than Communist ideology as the motivating force behind the peasant leaderships' mobilization of the lower classes, though a definitive position would require a larger and more explicit survey. As the dominant elite is pro-Congress, it is natural for a rival faction not only to mobilize the lower classes against it, but to try to get outside patronage and support from the state opposition party

[24] Biplab Dasgupta, "Agricultural Labour under Colonial, Semi-Capitalist and Capitalist Conditions: A Case Study of West Bengal," *Economic and Political Weekly*, September 29, 1984, p. A146.
[25] Hamza Alavi, "Peasants and Revolution" reprinted from *The Socialist Register 1965* (Boston: New England Press).

whether it be the Lok Dal as in Uttar Pradesh or the Communists in West Bengal. Within the village, however, party affiliations appear less important than factional rivalries and alliances, and party influence is used primarily in obtaining outside patronage needed to strengthen factional positions in the village. The weakness of the village leadership's ideological commitment, observed in Indian village studies, appears also in the case of West Bengal. It would therefore appear that the Communists were in a weaker position than was at first apparent. Both in the villages and in the Communist parties, leadership was largely the prerogative of the traditional elite groups. There appeared to be a weak link between the party and class, with the lower classes largely under the control of dominant or rival factions of the traditional elite. The elite class composition of the party was less significant in that most could be assumed to have an ideological commitment to the lower classes despite their elite backgrounds. However, the same could not be said for many of their elite followers. The Communists as the main opposition party or the governing party, could naturally attract support from village elite factions attempting to displace the traditionally dominant elite factions which had allied with Congress. At most this pro-Communist elite represented a landed and middle-class leadership trying to enhance their own position at the expense of the traditional elite, with the help of the lower classes. This alliance was justified by the Communist parties as part of their multi-class alliance, but in practice left the hegemonic position in the hands of the propertied village elite leadership of this Communist-supported coalition.

### The Left Front Panchayats

When in 1977 the newly elected Communist government in West Bengal decided to restructure the Panchayat system in its state, attention was drawn to this attempt at devolving power to the rural poor.

Many observers feel the CPM has a realistic chance of bringing about genuine reform of local governments in the West Bengal countryside. The party is probably the best disciplined in India, has obviously made its new rural thrust its highest priority for the next five years, and has enormous incentive to succeed ... Should the CPM be able to demonstrate that it can rule effectively and bring about meaningful reform at the local level in the West Bengal countryside, its appeal to the downtrodden in most Indian states would be considerably enhanced.[26]

This experiment appeared to have greater potential for success as a Communist government could be expected to override the rural vested interests and use its rural cadre organization to ensure that not only was development aid

---

[26] Franda, *India's Rural Development*, pp. 142–3.

actually delivered, but that it got to those most in need. Where previously Panchayat elections were held on the basis of individual nominations, now for the first time official party slates would compete against each other, bringing party politics formally to village government. The village Panchayats could give the Communists an organizational base from which to resist possible central government repression in the future. Decentralizing the administrative apparatus would make it more difficult for the central government to impose Presidential Rule effectively, as much of the state powers would rest in Communist-controlled village organizations which, if self-supporting, could not be readily supplanted. As control of the village meant effective control of the state in electoral terms, no party could rule democratically without eliminating the Communist organization in the villages. These partisan political objectives had important implications for the restructuring of Bengal politics.

The thirty-six-point program of the Left Front in the 1977 assembly election stated that "elections to the Panchayats should be held immediately on the system of proportional representation with measures to be taken to confer more powers and resources on all local bodies."[27] After the Panchayat election during the floods at the end of 1978 the potential of the Panchayats for rural reconstruction was realized in its flood relief program. Unlike in the past the relief work undertaken through the Panchayats prevented the usual rural migration to Calcutta normally associated with such natural calamities.[28] Their success in relief work prompted the Left Front to allocate more resources and responsibility to the Panchayats.

Though the conception was promising and the public was told that the Panchayat would receive increased power and financial resources, its success as an agency for rural transformation would depend on the type of people elected to the village Panchayats and the direction the Left Front would give these bodies.

The 1978 Panchayat election gave the Left Front an overwhelming mandate. At the village level, out of 46,700 seats the CPM got 28,105, the Revolutionary Socialist Party (RSP) 1,674, the Forward Bloc (FB) 1,539, the opposition Congress-I 4,536, Congress-S 580, Communist Party of India (CPI) 825, and the independents 9,436. The Panchayat Samiti, grouping several village Gram Panchayats, gave the CPM 5,596 out of 8,454 with the Congress gaining only 623, the RSP 353, FB 320, CPI 132, and Congress-S 105. The only substantial non-CPM group in the Samiti were independents who got 1,323. Of the 647 district level Zilla Parishad seats, CPM got 488, RSP 30, FB 44, CPI 5,

[27] Anjali Ghosh, *Peaceful Transition in Power* (Calcutta: Firma KLM, 1981), p. C-40.
[28] West Bengal, Directorate of Panchayats, *Panchayats in West Bengal* (Calcutta: 1981), p. 14.

Congress-I 23 and independents 53.[29] The Communist mandate was clear but the nomination of the Left Front's candidates was rather hastily and haphazardly done. Though the Panchayat election was held in June 1978, a full year after the Left Front came to power, the Left Front including the powerful CPM lacked the cadre to nominate experienced party members to most of the posts. The CPM had only 38,889 members in 1978, 10,000 having joined since the return of the Left Front to power in 1977.[30] In the selection the local influence of the candidates was often the prime consideration rather than political conscious-ness, and many relatives of CPM members were chosen as party candidates.[31] In the scramble to get nominations from the ruling state parties many influentials and even former Congressmen jumped on the Communist bandwagon and succeeded in obtaining seats.[32] The inclusion of these opportunists disgruntled some of the traditional Communist supporters who were left out of the nomi-nations. The divisions among the Left Front partners resulted in their contesting against each other in about 6,000 seats.[33]

An independent survey by the National Institute of Rural Development in Hyderabad on one Gram Panchayat each in the districts of Nadia, Midnapore, and Jalpaiguri found the educational level of Panchayat members "high enough to justify appreciation of the voters' judgement. There is no illiterate" Panchayat member.[34] Farmers made up 47 percent, 24 percent were professionals, 22 percent businessmen, and 4 percent service holders.[35] Only one person was a laborer, indicating that it was the village middle and elite class which controlled these Panchayats. The study found that while the Scheduled Castes and Tribes continued their traditional occupations, the upper castes which had dominated during the zamindari period had now branched out from their landed base into the services and professions where "their traditional literary skills, higher educational levels, and better linkages with urban areas (an aspect of the *bhadralok* syndrome) must have stood them in good stead."[36] It was this occupational and educational elite which controlled the Panchayat government in these villages.

[29] M. Shiviah, K.B. Srivastava and A.C. Jena, *Panchayati Raj Elections in West Bengal, 1978* (Hyderabad: National Institute of Rural Development, 1980), p. 134.
[30] Communist Party of India – Marxist, *Report and Resolution on Organisation* adopted by the Salkia Plenum, December 27–31, 1978 (New Delhi: May 1979), pp. 12, 49.
[31] Shiviah *et al.*, *Panchayati Raj Elections*, p. 51; Bhabani Sen Gupta, *CPI-M: Promises, Pros-pects, Problems* (New Delhi: Young Asia Publications, 1979), p. 137.
[32] West Bengal State Conference, CPM, *Rajnaitik-Sangathanik Report* ("Political Organisational Report"), 14th Plenary Session, December 27, 1981–January 1, 1982 (Calcutta: West Bengal State Committee, CPM, March 1982), p. 91; Shiviah *et al.*, *Panchayati Raj Elections*, p. 51.
[33] *Ibid.*, p. 136.
[34] *Ibid.*, p. 51.
[35] *Ibid.*, pp. 116–7.
[36] *Ibid.*, p. 127.

Table 4.1. *Distribution of Gram Panchayat members by occupations*

| Occupation | Number | Percentage |
|---|---|---|
| Owner cultivator | 743 | 50.7 |
| Teachers | 206 | 14.0 |
| Unemployed | 110 | 7.5 |
| Landless laborers | 70 | 4.8 |
| Sharecroppers | 26 | 1.8 |
| Artisans | 23 | 1.6 |
| Shop owners | 20 | 1.4 |
| Technical workers | 19 | 1.3 |
| Doctors | 16 | 1.1 |
| Tailors | 8 | 0.6 |
| Students | 8 | 0.6 |
| Fishermen | 6 | 0.4 |
| Others | 211 | 14.4 |
| Total | 1466 | 100.0 |

A larger sample survey of 100 village Panchayats by the Development and Planning Department of the West Bengal government found a similar occupational and educational distribution.[37] Only 4.8 percent of the Panchayat members were landless laborers and 1.8 percent were sharecroppers though 44.28 percent of agriculturists in Bengal were landless laborers (see table 4.1).[38] Over half were owner cultivators, 71 percent with less than 5 acres of land (see table 4.2).[39]

The dominance of the relatively well-educated section of the village community in the Panchayat was confirmed by the survey. The education of 78 percent of members was between the primary and higher secondary level while 14 percent were graduates. With only 8 percent below primary graduation level, the underrepresentation of the illiterates, who form 67.03 percent of West Bengal's rural population but 1 percent of Panchayat members, was marked (see table 4.3)[40]. In spite of this, on the basis of the above survey the West Bengal Left Front government concluded that "judging by the evidence of this survey the members of the Panchayats by a significant majority, can be taken to

[37] West Bengal, Department of Panchayats and Community Development, *The Working of Panchayat System in West Bengal* (Calcutta: March 1980), pp. 42–3.
[38] Ajit Kumar Ghose, *Agrarian Reform in West Bengal* (Geneva: International Labour Organisation, 1980), p. 8.
[39] West Bengal, *The Working of Panchayat System*, pp. 42–3.
[40] India, Registrar General and Census Commissioner, *Census of India, 1981, Provisional Population Totals: Workers and Non-Workers*, Series-1, Paper 3, 1981, p. 177.

Table 4.2. *Land holdings of owner cultivator Gram Panchayat members*

| Acres | Percentage of distribution |
|---|---|
| Below 2 | 42.9 |
| 2–5 | 28.2 |
| 5–8 | 13.0 |
| 8–10 | 8.1 |
| Over 10 | 7.8 |
| | 100.0 |

*Source:* Government of West Bengal, Department of Panchayats and Community Development, *The Working of Panchayat System in West Bengal: A Review of Main Events and Activities* (March, 1980), pp. 42–3. From survey of 100 Gram Panchayats.

Table 4.3. *Distribution of Gram Panchayat members by education*

| Education standard | Number | Percentage |
|---|---|---|
| Non-literate | 10 | 1 |
| Just read and write | 57 | 4 |
| Below primary | 49 | 3 |
| Primary | 214 | 14 |
| Middle level | 499 | 34 |
| High/higher secondary | 436 | 30 |
| Graduate level | 161 | 11 |
| Post graduate | 30 | 2 |
| Technical degree | 10 | 1 |
| Total | 1466 | 100 |

*Source:* Government of West Bengal, Department of Panchayats and Community Development, *The Working of Panchayat System in West Bengal: A Review of Main Events and Activities* (March, 1980), p. 42, from survey of 100 Gram Panchayats.

represent the interests of the poorer sections in villages."[41] Given the class composition of contemporary Bengal villages this would appear to be something of a distortion, the opposite being closer to the truth. Using the same government statistics, P. Roy Choudhury argues that the Panchayats are dominated by "the same old class of rural vested interests including money

[41] West Bengal, *Economic Review 1980–81* (Calcutta: West Bengal Government Press, 1981), p. 21.

Table 4.4. *Political and class profiles of Gram Panchayat members*

| Political profile | | Vocation | |
| --- | --- | --- | --- |
| Relationship with the CPM | Distribution percentage | Type of work | Distribution percentage |
| Opportunists[a] | 13.3 | Agriculturalist | 60.1 |
| Sympathizers[b] | 58.3 | Landless agricultural labor | 8.3 |
| Part-time members[c] | 21.7 | Non-agriculturalist | 31.6 |
| Full-time members[d] | 6.7 | | |
| Land ownership[e] | | Mode of land use[e] | |
| Size of holding (acres) | Distribution percentage | Land use | Distribution percentage |
| 0–2 | 8.3 | Only family labor | 0 |
| 2–5 | 69.0 | Use hired labor | 83.3 |
| 6–10 | 19.4 | Use sharecroppers | 16.7 |
| 10 and above | 2.8 | | |

[a] Less than two years of party involvement (after CPM came to power)
[b] Over two years of party involvement
[c] Over five years of party work
[d] Card-carrying members
[e] Breakdown for agriculturalists only
*Source:* Atul Kohli, "Parliamentary Communism and Agrarian Reform," *Asian Survey*, vol. 23, no. 7, July 1983, p. 793.

lenders."[42] "51 percent belong to the landowning classes; the rest are classified as 'others' but are themselves linked with landed interests."[43] He refers to the Land Reforms Commissioner D. Bandyopadhyay claiming only 6.54 percent of Panchayat members belong to the rural poor.[44]

Atul Kohli, from a sample of sixty Gram Panchayat members, takes an intermediate position that "institutional power has, at least for now, been transferred from the hands of the dominant propertied groups to a lower middle stratum."[45] As with all surveys which attempt to determine class land holdings, underestimation of holdings by landowners tends to place them in a lower class than is actually the case. In the Kohli survey (table 4.4) 8.3 percent of

---

[42] P. Roy Choudhury, "Land Reforms: Promises and Fulfilment," *Economic and Political Weekly*, December 27, 1980, p. 2173.
[43] *Ibid.*
[44] *Ibid.*
[45] Atul Kohli, "Parliamentary Communism and Agrarian Reform," *Asian Survey*, vol. 23, no. 7, July 1983, p. 794.

agriculturalist Gram Panchayat members have less than 2 acres, 69 percent 2–5 acres, 19.4 percent 6–10 acres, and 2.8 percent over 10 acres of land. Yet in this same group none use only family labor on their land, 83.3 percent use hired labor, and 16.7 percent use sharecroppers. While reporting use of outside labor hiring is presumably considered safe to reveal, land holdings are not, as the stated small size of holdings would indicate that some at least would more efficiently use family rather than hired labor. Under-reporting of landholdings from fear of confiscation is more clearly revealed in an ILO study in West Bengal, where listing and agriculture schedules of leased lands revealed a close correlation of 4,645 and 4,436 acres of leased-in land but only 1,408 and 312 acres of leased-out land. As the figures of leased-in and -out land should be identical, landowners are clearly understating their ownership, a discrepancy which is too large to be attributed solely to landowner absenteeism.[46] For this reason in-depth village studies by anthropologists are better able to reveal the true picture than large interview sample surveys by transitory outsiders, particularly on topics as sensitive as landownership and political affiliations. The in-depth studies would indicate that Communist leadership is rather more elitist than the lower-middle-class composition revealed by sample surveys. On the other hand the leadership is in conflict with the traditionally dominant village leadership, and it is therefore a fair assumption that it represents less economically powerful interests than the traditional village elite. It is therefore probably not quite the "same old class of rural vested interests" attributed to it by Roy Choudhury but rather more elitist than the lower-middle-class dominance found by Kohli.

Whatever the differences in class composition, the similarities appear to be closer to that of the class–caste composition under the previous Congress government. A 1974 village study of Panchayat leadership in Hooghly district showed that leadership in the Anchal and Gram Panchayats were respectively, rich holding over 15 acres, 25 and 11 percent, upper-middle class with 7–15 acres, 50 and 56 percent, and middle class with 2–7 acres, 21 and 25 percent. There were no positions held below this level except for an 11 percent landless share in the Gram Panchayat. In caste composition, the Anchal and Gram Panchayats were composed respectively of 25 and 11 percent high caste, 50 and 67 percent dominant agriculturalist caste, and 25 and 22 percent other middle castes. There were no members outside these categories.[47] In the Davis study, even though government requirements for ward representatives gave the low castes three of the nine seats, the members were nominees of the dominant

[46] Tares Maitra, *Expansion of Employment Through Local Resource Mobilisation* (Bangkok: Asian Employment Programme, ILO, 1982), p. 9.

[47] Rajatasubhra Mukhopadhyay, "Resource Distribution and Power Structure: A Case Study of a West Bengal Village," *The Eastern Anthropologist*, vol. 35, no. 1, January–March 1982, p. 70.

faction on whom they were dependent.[48] Thus class–caste composition alone can often disguise the political controls exercised by the dominant elite over lower-class members who are their nominees. The Communist government exacerbated this tendency by changing the law to make appointments of Scheduled Castes and Tribes and women by the state government dependent on the nominees recommended by the local Panchayats, thereby increasing the control of whichever faction is locally dominant.[49] Thus even this small proportion can be assumed to represent some poor Scheduled Caste and Tribe members nominated by the richer landowners to fill the reserved quota and, therefore, cannot automatically be assumed to represent the interests of their class as they are indebted to and under the influence of the richer landowners.

Though not dominated by the biggest landowners who are few in number and allied more closely to the Congress, the Panchayats are composed of the middle strata of village society, whose interests are by no means synonymous with those of the poorer sections of the villages. The heavy bias towards small propertied owners, and the gross under-representation of the landless, however, was only to be expected, given the middle peasant and rural middle-class dominance in the CPM rural membership. As the question of the landless organizing and representing themselves through the Panchayats did not arise, given their token membership in the Panchayats, it would be up to the rural middle class to represent their interests. Since according to Panchayat and Party officials 60–70 percent of the CPM's own Gram Panchayat appointees have no grasp of leftist theory, their ideological commitment to leftist mobilization of the poorest classes was limited. In tours with government officials to a number of Panchayats, the relative prosperity of members was obvious and most of their projects were of dubious value for the lower classes.

While the rural propertied classes failed to effectively represent the poorest classes, the poorest classes themselves were often unable or unwilling to assert themselves politically, making the task of the Communists more difficult. Their lack of education, indebtedness to the propertied classes, and their strenuous preoccupation with making a living gave the propertied and middle classes a significant political advantage. The organizers who came from outside the poorer classes were often unsuited to being their spokesmen and found greater affinity and ease of mobilization among the rural middle class.[50]

While in 1977 only .08 Rupees per capita was spent through the Panchayats,

[48] Davis, *Rank and Rivalry*, p. 185.
[49] Government of West Bengal, Legislative Department, *The West Bengal Panchayat Act, 1973 as modified up to November 1980* (Alipore: West Bengal Government Press, 1980), p. 96, section 210.
[50] T.M. Vinod Kumar and Jatin De, *Basic Needs and the Provision of Government Services: An Areas Study of Ranaghat Block in West Bengal* (Geneva: International Labour Organisation, World Employment Programme Working Paper, February 1980), p. 21.

over the next three years per capita annual expenditure was over 10 Rupees for the rural population.[51] From 1979 to 1981 300 crore Rupees were routed through the Panchayats by government departments, a substantial sum considering the neglect of the Panchayats under the Congress government and the limitations of an annual state budget of about 1,000 crores.[52] By the end of the five-year term in June 1983, 600 crores had been distributed through the Panchayats.[53] The major project assigned to the Gram Panchayats by the Relief and Welfare Department was the "Food-for-Work" program with food and funds supplied by the central government. From December 15, 1980 this was replaced by the National Rural Employment Programme.[54] The Rural Reconstruction Programmes of the Relief and Welfare Department and the Rural Works Programme of the Development and Planning Department both financed by the central government, created 56.63 million man-days of employment in 1978–79 reaching 70 million by December of 1979.[55] If spread over all 4 million farm laborers in West Bengal, this represented 17.5 man-days per capita. Considering that agricultural laborers are without work at least seven months or 210 days a year the program was inadequate.[56] Though minimum wage was fixed at 8.10 Rupees per day, the Food-for-Work program paid only slightly over 4 Rupees in both food and cash per day. However, as the labor was utilized in the off-season this exceeded the prevailing local wage rates. Certainly these laborers were better off than in some other states where corruption was rampant. An IAS officer from Bengal who visited a Food-for-Work program in another state found that the recipients were not even aware there was a food component to the payment, as the program administrators had misappropriated it.

The Final Report of the Programme Evaluation Organisation of the Planning Commission found shortcomings in the Food-for-Work program. In taking a sample based on one good district and one average district in ten states including the districts of Burdwan (good) and Nadia (average) in West Bengal, this positively biased survey found West Bengal had created the highest number of man-days in both years of the program covering 1977–79.[57] However, this was

[51] Franda, *India's Rural Development*, p. 140.
[52] B.C. Mukherji, "The Impact of Panchayats on Socio-Economic Development of Rural Bengal" in *Panchayats in West Bengal From 1978–79 to 1980–81: A Review* (Calcutta: Department of Panchayats and Community Development, Government of West Bengal, January 1982), p. 13.
[53] Sumanta Sen, "Grassroot Power," *India Today*, June 15, 1983, p. 50.
[54] West Bengal, Department of Panchayats and Community Development, *Panchayats in West Bengal from 1978–79 to 1980–81: A Review* (Calcutta: January 1982), p. 53.
[55] West Bengal, *Panchayats in West Bengal*, p. 14. Roy Choudhury, "Land Reforms."
[56] *Ibid.*
[57] Government of India, Programme Evaluation Organisation, Planning Commission, *Evaluation of Food for Work Programme, Final Report* (New Delhi: Government of India Press, 1981), pp. 2, 56.

generated in part by cheap labor paid below the West Bengal government's own legal minimum wage. As six districts in other states paid the legal wage and five paid above it, the eight districts including the two in West Bengal paying below were in a minority.[58] In the poorer district of Nadia the program had a positive effect on market wage rates but in more developed Burdwan it had no effect.[59] The forty beneficiaries interviewed were unanimous that the wages were insufficient to meet daily requirements compared with only twelve out of forty in Nadia. Half of the Nadia beneficiaries interviewed found the wage above prevailing market rates while thirty-five of the forty from Burdwan found it below.[60] The program only contributed a 5.6 and 8.4 percent increase in employment to its beneficiaries in Burdwan and Nadia respectively.[61] The responses of beneficiaries indicated the quality of foodgrains distributed in the two districts in West Bengal was worse than in the other states, 33.75 percent in West Bengal compared with 14.6 percent in the whole survey. Half the Burdwan respondents found the grain mixed with sweepings as did two of the forty in Nadia, where two others found it stone-ridden.[62] In one block in Nadia the investigators found that

although checks were officially applied at every stage still malpractices like false entries of names in the muster rolls, insufficient work than prescribed were reported by the local people. Even if some workers did not work up to the prescribed extent, they managed to get the certificate of satisfactory work. It was also reported that at times the modified Ration Shop dealer supplied very bad quality of wheat. It was doubted [suspected?] that the dealer sold out the actual foodgrains in the open market and distributed the worst quality of grains purchased at lower prices.[63]

In Burdwan on the other hand, in distribution of foodgrains "there was no scope for malpractice as it was done in the presence of Panchayat members and other villagers, including rival political party members."[64] Under the conditions of the program, foodgrains supplied free to the states had to be matched by a specified cash component by the state government. During 1977–78 West Bengal was the only state not to match the additional sum required making the 20,301,000 Rupee shortfall recoverable from the state government by the central Ministry of Rural Reconstruction.[65]

A World Bank commissioned study by the Institute for Financial Management and Research found the National Rural Employment Programme

[58] Ibid., p. 29.
[59] Ibid., p. 41.
[60] Ibid., p. 77.
[61] Ibid., p. 69.
[62] Ibid., p. 65.
[63] Ibid., p. 16.
[64] Ibid., p. 16.
[65] Ibid., p. 22.

implementation in West Bengal had been "perhaps the best" of all the Indian states and union territories.[66] However, its own statistics in the report indicated West Bengal had the third highest amount of allocated but unutilized funds and foodgrains in the country totaling 182,622,000 Rupees as of April 1981 and the second most unutilized grains and funds of 258,738,000 Rupees by April 1982.[67] Despite these considerable funds and grains available, employment generation was only 40–60 percent in 1981–82 of what it had been in 1980–81.[68] During 1980–81 employed beneficiaries in West Bengal received twenty–forty days of work which fell in the following financial year to less than twenty days which the report considered "very unsatisfactory."[69]

The Institute for Financial Management and Research study commissioned by the World Bank dealt in detail with the implementation of the Integrated Rural Development Programme in four states including West Bengal. Unlike the implementation in West Bengal of the National Rural Employment Programme which it had also studied, the IRDP came in for serious criticism. West Bengal achieved just 18.6 percent of its target in the first year and 33.5 percent in its second year. "This achievement rate was the lowest of all the states in the country."[70] Less than 5 percent of the target group was covered (table 4.5).[71] Investment per family was the worst in India and "declined disturbingly" from 1,287 Rupees in 1980–81 to 941 Rupees in 1981–82.[72] The subsidy of 314 Rupees was the lowest of all the states and territories. This low level of assistance was due to West Bengal spending less than envisioned in the IRDP guidelines, 39 percent in 1980–81 and only 10.5 percent in the following year.[73] The reason was that "the Centre released very small sums to West Bengal in both years," amounting to just 5.02 and 3.96 percent of central allocations in the first and second years.[74] "The blame for the poor Central release is apparently to be laid at the door of implementing authorities of the IRDP and the administrative machinery of the State."[75] Between 1977–78 and 1980–81 80

[66] Institute for Financial Management and Research, *An Economic Assessment of Poverty Eradication and Rural Unemployment Alleviation Programmes and their Prospects* (Madras: Institute for Financial Management and Research, April 1984), Part III, p. 463.
[67] *Ibid.*, p. 447.
[68] *Ibid.*, p. 444.
[69] *Ibid.*, pp. 455–6.
[70] Institute for Financial Management and Research, *An Economic Assessment of Poverty Eradication*, Part I, p. 150.
[71] K. Sundaram and Suresh D. Tendulkar, *Integrated Rural Development Programme in India* (Kuala Lumpur: The Asian and Pacific Development Centre, May 1984), p. 27.
[72] Institute for Financial Management and Research, *An Economic Assessment of Poverty Eradication*, Part I, p. 150.
[73] *Ibid.*
[74] *Ibid.*
[75] *Ibid.*, p. 151.

Table 4.5. *Integrated rural development program implementation during 1982–83*

| State | No. of blocks | Physical targets | | Percentage of total to target |
| | | Target (nos) | Achievement total | |
| --- | --- | --- | --- | --- |
| Andhra Pradesh | 324 | 194400 | 284783 | 146.49 |
| Assam | 134 | 80400 | 39588 | 49.24 |
| Bihar | 587 | 352200 | 362354 | 102.88 |
| Gujarat | 218 | 130800 | 173790 | 132.87 |
| Haryana | 87 | 52200 | 158678 | 303.98 |
| Himachal Pradesh | 69 | 41400 | 45755 | 110.52 |
| Jammu and Kashmir | 75 | 45000 | 35435 | 78.74 |
| Karnataka | 175 | 105000 | 178856 | 170.34 |
| Kerala | 144 | 86400 | 127798 | 147.91 |
| Madhya Pradesh | 458 | 274800 | 313870 | 114.22 |
| Maharashtra | 296 | 177600 | 219690 | 123.70 |
| Orissa | 314 | 188400 | 252453 | 134.00 |
| Punjab | 117 | 70200 | 98435 | 140.22 |
| Rajasthan | 232 | 139200 | 183402 | 131.75 |
| Tamil Nadu | 377 | 226200 | 271563 | 120.05 |
| Uttar Pradesh | 876 | 525600 | 554980 | 105.59 |
| West Bengal | 335 | 201000 | 95607 | 47.56 |
| All India | 5011 | 3006600 | 3455447 | 114.93 |

*Source:* Institute for Financial Management and Research, *An Economic Assessment of Poverty Eradication and Rural Unemployment Alleviation Programmes and their Prospects* (Madras, Institute for Financial Management and Research, April 1984), Part I, p. 91.

million Rupees out of an admissible outlay of 90 million Rupees had been left unutilized.[76] "The Government of India after reviewing this expenditure trend decided not to make any allocation for the two years 1980–81 and 1981–82."[77] Though this may have been justifiable, a political motivation by the newly elected Congress government cannot be ruled out. The study concludes, however, that "compared to what the State got from the Centre for the years 1980–81 and 1980–82, it has done well," spending about 530 percent of what the Centre allocated to it. "Nevertheless, in absolute terms, the performance of West Bengal in the first two years is poor, ... much below the national average in all aspects of the IRDP."[78] The study attributes this to the state government channeling the program through the Panchayats rather than through the state bureaucracy as was done in other states. As the object of the program was to

[76] *Ibid.*
[77] *Ibid.*
[78] *Ibid.*

assist families below the poverty line, the state government argued that the lower-level bureaucracy exercised favoritism in giving aid to the better-off classes or at best to those already near the poverty line. The additional subsidy would allow them to cross the poverty line thereby enabling the administrators to claim success in achieving their targets for removing poverty in recipient families.[79] The West Bengal government felt the target groups should be the very poorest families who would receive smaller subsidies which they would be better able to utilize in sustainable projects rather than more expensive ones that were beyond their resources and expertise to sustain after termination of the aid.[80] The vested interests who had received this aid from the administration in the past could be avoided by giving the aid to the Panchayats to distribute. As local elected representatives they would be best able to select recipients and administer the program. The commercial banks supported the West Bengal government position since distribution through the Panchayats would give them fewer accounts to deal with and greater collateral than individual poor families could provide.[81] This approach, however, was not acceptable to the Central government and "the disagreement between the two governments persisted for four years, beginning with 1977–78, and threw the implementation of the IRDP in disarray in the State. Consequently, very little was done in assisting the poor families or utilizing the national funds made available to the State."[82] In accordance with the state government policy:

the Panchayats were given comprehensive powers for implementing the IRDP, and Government officials at the block level were made completely subservient to them. The West Bengal Government feared that if bureaucracy is given more powers and the Panchayats become subservient to it, there would be a collusion between bureaucracy and vested interests and the benefits would be cornered by the well-off rural families through wrong identification ... Hence neutralising the bureaucracy was felt to be absolutely essential for ensuring that the benefits would go to the most needy.[83]

As the Panchayats were under Left Front control while the bureaucracy was nominally independent, it made good political sense to distribute aid through the Panchayats where it could be used to create political goodwill for the Communists if not also enabling distribution of political largesse in the form of development aid. This might have been the real reason why the state and central governments were in disagreement over distribution channels. When aid was

---

[79] *Ibid.*, p. 154.
[80] Sundaram and Tendulkar, *Integrated Rural Development Programme*, p. 49; Institute for Financial Management and Research, *An Economic Assessment of Poverty Eradication*, Part I, p. 158.
[81] *Ibid.*, p. 153.
[82] *Ibid.*
[83] *Ibid.*, p. 154.

distributed through the Panchayats numerous problems arose. One senior West Bengal IAS official who happened to look at the files of IRDP beneficiaries was surprised to find that the flocks of goats were dying of disease or accidents. On investigation it was found that the beneficiaries would take the goat flocks along with the subsidy, and then sell the flocks, bribe the veterinarians to give false death certificates and with this collect the insurance money. They were thus better off than if they had kept the flocks as the program intended, without having to do any work or entail any risk.

The World Bank-commissioned study noted that in West Bengal:

The village Panchayats lacked administrative expertise, and found the task of decision making tough. Since the bureaucracy was prevented from taking any part in the Panchayats' activities as a matter of policy, the implementation of anti-poverty programmes ground to a halt. Besides, the Panchayats in the States were entrusted with many other activities and made responsible for implementing a variety of schemes and programmes. Under the burden of these numerous responsibilities, lack of bureaucratic support, communication gap, etc., the whole setup nearly collapsed. No decisions could be made, no activities could be undertaken and no programme was implemented. This explains the poor performance of the State in IRDP.[84]

A total of 18,000 loan applications for IRDP families were pending with Bengal banks in 1982–83, and performance in that year was less than 50 percent of target.[85] Only one district exceeded the target, four achieved over 75 percent of the target and six were unsatisfactory.[86]

By the 1990s a number of government evaluations and academic village-level surveys indicated that the performance of the West Bengal IRDP was unexceptional. The Indian government Department of Rural Development in its periodic Concurrent Evaluation of IRDP found the West Bengal performance fairly average though the numerous criteria make any aggregate state ranking order impossible to accurately determine[87]. More limited academic village surveys did not find significant differences in the quantities of aid given. A comparison of West Bengal with Tamil Nadu found assets accumulation not significantly different between the states and noted that the failure of specific schemes in both regions was due to the "absence of serious and imaginative local level planning."[88] The assets were found to go disproportionately to the more propertied classes, though local participation was greater than in Tamil Nadu due

[84] *Ibid.*, pp. 154–6.
[85] *Ibid.*, p. 160.
[86] *Ibid.*
[87] Government of India, Department of Rural Development, Ministry of Agriculture, *Concurrent Evaluation of IRDP: The Main Findings of the Survey for January 1987 – December 1987* (New Delhi: August 1988).
[88] Madhura Swaminathan, "Village Level Implementation of IRDP: Comparison of West Bengal and Tamil Nadu," *Economic and Political Weekly*, March 31, 1990, p. A-25.

to the involvement of the Panchayats. A comparative village level study of West Bengal, Uttar Pradesh, and Gujarat found that while the poor in West Bengal received IRDP assistance, in the other two village samples, no landless poor received IRDP benefits. However, though the poor received assistance in West Bengal, benefits tended to be taken by CPM supporters. Thus party rather than class appeared to be the key determinant of benefit receipt in Bengal, in contrast to the propertied class bias in the two other states.[89] This party patronage helps provide local electoral durability, while excluding many from development benefits and creating a polarization between beneficiaries and non-recipients.[90]

The Panchayats' priorities were often misconceived or oriented to benefiting the richer sections. The larger share of funds went to infrastructure development mainly through road and building construction which created off-season employment for agricultural labor but contributed little else to the poorest sections.[91] Programs of direct relevance to the landless tended to be ignored, with agricultural laborers receiving only the remuneration of food and wages for their work. The Panchayats generally gave a lower priority to minor irrigation works which would have been more productive. Though West Bengal has over 1.1 million ponds and tanks, most of which are derelict, the Food-for-Work program did insufficient work to make these water resources effective. In other works, such as embankment repair after the 1978 floods, the repairs were unsatisfactory. The Left Front Irrigation Minister, Provash Chandra Roy complained that most repairs were useless and would have to be redone. The same was often said regarding buildings and roads.[92] The case of the Panchayat constructing a bridge without any access road was, however, an extreme example of inappropriate construction.[93]

The program tended to reflect the demands of the rural middle class represented in the Panchayats. Through the CPM-dominated Panchayats they were able to consolidate their political and economic control of the villages and create new vested interests opposed to the interests of the landless. The new vested interests undoubtedly represent a less-prosperous and more-numerous class than the Zamindars of the colonial period or *jotedars* of the post-independence Congress Party, but often they are just a different faction of the same class. "Socially the leftist leadership in rural areas are connected with the Rural Power

[89] Jean Drèze, "Poverty in India and the IRDP Delusion," *Economic and Political Weekly*, September 29, 1990, p. A-99.

[90] Satadal Dasgupta and Rajat Subhra Mukhopadhyay, "Party Politics, Panchayat and Conflict in a West Bengal Village," *Man in India*, vol. 69, no. 1, March 1989, p. 37.

[91] West Bengal, Department of Panchayats and Community Development, *The Working of Panchayat System*, p. 37.

[92] Roy Choudhury, "Land Reforms," p. 2173.

[93] Arun Ghosh, *West Bengal Landscapes* (Calcutta: K.P. Bagchi & Co., 1989), p. 56.

Structure by Kinship and affinity; they were not strangers elevated to power. Often the family struggle took a political shape and often it was within the Rural Power elite a struggle for power between two relatives."[94]

The Board of Revenue publication for government officials on *The Dynamics of the Rural Situation in West Bengal – Panchayati Raj* notes the difficulties involved in trying to benefit the poor through the Panchayats.

The Zilla and Panchayat Samitis are filled with rural elite – the larger surplus farmers and the leaders of dominant lineage or patronage groups ...

Far from establishing or introducing a territorially based structure at odds with traditional village power relations, the administrative system at its lowest level becomes an instrument of the traditional village power relations. As a result of this capture of the local system by the rural elite, their interests, and not those of the average farmer, or those proclaimed by the national government, continue to dominate the rural scene ...

If attempts to create an effective administrative structure independent of the local elite have thus foundered, most government programmes to directly promote rural development have met with a similar fate ...

Government attempts to impose outside organisation and direction have for the most part been taken over by traditional forces, which have diverted them to their own ends.[95]

Given the vested interests represented in the Panchayats, the aim of the Panchayat program in distributing the benefits to the lowest strata of society would face a formidable obstacle, which could only be overcome if the political parties ensured that their local organizations directed the resources in an appropriate manner. The Board of Revenue handbook concluded that "it will need strong political and social will in the Panchayati Raj structure to bend these opposing forces into making available the bulk of the social product to those that are in most need."[96] The bureaucrats who had to administer the Panchayat program, however, found this political will lacking in the Left Front government. They complained they had to do everything "from A to Z" in the Panchayat program with the Left Front claiming all the credit but doing little to fulfil its role. While the poorest sections were neglected, the middle peasants established their own interests with the acquiescence of the Communist leadership and the support of the local party membership. The leftist bureaucrats complained that the ideological work and consciousness-raising which could only be done by the party was never undertaken. The work of political education in the villages was neglected by the Communists and the administrators could do nothing about this as it was beyond their jurisdiction. As a result, the

---

[94] Ranjit Kumar Gupta, *Agrarian West Bengal, Three Field Studies* (Calcutta: Institute of Social Research and Applied Anthropology, August 1977), p. 45.

[95] West Bengal, Board of Revenue, *Dynamics of the Rural Situation in West Bengal – Panchayati Raj* (Calcutta: West Bengal Government Press, 1979), p. 20.

[96] *Ibid.*, p. 17.

Panchayats could not be an effective organ of support in the event of repression, as politically opportunist people had taken over. A small minority of about 5 percent of the Panchayats are even believed to have misappropriated funds. This corruption often had the backing of leftist political parties. The RSP Panchayat Minister Debabrata Banerji was very critical of corruption in CPM-controlled Panchayats but prevented action being taken against corruption in RSP-controlled Panchayats. It is now questionable whether these new vested interests can be removed. Even if they are not given party tickets they could run as independents using their local following and patronage resources to defeat party candidates. If there is changing of Panchayat members at the party nomination, the party may find the Panchayat moving out of their control. At the beginning it would have been easy to correct the defects. Despite repeated warnings from the bureaucracy, they were left alone to carry out the work without complementary support from the leftists. What might have been an asset to the peoples' struggle is in danger of becoming a liability to the Communists due to lack of party work in the villages. Now if resources are not continually allocated to the Panchayats it will create opposition to the Leftist government from the Panchayat vested interests but if the funds are given or increased, the patronage and entrenchment of these interests will increase also. The CPM Chief Minister of West Bengal, Jyoti Basu, noted with disappointment that:

Those supporters of ours from whom we expected so much have not come up to expectation. The sincere application and selfless will which may solve many of the problems, we have not been able to notice in some important matters ... That political consciousness which should have been expanded or implemented has not taken place ... I cannot say that in the state we have been able to achieve noticeable progress in controlling and ending corruption. We have to keep a vigilant eye on party workers and supporters conscious that before the ruling party there is a great temptation ... From the point of view of our party and its organisation it is essential to maintain a clean image and we attach great importance to this work.[97]

Bhabani Sen Gupta's book published in 1979 on the CPM has a chapter devoted to a sympathetic examination of the organization and work of the "Red Panchayats."[98] By 1982, however, the author's perspective has changed. "The CPM in West Bengal has, in fact, no concrete plans to take the peasantry through the Panchayats to a higher level of mobilisation for political or development purposes. Hence the stagnation of the Panchayat system."[99]

Atul Kohli comes to a more positive conclusion that:

---

[97] Jyoti Basu, "Tin Bajhar Bamfront Sarkar Parichalanar Avigyata Samparkay Kichhu Bak-tyavba" ("Something to Say Regarding the Experience of Running the Left Front Government for the Last Three Years") *Deshitaishee*, annual Puja issue 1980, pp. 19, 23.

[98] Bhabani Sen Gupta, CPI–M, pp. 118–39.

[99] Bhabani Sen Gupta, "Time to Take Stock," *India Today*, December 31, 1982, p. 115.

the CPM's organisational arrangements allow it to penetrate the countryside without being captured by the propertied groups. In part because of the democratic-centralist nature of the party organisation and in part because of the carefully reorganised local government, the CPM can now reach the lower peasantry without landlord mediation. This feature of the CPM distinguishes it from all other organised political alternatives in India. It allows the regime to channel some developmental resources directly to the rural poor, as well as to mobilize them for occasionally fulfilling reformist goals.[100]

This contradicts the conclusions of many independent observers of the Panchayat program. However, his conclusion that "the CPM has moved away from a revolutionary to a reformist orientation" would find general agreement, and the Panchayat experience in West Bengal is indicative of this general tendency.[101]

There was a feeling among the leftist bureaucrats that the Panchayats were a good experiment that had gone bad for lack of proper support and cooperation from the parties, and that the effort had been a waste of work. The feeling was confirmed by the CPM cadre who complained that the party was leaving everything to the administration to undertake rather than depending on local party organizations and the people themselves.

Partly as a result of these lapses, in the June 1983 Panchayat elections the Congress increased its seats from about 4,000 in 1978 to over 14,000 Gram Panchayat seats. The CPM decreased slightly to about 24,000 seats from 28,105. The biggest losers were the smaller Communist parties including the CPI which together with other parties received less than 2,000 seats.[102] The Left Front parties had run candidates against each other in about 10,000 seats as against 6,000 previously, indicating lack of the Front's cohesion at the local level.[103]

The deficit financing that had helped to fund the Panchayat development program could not survive the return of the Congress to power, with the financial restrictions it imposed on state governments. Whereas the Left Front spent 43 crore Rupees and distributed 150,000 tonnes of foodgrains under the Food-for-Work and Rural Works programs in 1978–79, central government cutbacks resulted in only 14 crore Rupees and 15,000 tonnes of foodgrain being distributed in 1983–84.[104] Gradually, as the funds dried up, development aid dwindled or was postponed by chronic financial crises. Though the programs formally continued, the Panchayats lost much of their reforming impetus. Though it has succeeded to a certain extent in devolving power in the villages to the next

---

[100] Kohli, "Parliamentary Communism," p. 806.
[101] *Ibid.*, p. 805.
[102] Saumitra Banerjee, "CPI(M) Maintains Supremacy," *Sunday*, June 12–18, 1983, p. 52.
[103] Sumanta Sen, "Grassroot Power," p. 50.
[104] S.K., "Diminishing Returns from Blaming the Centre," *Economic and Political Weekly*, April 13, 1985, p. 633.

lowest rung of more numerous middle-class elements and consolidating their position, it has not increased the bargaining power of the lowest classes to any appreciable degree. By bringing a more numerically strong landed and professional middle class to a dominant position in village life, it may make further mobilization and radicalization of the lower classes more difficult. Though the Communists' conception was for an alliance of the middle and lower classes, there is no evidence that this will further the interests of the lower classes that the middle class Panchayat members supposedly represent. Though undoubtedly a more efficient and honest Panchayat system than in some other states, there is no evidence that they represent a qualitative or revolutionary break with traditional methods of operation. The failure of the Panchayats to deliver the goods to those most in need reflected the failures of the Left Front government in general to alter the balance of power in rural Bengal in favor of the lower classes. In the event that the Left Front is defeated in an election or removed by the central government, there is no evidence that the Panchayats will be able or willing to put up resistance to a new state government.

## The rural reform impasse

The failure to attempt a socialist transition was not caused by lack of understanding of the issues involved. In fact the issue was a matter of long historical debate in the Indian Communist movement. The policy of passing radical land reform legislation and then going ahead with local redistribution regardless of central government opposition had been advocated previously by elements in the Kerala CPM. According to Ronald J. Herring in his *Land to the Tiller*:

Within the CPI(M), both national and local leftist forces urged the government [Kerala State Communist government] to cease placating conservative elements in the coalition, legal scholars, and the Center. They urged that a truly radical land reform be legislated; if struck down by Delhi or the courts, the situation would dramatically illustrate to the people the impossibility of fundamental change within the existing structure of power. The analysis was that there was more potential for politicizing and mobilizing the rural masses in an abortive radical reform than in meticulous compliance with existing constraints ... In retrospect, the leftist analysis appears compelling; however, the CPI(M) leadership took the strictly parliamentary path on land reform. That stance strained party cohesion and contributed to the formation of leftist splinter groups.[105]

The Left Front leadership, though aware of what happened years before in Kerala, did the same thing in Bengal. As in Kerala the argument could be made of there being "a danger in the *embourgeoisement* of the poor peasantry, creating

[105] Ronald J. Herring, *Land to the Tiller: The Political Economy of Agrarian Reform in South Asia* (New Haven: Yale University Press, 1983), p. 192.

a conservative class in the place of a revolutionary one" through radical land redistribution, but this was little more than a sophisticated rationalization for doing little or nothing.[106] The Left Front had more immediate worries about opposition among its rich peasant supporters than to be concerned over long-term peasant *embourgeoisement*, real as this might be.

It is true that "not all reforms are conducive to new reforms."[107] Whatever reforms the Left Front undertook initially in the rural areas tended to consolidate new elites or rival factions of the old elites, which would resist a further radicalization that benefited the lower classes. In this sense the Left Front experiment was decidedly not a transition to socialism but to something altogether different. The reason for this lay in the Communists' approach to rural transformation, an approach based on incremental change rather than a revolutionary break. While worker takeovers of West Bengal industries were unrealistic given the complexities of the organizations involved and lack of financing available, in the rural economy the assets were largely immobile, easily secured, and simple to operate efficiently. This gave ordinary agricultural laborers the skills needed for a takeover of the means of agricultural production unavailable to the industrial proletariat, dependent as it was on the skills of middle and upper management and the capital of the enterprise owners. This does not mean such agrarian takeover would be easy, even without central intervention, but it was a practical economic possibility in a way that industrial workers' control was not.

It is well-known that land reform in South Asia has been unsuccessful in helping the poor majority.

There are many more people in rural areas of South Asia who are nonprivileged than privileged by the land-tenure system, suggesting that genuine land reform would be politically expedient ... Yet land reforms in most of the region have redistributed very little to those at the bottom of the agrarian hierarchy. Part of the explanation, as usually recognized, is that ruling elites are typically beholden politically to landed classes.[108]

This political influence of the landed classes prevents radical land reform. As a result political parties are forced to tinker with incremental legislation whittling down the land ceiling over a period of decades. This gives ample time for landowner evasion of ceiling limits and provides precious little to the poor who are too numerous to benefit from the minuscule amounts of land confiscated. To make matters worse the poor are dependent on the rich for work, which discourages them from taking action against their employers whose loans save them from starvation in lean years. It would therefore be the height of

[106] *Ibid.*
[107] Adam Przeworski, *Capitalism and Social Democracy* (Cambridge: Cambridge University Press, 1985), p. 242.
[108] Herring, *Land to the Tiller*, p. 217.

irrationality for the really poor to engage in class struggle without an independent income to fall back on. It is for this reason that the middle classes tend to be most active in dissident politics and usurp incremental land-reform policies for their own benefit. This is why land redistribution has succeeded only through revolution as in China, or through alien occupation by a reforming power such as America in Japan. Land reform cannot significantly benefit the poor through half measures; it must be sufficiently radical to provide all the poor with an independent means of livelihood.

The CPM's land reform in Kerala presents evidence of the disastrous long-term effects of half measures. Though over the years some cultivated land was distributed to 43.3 percent of agricultural households, effectively eliminating the old style landlordism, the redistribution was skewed in favor of those already better off. A sample survey found that 15.8 percent of households with more than 5 acres received 63.8 percent of redistributed land while those with less than 5 acres received only 36.2 percent of redistributed land though they were 84.2 percent of the sample. Self-cultivators with less than 1 acre constituted 16.6 percent of the survey but received only 0.9 percent of the land.[109] Though no equivalent sample survey has been made of the West Bengal Left Front reforms, there is every reason to assume a similar outcome may have occurred. Given Kerala's greater lower-class literacy and political involvement, the social situation would seem to suggest fairer redistribution in Kerala than in Bengal, though this must remain speculative.

It would be a mistake to attempt to apply the lessons from other parts of India too closely to West Bengal. The diversity of India's cultures and castes makes these parallels inexact. However, reformism is a national Communist policy and both Marshall M. Bouton and Kathleen Gough conclude in their studies of Thanjavur District that the Communist parties have moderated lower-class agitation and moved them "in a progressively reformist direction ... Especially in the case of the labor organizations, the parameters of organizational activity were set by the political parties on which they were almost wholly dependent."[110]

Already in 1953 ... we have seen that Communist policy was to curb the labourers' militance, persuade them to rely on constitutional channels for redressing grievances, and even confine them to strikes within their own villages. Over the next two decades, the stress on small increments in agricultural wages at the expense of wider revolutionary change was to deepen the rift between the Adi Dravidas and other castes in the countryside, eventually to the Harijans' own detriment.[111]

[109] *Ibid.*, pp. 211–12.
[110] Marshall M. Bouton, *Agrarian Radicalism in South India* (Princeton: Princeton University Press, 1985), p. 252.
[111] Kathleen Gough, *Rural Society in Southeast India* (Cambridge: Cambridge University Press, 1981), p. 240.

On the state level there have been a number of books dealing with the Communists in Kerala, including recent studies by Herring and Sathyamurthy.[112] Both conclude that the Communists have failed in Kerala in achieving expected objectives. According to Sathyamurthy "the end of the electoral road may indeed have been reached, and a major change of strategy based on a detailed knowledge of facts and analysis of the social, political, and economic forces in the country may be necessary in order that it may recoup its fortunes as a party of power."[113] Noting the CPM's "indecisive approach to the correct level of tension that ought to be maintained between 'administration' and 'agitation'" he concludes "it is hardly likely that its popular base as a political party on the electoral scene will expand further."[114] Though the Communists have failed to radicalize either state, their prospects are if anything bleaker in Kerala than in West Bengal.

In Kerala both Sathyamurthy and Herring argue that the *embourgeoisement* of the peasantry is well advanced. "The formerly radical core of the peasant movement which has now become a relatively privileged stratum" comes into conflict with the unprivileged.[115] "The CPI (M) is a victim of its own success ... As party leaders, local cadres, and peasant association activists recognize, the political loyalty of the tenants has become problematic since the land reform."[116] The party has been caught between the new beneficiaries fearful of losing their newly acquired property through more radical land reform, and the landless demanding their fair share too. "The former tenants quite naturally fear that further land and labor reforms will threaten their new status and privilege, and thus feel more comfortable with parties of property than with parties of redistribution."[117] What is more, these new beneficiaries treat the agricultural laborers worse than the old landlords did. The landlords, having greater wealth, could afford to be more generous to their employees during lean periods, and being unable to cultivate their own large holdings had to bargain with laborer demands. The new smaller holding beneficiaries, however, can substitute their own family labor for hired labor when pressed for concessions and, being more numerous, are more influential politically as a class.[118]

The same situation can be presumed to be taking place in Bengal. The Left Front is painting itself into a corner; its reforms are its own worst enemy, effectively making its own conservative supporters stronger. The reforms,

---

[112] T.V. Sathyamurthy, *India Since Independence – Centre–State Relations: The Case of Kerala*, vol. I (Delhi: Ajanta Publications, 1985), p. 454; Herring, *Land to the Tiller*.
[113] Sathyamurthy, *India Since Independence*, p. 322.
[114] *Ibid.*, p. 436.
[115] Sathyamurthy, *India Since Independence*, p. 290.
[116] Herring, *Land to the Tillers*, p. 214.
[117] *Ibid.*, pp. 214–15.
[118] *Ibid.*, pp. 215–16.

instead of building towards revolution, are creating obstacles to it. The transition, if it is a transition at all, is to farmer capitalism not socialism. The Left is indeed undertaking the bourgeois democratic reforms the capitalists have been unable or unwilling to carry out, but this path does not lead to socialism; it leads to agrarian capitalism. Land reforms that leave a substantial agricultural labor underclass, and create a richer cultivator class, only exacerbate class divisions, making a polarization of reform versus anti-reform interests more evenly balanced in favor of the new richer landowners. Indeed the more extensive these reforms the stronger the opposition to reform will be later, should the Communists attempt to help the poorest classes. It is for this reason that the Left Front reforms have ground to a halt. Having disposed of the unpopular landlords, any further reforms will alienate the Communist rich peasant base. The party now has to choose between its rich peasants and the landless and poor peasantry. Rather than take a stand it has adopted a do-nothing policy. This option for the status quo, which the Communists have helped to create, is by default in favor of the rural rich.

There are sound policy reasons for the Left Front's stepping back from land reform. They do not wish a repeat of what has happened in Kerala. "Fears of *embourgeoisement* expressed by Lenin, ... and a section of the CPI (M) has come to pass" with agrarian capitalism succeeding, leaving the Communists to press only for reformist demands.[119] Already there are signs that the poor are leaving the CPM fold in Kerala.

For a very long time, the Communists alone stood consistently for the poor against the wealthy. Their electoral successes have drawn other parties to champion the cause of the laborers and small farmers ... Organizationally, this process is reflected in the proliferation of peasant and laborer unions sponsored by parties all across the political spectrum, including those which historically opposed interference with property privilege.[120]

This process has not yet happened in Bengal. Unlike Kerala where party coalitions are required to form majority governments, in Bengal the CPM requires no allies. While the Bengali laboring classes are less educated and politicized than those in Kerala, this Kerala phenomenon could well be in Bengal's future. The CPM base cannot be taken for granted indefinitely, as the Kerala experience shows. The Left Front's current policy of doing nothing to disturb the status quo therefore may not be a viable option in the long run. In a democratic environment it cannot prevent other parties on the right or left from mobilizing the lower classes. This has not yet happened very effectively but, for a government intent on staying in power indefinitely, this possibility cannot be overlooked.

---

[119] *Ibid.*, p. 215.
[120] *Ibid.*

If the Left Front is to avoid the *embourgeoisement* observed in Kerala and yet satisfy its lower-class constituency, it must devise a rural policy that can accomplish both objectives. Any policy which provides substantial benefits and opportunities to one group, but leaves a larger group with no improvements, is inviting further class conflict. In other words, the CPM is strengthening an enemy they will have to fight against later on when they promote lower-class interests. Creating a more powerful enemy is not advantageous to the Communists or the dispossessed. It is for this reason that there can be only one land reform policy, that of equalization of land holdings on a per capita basis for the entire agricultural population, landed as well as landless. How it is implemented depends on the reaction expected from the central government.

Opposition governments like the Communist state governments are particularly subject to central government pressures, not only in the allocation of central revenues and investment, but in the threat of removal by the central government through imposition of Presidential Rule. This destabilization strategy was undertaken by the center when the Communists first came to power in Kerala in 1957 and subsequently during the Bengal United Front governments. If the Communists wish to remain in power they cannot push measures that are too radical. On the other hand, imposing Presidential Rule makes the central government and its state party unpopular in regionally conscious states and this measure has always rebounded against the central government in subsequent fair elections. Therefore the central government in recent years has always been reluctant to impose Presidential Rule in the face of mobilized regional opposition. This provides the boundaries of an alternative CPM strategy that might have been adopted. The Left Front could have pushed radical reform up to the limit likely to lead to Presidential Rule but stopping just short of the brink. This limit is not clearly defined and requires political calculation.

What would be sufficient to force central intervention is difficult to determine. Sathyamurthy puts a narrow limit on state autonomy in this regard. "The central government, the national Congress party, and the court system as well as the state bureaucracy are powerful forces keeping a close watch over developments taking place in the field of agrarian reform and would not allow anything like a revolutionary transformation of the prevailing structure of agrarian relations in Kerala."[121] The mainstream Communists therefore work within "the possible ... to remove feudalism and not capitalism."[122]

These limitations on provincial autonomy are not constant over time. For instance when Indira Gandhi returned to power after the Janata government many thought Presidential Rule would be imposed. That clearly would not have

[121] Sathyamurthy, *India Since Independence*, p. 289.
[122] *Ibid.*

been an appropriate time for radical action. On the other hand when the central government is vacillating and facing the possibility of electoral defeat more reforms may be possible. With current problems in the Punjab and elsewhere it would be loath to add another insurrectionary state to its agenda. A weakened central government might find armed intervention in Bengal more difficult once mobilization had reached a certain level. An equalization strategy might succeed if the central government is otherwise occupied with Punjab, Assam, Kashmir, or a general election. It would then be reluctant to send in the armed forces which are the only forces capable of stopping the mass movement. In that event the Left Front, with a solid mandate for another term in office, could be pushing forward with reforms. This it is decidedly not doing. As Ronald Herring notes: "There is thus a delicate tension between policy as a potentiating force and policy as impracticable utopianism, between underestimating and overestimating potential for change."[123] The Left Front has been consistently underestimating this potential.

A radical approach could be applicable if there were the necessary political will among the CPM leadership. As the Communists are in state power, the landlords lack the coercive apparatus needed to repress the peasant movement which can now only be done by the central government. A first step in a radical strategy might involve passing an equitable land ceiling law in the state assembly and sending it for approval to the central government. In the likely event that this is stalled, a mass movement by the Left Front parties would be launched to present the center with a *fait accompli*. All land over a variable land quality based ceiling would be occupied by the landless and redistributed. The central government at this point would either have to impose Presidential Rule or accept the action. If Presidential Rule is imposed, the Left Front avoids the acutely embarrassing defeat at the polls which would be a serious setback for the Communists in India. The Left Front government will thereby go out of power at the head of a mass movement, which will preserve its radical image in the country, and give it a chance of winning the next democratic election. If fraudulent elections are held, the replacement of a democratic environment with a repressive one could result in longer Congress rule. However, since the Left Front was not doing anything in office, it would be better for them to be inactive in opposition where they could not be blamed for all their shortcomings by a frustrated public.

A land reform that the Communists are in a position actually to implement in the field must be on the basis of equality. *Embourgeoisement* occurs only when there is a proletariat left without land but desirous of acquiring that of others. Equalization with a variable land quality based ceiling averaging 1/3

---

[123] Herring, *Land to the Tiller*, p. 281.

acre per person eliminates the need for hired agricultural labor and turns the agricultural population into self-cultivators. While this will take away the major grievances of the lower classes, it will leave no privileged class that would feel threatened by the lower classes. The Communists will take all the credit for the reforms, receive the support of the majority of the rural population which benefits, and provide an example to the rest of the country that no other party or state can match. Fear of other parties taking away their land if they return to power will ensure the Communists a support base for years to come. As the non-Communist parties will oppose the reform, their opposition will serve to strengthen the Communist base among the lower classes. In this policy the law courts are largely irrelevant and the mass movement would be launched with or without legal sanction on passage of the legislation in the state Assembly. Only central armed force could stop the movement which the central government has the legal power to do at any time.

It is many years since the Communists have shown such revolutionary courage, but assuming this equalization could be carried out, it would have to be done in one quick movement to prevent disinvestment and the removal or destruction of farm machinery and crops. Rural bank assets could be frozen through Communist bank employee unions to prevent withdrawal or transfer of capital by the landed elite. As the Green Revolution has already made substantial inroads with high-yielding varieties and fertilizer, agricultural inputs and capital to purchase them would be required. It is at this point that the real test of the reforms will take place. Though the state can meet some of the requirements, much of the rural credit would dry up with the confiscation of the larger holdings. The peasant would then have to fall back on traditional farming methods without the more expensive inputs. This could cause a temporary fall in output, particularly if assets and inputs seized from the rural elite are of limited value. As most of the lower classes suffer from malnutrition it might be expected that their own increased consumption would reduce the surplus available to the urban population. The state thus might have difficulty meeting its food requirements. On the other hand, the peasants' acquisition of new land and its more intensive cultivation could lead to production increases. Whether short-term production will increase or decrease is impossible to predict accurately in advance, though in the long term with the development of alternative credit sources and co-ops, production might conceivably increase.

As can be expected, land redistribution is the most politically difficult, but once completed its success or failure will depend on economic factors such as availability of inputs and credit rather than on holding size, since the land will stay in production regardless of ownership. As the Indian surplus has been at the cost of malnutrition for perhaps a third of the population, even a drop in production that was more evenly distributed among newly landed agricultural laborers might improve living conditions more than the present strategy of

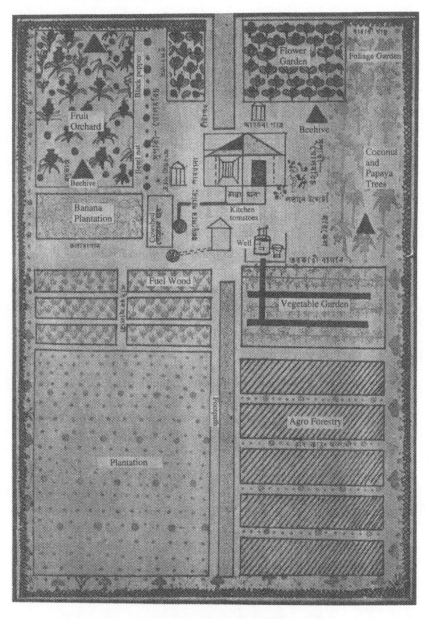

Fig. 4.1. Plan of household plot of 1/3 acre (100′ x 150′)

Table 4.6. *Yield on 1/3 acre of agricultural land*

| Yearly income and description of the yield of each tree and plant | | | | | | | | Year | | | | | | | |
| --- | --- | --- | --- | --- | --- | --- | --- | --- | --- | --- | --- | --- | --- | --- | --- |
| | 1 | 2 | 3 | 4 | 5 | 6 | 7 | 8 | 9 | 10 | 11 | 12 | 13 | 14 | 15 |
| Lemon tree rate 20p/lemon | — | — | — | 90 | 90 | 90 | 120 | 120 | 120 | 120 | 300 | 300 | 300 | 300 | 300 |
| Banana 20 Rupees/bunch | — | — | 300 | 400 | 400 | 400 | 400 | 400 | 400 | 400 | 400 | 400 | 400 | 400 | 400 |
| Vegetables | 500 | 700 | 700 | 700 | 700 | 700 | 700 | 700 | 700 | 700 | 700 | 700 | 700 | 700 | 700 |
| Bamboo 7 Rupees/stick | | | | | 280 | 280 | 840 | 840 | 840 | 840 | 1400 | 1400 | 1400 | 1400 | 1400 |
| Black pepper, pan | | | 250 | 250 | 250 | 250 | 250 | 250 | 500 | 500 | 500 | 500 | 500 | 500 | 500 |
| Honey | | | 100 | 100 | 200 | 200 | 200 | 200 | 200 | 200 | 500 | 500 | 500 | 500 | 500 |
| Fruit from 20 trees | | | | | 300 | 300 | 300 | 800 | 800 | 800 | 1500 | 1500 | 1500 | 1500 | 1500 |
| Fuel from plantation | | | 200 | 300 | 400 | 400 | 400 | 400 | 400 | 400 | 400 | 400 | 400 | 400 | 400 |
| Betel nut | | | | | 500 | 500 | 750 | 750 | 750 | 750 | 1000 | 1000 | 1000 | 1000 | 1000 |
| Papaya | | 400 | 400 | 400 | 400 | 400 | 400 | 400 | 400 | 400 | 400 | 400 | 400 | 400 | 400 |
| Coconut | | | | | | | | | 600 | 600 | 600 | 600 | 600 | 600 | 1500 |
| Boundary trees | | | | 100 | 200 | 400 | 100 | | 400 | 400 | 400 | 400 | 500 | 500 | 800 |
| Tree orchard and miscellaneous | | 400 | 300 | 200 | 100 | 100 | 100 | 100 | | | | | | | |
| Agro forestry and plantation | | | | | | | | 500 | | 1000 | | 1200 | 1200 | 1200 | 1200 |
| Total income | 500 | 1500 | 2250 | 2540 | 3820 | 4020 | 4560 | 5460 | 6110 | 7110 | 8100 | 9300 | 9400 | 9400 | 10600 |
| Expenses | 1500 | 500 | 500 | 500 | 500 | 500 | 500 | 500 | 500 | 500 | 500 | 500 | 500 | 500 | 500 |
| Net income | −1000 | 1000 | 1750 | 2040 | 3320 | 3520 | 4060 | 4960 | 5610 | 6610 | 7600 | 8800 | 8900 | 8900 | 10100 |

*Source*: Government of West Bengal, "*Adarsh Gramin Abash*," (Ideal Village Habitation).

maintaining artificially high food prices for surplus farmers. A free market in food produce could help the urban sector as well as alleviate the financial drain of government farm subsidies.

The enclosed-plot map and cost-benefit table published and circulated to farmers by the West Bengal government indicate that an equitable land redistribution, which would give a per capita land holding of 0.33 acres, can be profitable and increase the income of the lower classes. It is political constraints rather than economic impracticability which have prevented this. As the rural rich attain their wealth at the expense of their poor tenants and their debtors, it can be expected that credit will dry up as they seek urban outlets for their capital. As they provide most of the current capital requirements, it will be imperative that the peasants themselves generate their own capital through production on their newly acquired land. State loans could meet many of these initial capital requirements through the savings from cutting back on non-productive public enterprises and staff. Should the reforms be successful, they will provide increased demand for urban products such as fertilizers and irrigation equipment.

This would only present a medium-term solution however. Over generations, changing land productivity and unequal family size will create inequality even where it was not present at the initial land equalization. This could be avoided by making land tenable only on an individual basis rather than by family units, and only by actual tillers of the land. This would make family land inheritance impossible in many instances and discourage major investment in land improvement. To ensure equality, land could not be mortgaged to secure loans, which would have to be guaranteed on the basis of collective responsibility by the village for default of payments by individuals. This has already been done by the Grameen Bank in Bangladesh with success.[124] Without population control the land–person ratio will continue to deteriorate, and there is no immediate prospect of improvement in this. Industrialization that would absorb surplus rural labor is even less likely to occur, so whatever the solution, it must be found within the villages themselves. Even with these safeguards some farmers and castes will prove to be better farmers than others, and become richer as a result. The differentiation was observed under the New Economic Policy (NEP) in the Soviet Union and is likely to occur under the current reforms in China and the former USSR. The failure of the Communist bloc in collective agriculture, however, points to the difficulties of trying to implement an "ideologically correct" Marxist solution. Peasant land hunger for private plots has not proven amenable to collective land ownership, which may tell more about human

---

[124] David Stewart-Patterson, "Bank lending to Bangladesh poor a trail-blazer," *The Globe and Mail*, July 9, 1987, p. B19.

nature in general than the peasant economy in particular. However, for the Left Front government no permanent solutions are required. What the reforms need only do is provide an example to the rest of India and an experimental model for Communist expansion to the rest of the country. Land equalization as a medium-term goal would help to accomplish this, leaving a permanent solution to a more opportune time. The political benefits for the mobilization of the lower classes in the rest of India and for the Communist movement could be great, if the central government is willing to tolerate the changes. While initially the Left Front might have been wary about provoking President's Rule they now have nothing to lose by such a radical strategy as their present course is leading nowhere. However, this is unlikely to be sufficient to motivate the Communists to adopt such a radical strategy. The vested interests have become too much a part of the Communist movement to be easily shaken off.

In short, a provincial government strategy can at most be social democratic in the urban areas, while in the rural areas it can be revolutionary. An essentially conservative urban strategy reduces the risk of central intervention when a revolutionary land reform is undertaken. Since landowner influence over the central government is generally regarded as less significant than it is over provincial governments, there would be less temptation to intervene than if the local interests of the national bourgeoisie were threatened or urban economic collapse occurred. Nevertheless central intervention cannot be ruled out and so timing the radical reforms to reduce the risk of intervention is critical. On taking power the government would have to neutralize the state police as far as possible, which the Left Front did through its union activities. However, it is the mass movement that must carry the struggle forward. The Communist government can only facilitate the process by converting or neutralizing the police and administration, and passing progressive legislation to legitimize and popularize the revolutionary measures taken by the masses in the countryside.

When this policy is examined it is easy to see why the Left Front backed off from introducing real land reform. The policy was a high-risk one because the political and economic outcomes in the countryside were to a large extent unpredictable. The replacement of a democratic environment by "semi-fascist terror" after the United Front governments were removed from power was all too vivid a memory to be forgotten. Being driven underground offered few opportunities for mass mobilization even though popular sympathy had not been forfeited. It was far easier to do nothing while in office and hope for more favorable opportunities to develop in the fullness of time. The problem with doing nothing is that it is better done in opposition where no public responsibility is assumed. The Kerala situation parallels the West Bengal CPM situation in this regard. "If it continues to pursue the path of electoral politics wholeheartedly in such a static situation, its revolutionary credentials are bound to become diluted; and its decline as a party of the people and a party of principles may indeed be difficult to arrest."[125]

Once the state government has been used to introduce the reformist and revolutionary policies, a way out of government must be found that avoids electoral defeat and places the popular blame for its removal on the local opposition and the central government. This can be done only by provoking central intervention through radical measures that are popular. This is essentially what happened during the earlier United Fronts. This time the movement would be even more unified given the CPM's dominance in villages throughout the state. While urban opposition is relatively easy to control by force, a rural movement on a statewide basis is much more difficult to deal with, particularly if the state government and its ruling party has organized for it beforehand. When based on the promise and prospect of new land for the majority of the agricultural population, the movement could quickly become so overwhelming that the center might choose not to use force. This would have been better done before Left Front land reforms had helped consolidate new elites, but given the still highly skewed land distribution of the 13 percent controlling 44 percent of the land, it is still viable. However it is extremely doubtful that the current CPI and CPM would ever even contemplate such a drastic move. Only a purge in these parties against the current leadership could achieve it, and no such alternative leadership appears to be present. In the end the Communist experiment in West Bengal government was defeated as much by the leadership's lack of boldness as by unfavorable circumstances. It is quite possible that the radical strategy would have failed as well, but since it was never attempted, this will never be known. What is known is that the reformist, and finally the do-nothing option, has been a total failure, except in keeping the party in office.

Sathyamurthy has argued that the center "would not allow anything like a revolutionary transformation of the prevailing structure of agrarian relations."[126] If that is the case, then it is difficult to see how a Communist provincial government can be part of a transition to socialism. No radical change on the path to revolution is possible because the state government will be removed and the movement repressed by the center. At most this removal will be an educative process exposing the hollowness of the central government's democracy, but nothing of substance could be achieved. If central intervention is inevitable, then only two options are left: (1) follow the policy of the present Left Front government in distributing patronage among supporters while doing nothing to further a socialist transition that might bring central intervention or (2) adopt the Maoist approach of refusing to take office, or take office only to prove to

[125] Sathyamurthy, *India Since Independence*, p. 322.
[126] *Ibid.*, p. 289.

the people the futility of doing so, and hence the need for an extra-parliamentary approach at the state and local level. To accept the first policy is to admit that the Left Front has done about as much as was possible in the circumstances. Since what was done was practically nothing, one is left with the inescapable conclusion that only the radical approach towards local government is possible. Therefore: (1) power can be transferred only at the national level, (2) parliamentary activity at lower levels is for educative purposes only, and (3) if power is obtained it is to be used as an adjunct to revolutionary activities, which will inevitably lead to its early overthrow. The underlying assumption behind this second strategy is that a peaceful transition to socialism is impossible and confrontation begins from day one of the socialist government. The Left can govern securely only after it controls the coercive apparatus of the state.

Since it can be argued that a regional government revolutionary strategy is impossible in industrial society, it follows that only a revolutionary agrarian strategy can justify a state government's retention of office. If even this is impossible because central intervention is inevitable, then the implications for the transition to socialism are profound. Urban governments cannot adopt measures that advance the cause of revolutionary socialism without an economic collapse. This holds for Third World urban industrial centers but even more for advanced capitalist ones where the whole of society is part of the urban industrial nexus. The only justification for staying in office then is to await the arrival of favorable circumstances at the national level. Doing nothing but staying in power as long as possible until favorable circumstances arise nationally, is therefore the only possible strategy once the taking of office is accepted as legitimate. Since this will inevitably lead to demoralization, disillusion and the corruption of office over the long run, on balance it is better not to take office or to do so while being prepared to be removed from power when radical measures are not tolerated by the center. Clearly, staying in power while following a course towards socialism is an extremely difficult proposition for a state government.

Attempting revolutionary change through electoral state office has many limitations, but the alternative to electoralism appears no more promising. An insurrectionary strategy against the largest and best-equipped armed forces in the Third World is not likely to be viable in the foreseeable future. While the Left Front was a failure in terms of introducing reforms, it might not have succeeded even with a radical strategy. Though its reformism failed, a more resolute government could have achieved many more reforms, even within the constitutional system. Historically the Communists have moved back and forth between extreme reformism and armed struggle without seriously attempting a middle course. The Indian Communist movement's oscillation between reformist and revolutionary strategies is an understandable symptom of the difficulty in finding an appropriate path forward in a unique country, which has an institutional superstructure analogous to western democracies but an economic base often not far removed from feudalism. For the Left Front government to develop an appropriate strategy in such circumstances with so few parallel experiences elsewhere in the world to draw on is understandably difficult.

There was a second set of rural policy options which might have formed a strategy for a socialist transition that avoided Presidential Rule, yet advanced Communist goals. This would have accepted property ownership as essentially unchangeable prior to a national revolution. Rather than undertaking land redistribution with the creation of a potentially conservative yeoman class, struggles for wage increases from landowners might have been attempted. Unlike the fundamental changing of land ownership required in an equalization strategy, rural labor wage struggles are less threatening to both landowners and the central government. Wage increases could be enforced up to the level landowners were willing to pay them, but otherwise property would remain in their hands. In essence the village society is treated as analogous to urban industrial society, only with an agricultural working class to be unionized for wage improvements. Like their urban counterparts, workers would gain control of the means of production only after a successful revolution. This would allow the development of the most competitive and wealthiest farmers who were best able to meet labor wage demands. A progressive agricultural taxation would be adjusted to give an advantage to the smaller farmers employing labor, however otherwise agricultural business ownership would not be changed.

With half Bengal's agriculturalists now landless, proletarianization is well advanced. In terms of orthodox Marxism it would therefore seem probable an agricultural labor wage struggle rather than land redistribution would have been the Left Front priority. In fact, neither proved to be a priority. Major land redistribution threatened the Communist middle-class landed base, while wage increases would have made this same base uncompetitive with the largest and most prosperous landowners. The Left Front therefore had to placate labor with government distributed palliatives such as wages for working on development projects. Though not all development aid benefited the rural rich, essentially the function of aid was to help keep labor demands within the confines acceptable to the Left Front and its landed base. The failure of agricultural wages to keep up with wages in other states, combined with the demands for higher procurement prices and reduced agricultural taxation, is indicative of the power of these landed interests over the Left Front, even when the government was inclined to follow more radical policies. Though these reforms would have been much less confrontational than changes of property ownership, and could have avoided Presidential Rule, they were not undertaken for reasons of the Left Front's own propertied constituency. While radical land redistribution might have appeared a "revolutionary" strategy and therefore unacceptable to the center, the "reformist" strategy of incremental wage improvement could have been attempted without central interference as part of a larger long-term struggle for lower-class mobilization. A "reformist" wage policy could have been an initial mobilization issue for long-term revolutionary goals that would only be put forward at a later stage in the struggle. This "reformist" strategy like the "revolutionary" one was never seriously attempted.

In theory the CPM promoted both land redistribution and wage increases, but these two demands were contradictory. Why should one class be allowed to own land while another could only work on it? In practice, to promote land redistribution would threaten its own landed supporters, while pressing wage increases would threaten those small holders least able to pay higher wages. In essence the Left Front had to choose between agitating for land grabs or striking for higher wages, both demands which would entail attacking important segments of its own constituency. There were good reasons why the Left Front ultimately chose not to press for either demand and ended up doing nothing.

In retrospect, the period of Left Front government reveals no clearly thought-out policy in advance of implementation. It began policies and programs on which it later had to back down on when confronted with its own vested interests. The retreat indicates that the Left Front had no clear idea of its mission and tactics to begin with, but was flexible in adapting to changing circumstances and demands. It began potentially radical programs such as land redistribution and Operation Barga but retreated on them. It tried to increase taxation thinking this at least was practical only to back down at the last stage after going to the Assembly. This bill would never have reached the Assembly had the Cabinet had a clear idea of where its political interests lay and how its strategy should be followed. This *ad hocism*, while useful in adapting to important lobbies, has left the Communists with no clear policy direction. It can no longer promote reform without threatening its own supporters' interests. It has found no strategy to lead itself out of this dilemma. With no class enemy left in the countryside to struggle against, without narrowing its electoral class base, it must prevaricate and make capital out of secondary issues such as central government discrimination. Class issues can no longer be pressed with any vigor as it endangers electoral support. The previous removal of the old Zamindars and biggest landowners has left no convenient enemy to be attacked or expropriated. Incremental reforms with the gradual lowering of land ceilings has effectively made lower class struggles much more difficult than was traditionally the case. The polarized land ownership, which Bouton argues is conducive to agrarian radicalism, has been removed by incremental land reform, making a multi-class alliance against a common enemy no longer an easy proposition. The sides are numerically more evenly divided, and both sides are to be found as political supporters of the Left Front. With no class enemies convenient to attack, the Left Front has had to press non-class issues and adopt a "constructive" approach of development policies designed to improve village amenities. However, development without redistribution has limits and tends to be skewed in favor of those with the most political power.

The possibility of a transition to socialism in India appears to be dim. The limitations on provincial power imply that only a national transition is possible. However, the uneven development of the left movement in India makes this increasingly problematic. For many years the left has not significantly expanded beyond its old state bases gained during the colonial period. Rather the left has suffered a relative decline since independence, even while gaining power in its old pre-independence bases in Bengal and Kerala. Though it has made absolute gains, its relative position *vis-à-vis* rightist and communal forces has been weakened. If moderate secular parties are defeated they will likely be overtaken on the right rather than on the left, by communal and ethnic parties which could further disintegrate the country. The Congress Party and the Communists, both of whom advocated a transition to socialism but failed to implement it, promoting private enterprise instead, are now faced with centrifugal forces threatening national unity. Though everything in India works after a fashion, only the armed forces and private enterprise operate efficiently. Increasingly the left and center may have to rely on these sections to keep up economic growth and national unity. The centrifugal forces which the left promoted are now dominated by ethnic and religious groups who could marginalize the left if they came to power. Only class-based politics can overcome these barriers but the divisions of religion, caste, and ethnicity run so deep as to make this unlikely in the foreseeable future. The willingness of rightist, religious and ethnic groups to take up class-based issues means that the left no longer has a monopoly on using these grievances. Class grievances when combined with ethnic and religious overtones have proven more potent than strictly class issues in India, as the Gandhian and Islamic movements that caused the partition of the subcontinent have already shown. The left was powerless to have any impact on the events then and the situation is basically not much different today. In the present era at least, the left movement has missed whatever opportunities may have existed, and the momentum is with the right.

In this respect India is very much in tune with the rest of the world where the revolutionary left is being eroded. In Socialist as well as Capitalist states free enterprise is on the ascendancy, and whatever the economic imperatives, the fact that they are being promoted at all indicates that the revolutionary left has failed to provide workable government economic policies consistent with revolutionary socialism and communism. In the final analysis the Communist bloc has had to fall back on capitalist-type incentives to provide for renewed development. The implications for Marxist theory are profound but have yet to be adequately addressed. If Marxism is not the most efficient economic model for development then its long-term survival is problematic. Even national leftist movements that successfully use Marxist ideology to seize power, will have to revert to capitalism to develop or else become economic backwaters. The West Bengal experiment, though hardly proving the ineffectiveness of a whole system, nevertheless has profound implications for the possibilities of a socialist transition that cannot be wished away. The Left Front failed as a force for revolutionary change and its reformism was less impressive than that of "capitalist" parties in other states. The justification for its continued existence in office is therefore in serious doubt.

# 5    State, industry, and labor

### Public administration

In orthodox Marxist theory the bureaucracy represents the interests of the ruling class, hence the CPM's theory of the Indian "bourgeois-landlord" state. The experience in West Bengal indicated this is an oversimplified view. Rather the administration is an instrument in the hands of the ruling party which can be used by the Communists for implementing significant changes if they so desire. In fact the Communists did not have to obstruct the bureaucracy but could utilize it for Communist ends without necessarily becoming reformist. In the short term at least the bureaucracy was indispensable, as the Communists had no organization capable of performing its functions, and without these functions being performed the system, whether Communist or capitalist, would collapse.

The state in West Bengal is in a unique position in India, in being manned to a considerable extent at all levels by East Bengal refugees and their descendants, who are not tied to the propertied class and most importantly not to the rural landed class.[1] At the clerical level and also at the officers' level the Communists often had a dominant position. The extent of their influence is indicated by Congress charges that the CPM used its position as the dominant force among state government employees to pad and fabricate voter rolls deleting known Congress supporters. Though this support does not extend to the point where their Communist followers will undertake their jobs conscientiously as government employees, it does mean they are not actively hostile. If active at all it is on behalf of the Communist government, rather than working for the opposition. In the circumstances it would be difficult to argue that the bureaucracy represents any class interest except its own group interests, which relate to wage and bonus increases and supplementary benefits.

At the senior levels among the IAS cadre the Communists are also not without their supporters, many of the Congress supporters having obtained transfers to Delhi. The successor IAS has lacked the cohesion and power of the smaller ICS

---

[1]  D. Bandyopadhyay, Land Reforms Commissioner, *Land Reforms in West Bengal* (Calcutta: Information and Cultural Affairs Department, Government of West Bengal, 1980), p. 10.

and has been unable to resist the demands of politicians to any critical extent. On the other hand they have actively sought the backing of politicians for their promotions and transfers, and as a result have often become factionalized along party lines. While this has not happened to the same extent in West Bengal as in some other states, some of the more important programs under the Communist government were administered by leftist IAS officers.

The Left Front explains shortcomings in their reforms as being due to the constitutional requirement that state legislation receive Presidential assent before it becomes law, effectively giving the ruling party at the center a veto power over state legislation. However, this power has rarely been used by the central government against the West Bengal government. Of the 411 bills passed by the Left Front till mid 1984, assent was withheld from only ten bills.[2] In all these cases the bills were to acquire or take over the management of minor private educational institutions. The refusal may have been justified on grounds of preventing state control over higher education, which in any case was an issue of secondary importance in the Left Front program. The Communists could have chosen the tactic of deliberately passing radical legislation knowing it would not be assented to, and then organized mass movements on the basis of central obstruction. It chose however only to pass legislation acceptable to the center, which in itself was a measure of its acceptance of the constitutional system. Though the scope for reform may have been less under the Congress government than under the Janata and National Front governments, at no time did the Left Front approach the limits of constitutional reformism.

The only sector of the State government opposed to the Communists was the Calcutta High Court whose influence was somewhat offset by the more sympathetic liberal Supreme Court.[3] That the High Court was an effective obstacle to reform was somewhat surprising since the Court had no agency to implement its rulings, the police being supportive of the Left Front for its own reasons. The Left Front had improved the pay of the lower ranks and unionized an important segment of it, while the IPS officers like the IAS had to keep in favor with the ruling politicians. Nevertheless the Left Front was careful not to override the Calcutta High Court rulings and carefully kept within the bounds of legality. This was particularly surprising since the CPM in the past had never shown such regard for the law. It dismissed numerous criminal cases against its own followers including some well-substantiated murder charges. In the two United

---

[2] West Bengal, Department of Information and Cultural Affairs, *Left Front Government in West Bengal* (Calcutta: Government of West Bengal, 1984), p. 196; West Bengal, Information and Cultural Affairs Department, *Reply to Questionnaire: Commission on Centre–State Relations* (Calcutta: Government of West Bengal, July 1984), p. 9.

[3] Communist Party of India – Marxist, *Political Resolution*, adopted by the Eleventh Congress, Vijayawada, January 26–31, 1982 (New Delhi: March 1982), p. 33.

Fronts it had initiated land-grab movements with success, though these were in violation of the law. With the forces of law and order even more firmly under the CPM's control in the Left Front government, there was nothing the High Court could effectively do to impede another mass movement for popular demands if the CPM chose to organize it. Without the imposition of Presidential Rule and despatch of central police to the state, there was little the other institutions in West Bengal could do to oppose the CPM, and if the High Court had its way it was only because the Left Front chose not to pursue a radical strategy of mass mobilization such as had occurred previously. It obeyed the High Court out of choice as part of its policy of gradual change. The Maoists questioned what prevented grass-roots Communist organizations from mobilizing for passage of legislation.

When the Central Government delayed the signing of the amendment to the Land Reforms Bill, there was no attempt to mobilise the people in general and the peasantry in particular in massive demonstrations. Would not such steps have raised the consciousness of the people as regards the importance of the issue? But the Left Front government is committed to a policy of all talk and no struggle.[4]

Whatever the political perspective, no one disputes the fact that there has been nothing approaching a mass struggle since the United Front days, when the left was in a much weaker and more vulnerable position. This avoidance of struggle is not without an ironical twist, as the criticisms leveled by the leadership of the CPM at the time of the split against the right would now seem to apply equally to themselves.

The degree to which the bureaucracy as a whole has actively obstructed the Left Front government does not appear to have been significant. At the lower levels most of the state government employees support the Left Front and many at the middle and higher levels do also. Jyoti Basu, a CPM leader and the Chief Minister of West Bengal, stated that "although it is not possible to have radical change in administration now, many in the administration and police are quite alive to implementing our policies."[5] The CPM's State Committee Political-Organizational Report went further in stating that "with the Left Front Government in power the State administration and police has largely changed."[6] The Left

4 CPI, "The Left Front Government in West Bengal: From Class Collaboration to Class Capitulation," *For a New Democracy*, vol. 1, no. 10–12, December 1978–February 1979 (Calcutta: Provisional Central Committee of the Communist Party of India – Marxist-Leninist), p. 120.
5 Jyoti Basu, "Tin Bajhar Bamfront Sarkar Parichalanar Avigyata Samparkay Kichhu Baktyavba" ("Something to Say Regarding the Experience of the Running of the Left Front Government for the Last Three Years"), *Deshhitaishee*, annual Puja issue 1980, p. 19.
6 West Bengal State Conference Communist Party of India – Marxist, *Rajnaitik-Sangathanik Report*, "Political-Organisational Report" December 27, 1981–January 1, 1982 (Calcutta: West Bengal State Committee, Communist Party of India – Marxist, March 1982), p. 68.

Front's concessions to government employees have gone a long way towards preventing the state apparatus in Bengal from being used to actively subvert the Communist government. This is particularly noticeable in the State Police where the Communists have made considerable inroads. "The sympathetic consideration of police demands by the Left Front prevented the police force taking an anti-government part ... The Police are happy with this treatment compared with other states."[7]

Jyoti Basu wrote that "the future of West Bengal and the whole future of the political situation in India depends on ordinary government employees who through their dedicated work in government can implement progressive programmes benefiting the poor."[8] The tone of the new Communist government in the relations with the public would therefore be set by the CPM's own supporters in the State Employees Coordination Committee. The CPM has gained the support of most government employees at the middle and lower levels through judicious use of pay increments and support of trade union rights. Their supporters' political consciousness, however, is at a low level, being oriented to the material inducements that the Communists can deliver. A typical example was making 3,300 Tahshildars and Tahshildar peons full-fledged permanent government employees at an additional cost of 3 crores a year.[9] As a result of this they do not receive a commission on the land revenues they collect, the consequence of which has been a drop in its collection for the state exchequer. Though these employees are part of the rural landed interests, the assumption is that by making them permanent employees they will support the Left Front regardless of their class interests. On the contrary it has made them even less amenable to work now that their employment is secured, and costs the government an additional financial burden. The same financial inducements have been given to school teachers' by increasing pay to the level of the central government employees, something which has not been done in other states. There has been no improvement in teaching, however, and the expenditure on teachers' salaries has gone up from 59 crores in 1976–77 to 166 crores in 1984–85.[10] It is also said the Left Front has appointed its own supporters as school teachers and village health workers as a means of getting committed support in the villages.

As a result of such salary inducements about 22,000 million Rupees out of

[7] *Ibid.*, pp. 52–3.
[8] Jyoti Basu, "Party, Yukta Front O Sadharan Manush Gata Tin Dasaker Andolaner Avigyata" ("Party, United Front and Common Man: Experience of Movement for the last three Decades"), *Deshhitaishee*, annual Puja issue 1981, p. 43.
[9] West Bengal, Department of Information and Cultural Affairs, p. 7.
[10] West Bengal, Department of Information and Cultural Affairs, *School Education in West Bengal 1984* (Calcutta: Director of Information, 1985).

the 27,000 million Rupee Annual State Plan goes just in paying government salaries and little is left for development work. In spite of this largesse the lethargy of the bureaucracy has undergone no change since the coming of the CPM to power. Punctuality and dedication to work are with few exceptions observed in the breach. Hardly 30 percent of employees turn up on time in the Secretariat with most staff arriving 1/2 to 1 1/2 hours late and leaving work from 1/2 to 1 hour early. This despite appeals from the CPM-controlled Coordination Committee of State Government Employees, and substantial increases in pay which the Left Front awarded them.[11] Jyoti Basu admitted "the common man is not getting the help they should normally get from government. In this situation, those ordinary Government employees in the administration, a large majority of whom are supporters of the Left Front government, have a special responsibility."[12] The CPM's West Bengal State Committee *Political-Organisational Report* complained of "considerable weakness at all levels" of the administration, noting the need for "punctuality and quick decisions on files to maintain close contact with people."

In spite of many actions taken by the government organisation our supporters and sympathisers have not worked with punctuality and dedication but gone back to old traditional ways. These people forget that this sort of attitude brings down the government. ... From a large section of government employees we are getting support but even here their long standing habits of lack of total dedication, procrastination, malpractices and their indifference to the people have stood in the way of implementing government work programmes.[13]

By the time the second Left Front government came to power, the Communists had seen their mistake. The pro-CPI *Link* admitted Communist responsibility for the state of affairs among its Communist organized government employees.

This responsibility stems from the fact that none of the trade unions have ever talked of work principles in the past ... leading to a kind of cynicism and an attitude of work shirking among the workers and middle class employees. This attitude has seriously affected the CPI-M led coordination committee followers even in the Writers Building, the seat of the State Government ... Caught in this dilemma the CPI-M and the CPI today are stressing on work principles. Indeed, in a party letter for the members alone, the CPI-M has exhorted its ranks and followers to become model workers wherever they be and thus inspire and lead others ... The cumulative effect of all these factors, which the Left has not yet been able to combat successfully, is seriously tarnishing the Front's image among the urban population. It is easy to surmise that if this doldrum continues to dog the State for long, even the rural population will hardly remain well disposed towards the Left ... This is a big challenge for the Left, which calls for the establishment

---

[11] *The Statesman*, July 6, 1982.
[12] Basu, "Party," p. 43.
[13] Communist Party of India – Marxist, West Bengal State Conference, 1982, pp. 45–6, 52.

of work principles. In other words, unlike in its oppositional phase, the Left now has to insist that the democratic rights of the toilers do not preclude work ethics, responsibility and so on, but in fact include these factors. In the absence of work ethics and honesty democratic rights cannot be evoked and would cease to be legitimate.[14]

A *Statesman* editorial noted, however, that such observations and appeals had had no effect, but at least had shown that the CPM leadership was aware of the problem.

Why the Left Front has so far been disinclined to use its influence over the employees to ensure greater discipline at least in Government offices is not clear ... It is apparently making some effort to come to grips with problems it chose earlier to neglect. But it is widely felt that the opportunity it lost when it came to power with a massive mandate in 1977 cannot be re-created. The popular mandate is still in force, but the intervening years have exposed an unwillingness to take hard decisions and thereby weakened the Government's authority ... If appeals for greater discipline and harder work have been generally ignored, it is because the Government has never been seen to be determined to follow up its words with the necessary action, apparently for fear of losing its reputation of being a friend of the working class ... The overall effect has been a virtual breakdown of administrative control, whether in milk and power supply or in transport and hospital services. Even the latest directives may go unheeded unless the Left Front sheds its political and other inhibitions about punishing the guilty.[15]

Having totally failed by attempting moral incentives, the Left Front is left with no alternative but to enforce penalties for lack of discipline and punctuality. The Left Front has not been willing to do this. In attempting not to alienate any of its supporters, it has sacrificed the interests of the urban public, and to the extent that the state penetrates the villages, the rural public as well. Having constantly emphasized job security and wage and bonus increases over productivity, it now finds itself saddled with a lot of lazy undisciplined supporters who are a greater liability than an asset. Only with connections or money can individuals hope to receive prompt services from the state sector, and this trading of favors, influence peddling, and bribery has become such a way of life in India that it is taken for granted by the middle and upper classes. The officers spend a large amount of time doing favors for friends and contacts who can't get routine things done through the regular channels, which have long since ceased to function with speed and efficiency. The trading of favors and contacts has become a way of life for the middle classes; there is no other way to survive. Those without favors to dispense or at least friends and relatives willing to trade favors on their behalf, have to resort to bribery. It is said of Bengalis and Indians that "next to the interest of his family, the public interest does not exist."[16] However, in an

[14] *Link*, May 1, 1983, pp. 8–9.
[15] Editorial, "Words and Action," *The Statesman*, December 31, 1982, p. 6.
[16] Joseph Lelyveld, *Calcutta* (Hong Kong: The Perennial Press, 1975), p. 26.

extremely competitive situation, where even seemingly routine tasks can present insurmountable difficulties and inordinate delays, there is little choice for the individuals involved. The lower classes do not enter the picture and tend to view the bureaucracy with suspicion and cynicism at best and often as an exploiter. Not surprisingly a poll of rural voters at the time of the 1978 Panchayat elections found that 84 percent thought that the state and central governments do not care much for rural people.[17] One Secretary of the West Bengal government complained he had difficulty taking decisions because files would either be misplaced or incomplete and his staff could not be made to look for them. If previous correspondence is referred to in a letter there is a good chance it will be untraceable as no master file is kept.

According to the IAS officers, the whole state apparatus is manned by staff, most of whom are completely redundant and dependent on the remainder for whatever work is accomplished. If whole ministries and departments were abolished, it is doubtful if the lower classes would be in the least affected. Even in departments created for the benefit of these lower sections, their abolition or the retrenchment of large numbers of staff would have only a marginal impact on the people they were supposedly serving. The question must therefore arise as to why the Communists, on attaining state power, did not reorganize the state apparatus by abolishing redundant departments and staff or transferring them to new productive projects, and use the financial resources thus released for the benefit of the poorer sections. From the CPM's viewpoint, however, this was never an option, as one of their strongest bases was among state government employees, and the lower classes lacked any equivalent power or lobby in the party. The ponderous, largely redundant state apparatus was therefore accepted as one of the givens of the situation, which would continue to absorb a large part of the state budget. Whatever limited funds were left over for social transformation of the lower sections, were raised through tax increases and deficit financing from the Central Reserve Bank. Jyoti Basu claimed the Left Front Government had doubled the West Bengal Budget in the space of three years, but when the Indian government complained that Bengal had accumulated the highest State deficit of 4025.3 million Rupees by its borrowing from the Central Reserve Bank, the state government repeated the longstanding claim of central discrimination.[18] The Communists, however, refused to consider any radical ways of raising funds, thereby seriously curbing the resources available for social transformation.

---

[17] M. Shiviah, K.B. Srivastava, and A.C. Jana, *Panchayati Raj Elections in West Bengal, 1978* (Hyderabad: National Institute of Rural Development, 1980), p. 132.

[18] Basu, "Tin Bajhar," p. 19.

Rather than the party transforming the bureaucracy the party is itself becoming a bureaucracy. The IAS and WBCS officers who were sympathetic to the aims of the Left Front noted with apprehension the danger of the CPM becoming complacent in office, like the Congress before them. The CPM, by getting used to the perquisites and amenities of power, were in danger of becoming detached from the people. The tendency of having the people coming to them rather than going to the people was present. The defects of the existing state bureaucracy were being replicated to some extent in the party. Even in the three years from 1982 till 1985, there was a marked change. Corruption in the party which had previously been rumoured had come much more into the open. Even CPM party members were admitting the honesty of some of their own ministers could not be vouched for. They blamed this on the influence of a corrupting society. The senior IAS officers who had to work with the Ministers on a daily basis took a less charitable view, claiming most were corrupted by their positions. Only a few were considered competent ministerial administrators. At the district level the administration had to take cognizance of party affiliations even in criminal matters, including consulting local party leaders on the granting of bail. Two District Magistrates who tried to prosecute cases of corruption were transferred. The morale of the senior IAS officers was low and the ones with leftist leanings seemed the most disillusioned. The IAS and IPS as well as subordinate ranks had become factionalized by party interference. By creating a base in the bureaucracy, the Left Front had gone a long way to ruining its efficiency. Standards of administrative efficiency had slipped even from the Congress period as the Left Front ministers took a more lenient view of corruption and inefficiency, blaming it on the capitalist system rather than on the individuals concerned. When an old CPM leader stated "the attitude of the leadership is to remain in power at any price" he summed up the only consistently followed policy of the Left Front.[19]

## Public enterprises

When the Communists came to power in 1977 the State government undertakings were generally in a position of having a current and accumulated deficit. The accumulated losses were to the tune of 1254.4 million Rupees, while accumulated profits stood at only 11.3 million.[20] After three years of Communist government, the 1980 returns indicated accumulated losses of 1510.2

[19] Piyash Das Gupta, "CPI(M) Sangramer Madhye Janma O Briddi, Mahakaraner Kanke Prabesh O Siddi" ("The Birth and Expansion of CPI(M) – Formation of Government and its Fulfilment"), *Bartaman*, December 7, 1985.
[20] West Bengal, *Economic Review 1977–78* (Calcutta: West Bengal Government Press, 1978), pp. 28–30.

compared to profits of 39.3. Of twenty government-sponsored schemes and projects mentioned by the Finance Department, only two showed a profit in 1981–82.[21] As the 1980–81 state revenue receipts were 11,230 million Rupees, the net losses in that year represented 13.1 percent of the state budget. By 1984–85 the situation was considerably worse, with current profits of 151.7 million and 1,063.7 million in current losses. Of the twenty-eight enterprises for which statistics are available, accumulated profits were 139.7 million and accumulated losses 4,449.3 million Rupees. The net losses represented 24.7 percent of the increased state budget of 17,441.6 million Rupees.[22] Though many had been sick industries that the government took over to maintain employment, many were potentially viable and some should have been extremely lucrative. When compared with Central government enterprises the Left Front performance was poor. Current profits in 1982–83 of 25,201 million made by 110 Central government enterprises compared with 81 concerns making losses of 9,747, for a net profit of 15,454 million Rupees.[23] The fundamental question on assuming power was whether it should be the role of a Communist Party to operate the public sector as profitable entities in a capitalist economy or as public services with the state subsidizing the loss. In practice the government succeeded in doing neither. The public services these corporations provided were notoriously inefficient and could probably have been better run under private management. The Government proved incapable of running the firms on profitable lines and thus had to subsidize them as a drain on the state exchequer with money that might have been better spent elsewhere. The employees, secure in the knowledge that the government would absorb the losses, found no reason to apply themselves to serious or punctual work. Half of the employees of the state Dairy Industry are normally absent from work and those that bother to show up work only for about four hours.[24] The Calcutta State Transport Corporation is not much better, with 28 percent absenteeism in the first fortnight and 40 percent in the second fortnight of each month. On average only half of the 660 state buses ply the streets due to poor maintenance and absenteeism.[25] With 14,219 employees this represents over twenty-one employees per bus, or twice that if only operational buses are included. The company had current losses of 199.9 million and accumulated losses of

[21] West Bengal, *Economic Review 1980–81: Statistical Appendix* (Calcutta: West Bengal Government Press, 1981), pp. 119–25. *The Statesman*, March 9, 1982.

[22] West Bengal, *Economic Review 1984–85: Statistical Appendix* (Calcutta: West Bengal Government Press, 1985), pp. 134–41, 184.

[23] Tata Services Ltd., Department of Economics and Statistics, *Statistical Outline of India 1984*, p. 84.

[24] *The Statesman*, August 15, 1982.

[25] *The Statesman*, July 1, 1982; West Bengal, Department of Information and Cultural Affairs, *Left Front Government in West Bengal: Eight Years* (Calcutta: September 16, 1985), p. 96.

Table 5.1. *Installed capacity and potential demand for electricity in West Bengal (1980–84)*

| In MW | 1980–81 | 1981–82 | 1982–83 | 1983–84 |
|---|---|---|---|---|
| Installed capacity | 1,945 | 2,155 | 2,425 | 2,553 |
| Peak demand | 1,172 | 1,213 | 1,282 | 1,438 |

*Source:* West Bengal, Development and Planning Department, *Draft Seventh Five Year Plan 1985–90 and Annual Plan 1985–86*, Calcutta, January 1985, mimeographed, pp. XVIII–XIX.

729.8 million Rupees, despite the buses being so crowded with passengers as to force commuters to cling to the outside of the moving vehicles.[26]

No public sector enterprise has been the subject of as much criticism as the West Bengal State Electricity Board. In contrast to the private sector Calcutta Electric Supply Corporation which has maintained a reasonable standard of efficiency, the larger State government board has proved a failure. Though most cities of India suffer from power cuts, Calcutta is by far the worst affected of any major city due to the failure of the State Electricity Board to adequately supply the city. Aside from the discomfort felt by domestic consumers, the industrial production has been seriously affected by the power shortage and the overheads required to install their own inefficient generators as substitutes. The load-shedding has been partly responsible for the loss of support for the Left Front among urban middle-class voters.

In part the cause of the under-utilization of existing capacity lies in inadequate supply of spare parts and fuel. However, the primary fault appears to lie with the personnel employed by the State Electricity Board. Unlike other equally inefficient government organizations, the shortcomings of the State Electricity Board are immediately apparent to the general public whenever the power goes off. Though in 1983–84 the installed capacity of electricity in West Bengal is 2,533 MW and peak demand only 1,438 MW, the State Electricity Board generated only 35.9 percent of its own installed capacity.[27] This compares unfavorably with a national average of 50.1 percent, and with several Indian plants which generate over 70 percent of installed capacity.[28] West Bengal

[26] West Bengal, *Economic Review 1984–85: Statistical Appendix*, p. 135.
[27] West Bengal, Development and Planning Department, *Draft Seventh Five Year Plan 1985–90 and Annual Plan 1985–86*, vol. I (Calcutta: January 1985), mimeographed, pp. XVIII–XIX; Government of India, Power and Energy Division, Planning Commission, *Review of Performance of State Electricity Boards in the Sixth Five Year Plan Period* (New Delhi: June 1985), Annexure 4.
[28] Government of India, Ministry of Information and Broadcasting, *India 1984* (New Delhi: Publications Division, March 1985), p. 317.

Table 5.2. *State Electricity Boards' annual plant load factor (percentage) of thermal stations (1979–80 to 1984–85)*

| State/Board | 1979–80 | 1980–81 | 1981–82 | 1982–83 | 1983–84 | 1984–85[*] |
|---|---|---|---|---|---|---|
| Andhra Pradesh | 40.9 | 36.3 | 46.8 | 51.1 | 54.6 | 54.9 |
| Assam | 41.1 | 36.5 | 34.8 | 36.9 | 34.2 | 29.6 |
| Bihar | 37.8 | 31.4 | 35.5 | 38.5 | 32.8 | 30.4 |
| Gujarat | 48.4 | 50.0 | 53.6 | 53.9 | 55.3 | 54.0 |
| Haryana | 25.7 | 31.7 | 37.3 | 32.2 | 31.1 | 34.7 |
| Madhya Pradesh | 53.1 | 52.4 | 49.9 | 58.5 | 53.1 | 51.6 |
| Maharashtra | 55.0 | 52.8 | 49.4 | 50.2 | 51.0 | 46.6 |
| Orissa | 31.8 | 34.0 | 35.9 | 35.2 | 33.3 | 32.2 |
| Punjab | 29.6 | 37.8 | 41.3 | 51.0 | 72.3 | 57.4 |
| Rajasthan | — | — | — | — | 57.1 | 64.2 |
| Tamil Nadu | 38.8 | 34.5 | 37.8 | 44.0 | 39.4 | 49.2 |
| Uttar Pradesh | 43.8 | 36.5 | 37.6 | 39.6 | 35.1 | 31.6 |
| West Bengal | 43.5 | 42.1 | 37.6 | 38.5 | 35.9 | 36.5 |
| All India | 44.3 | 44.2 | 46.4 | 49.4 | 47.9 | 50.1 |

[*] Tentative.
*Source:* India, Power and Energy Division, Planning Commission, *Review of Performance of State Electricity Boards in the Sixth Five Year Plan Period*, June 1985, Annexure 4.

should therefore have been able to meet potential demand for electricity as shown in table 5.1. While the Plant Load Factor has improved for the country as a whole, in West Bengal table 5.2 shows there has been a decline since 1979. The failure to meet the demand for electricity was partly due to politically motivated overstaffing making the State Electricity Board inefficient. Of the 32,000 employees of the Board 10,000 are completely redundant Congress supporters whom Ghani Khan Choudhury, Congress Minister of Energy, had appointed at the behest of Sanjay Gandhi during the Emergency in order to increase employment of Congress followers throughout India, with each State Electricity Board in the country being given a quota of employees to be hired. These Congress workers have no functions but to obstruct the work of the new Left Front government and create a heavy financial burden on the Board. The security of tenure in government organizations has effectively prevented their dismissal. Though Jyoti Basu has blamed these workers for obstructing the work of the Electricity Board, the state government was able to maintain power supply in the days immediately preceding the 1982 elections, indicating that the government could exert control over the Board when the occasion demanded. In spite of this, many of the CPM candidates in Calcutta were defeated and load-shedding continued as usual after the election.[29] Though it takes five years

[29] Editorial, "A Look at Power Plants," *The Statesman*, August 18, 1982.

to develop new power sources, the advance planning was inadequate or unimplemented, and even when developed was behind schedule in installation. While management and the unions blamed each other for the problem, the CPM and Congress accused each other of political interference.

The Left Front had originally promised to solve the electricity problem before the end of its first term, but in its *Economic Review* for 1981–82 this had been revised to an expectation of "a significant narrowing of the gap between effective demand and the supply of power in the State by the end of the Sixth Plan (1980–85)."[30] By 1985 it was clear that these subsequent targets had proven illusory. Though the state governments knew in 1976 that in West Bengal "demand for power continues to grow even during a period of recession and only the rate of growth decreases,"[31] the Left Front singularly failed to anticipate and develop sources of power, resulting in much loss of production, discouragement of new investment and urban consumer dissatisfaction. Their belated attention to the problem did not produce an improvement in the situation.

The Association of Indian Engineering Industry (AIEI) noted the industrial structure of West Bengal had been nearly the same for the last twenty years and was now "witnessing a complete breakdown of infrastructure which, far from attracting fresh investment, is resulting in a massive flight of capital to other States and that too by companies who were firmly entrenched in this State for nearly a century."[32] While the flight of capital was a matter of dispute, new investment was marginal and would remain so until the power situation was resolved. The prevalent work attitudes and infrastructural deficiencies had proved beyond the ability or willingness of the Left Front to handle.

Whether in administration of the state bureaucracy or in public enterprises, the Left Front was totally unsuccessful in altering or even alleviating existing maladministration. However, improving administration of a capitalist economy was not the Left Front's top priority. The major objective was re-election.

### Industry

The Left Front victory placed the Communists in an awkward position in government. They had strenuously denounced foreign multinational penetration of the Indian economy and the role of Indian monopoly houses which

---

[30] West Bengal, *Economic Review 1981–82* (Calcutta: West Bengal Government Press, 1982), p. 32.
[31] N.K. De Sirkar, "Power Supply for the Industries in West Bengal" in *Industries in West Bengal*, vol. XXII, nos. 2 and 3 of *India in Industries*, edited by Parimal Sengupta (Calcutta: Oxford Book Company 1976), Sponsored by Commerce and Industries Department, Government of West Bengal, p. 65.
[32] *The Statesman*, January 31, 1982.

controlled most of the large scale private sector. However, the Communist electorate and the trade unions were interested in the employment which big business provided. Noting its own budgetary constraints the Left Front government stated:

Only the private sector can do something for industry here if they really want to do so. Because of this reason the Left Front Government is trying to encourage the private sector to come forward and invest here.[33]

The West Bengal government accuses the center of blocking or obstructing business investment, while crediting itself for whatever expansion takes place. It claims that this expansion takes place with the help of the state government in spite of central government obstruction. Much of this dispute is due to central government control over business investment. Under the *1951 Industries (Development and Regulation) Act* the central government alone decides on the setting up of large- and medium-scale industries, which have to receive licences to operate. This leaves only the small-scale industrial sector under state government control.

The Left Front accuses the center of encouraging businesses applying for licences to set up elsewhere in India, particularly in states where Congress is in power. It is perfectly understandable that Congress politicians would attempt to bring investment to their own states. In this sense any opposition government would be at a disadvantage, and perhaps a Communist government most of all. However, the Indian bureaucracy is so lethargic it is difficult to prove delays are politically motivated, particularly since the Left Front administration is no more efficient. Even the Left Front admits that investment in Bengal has been on the downturn since the 1950s when Congress was in power. Bengal in any case has neither the electoral numbers to exert political pressure nor the efficient infrastructure likely to encourage investment. If one looks at the issuing of licences by the center during both Congress and Communist regimes there does not appear to be any systematic discrimination against Bengal because of its Communist government (table 5.3). Though it does not receive the highest number of licences, it occupies a middle position commensurate with the investment opportunities it can provide. Certainly if a private investor wished to invest in Bengal he could do so eventually, despite the usual obstacles placed by the center on investment. Multinationals are usually required to operate as joint ventures with Indian companies, though substantial ownership may be foreign if new technology is being introduced or production geared for export. Investment in West Bengal has in fact been greater under the first five years of the Left Front than in the previous five years of Congress rule. (Rupees 2176

[33] Department of Information and Cultural Affairs, *Left Front Government*, p. 91.

Table 5.3. *Industrial licences issued to different states, 1974–84*

| State | 1974 | 1975 | 1976 | 1977 | 1978 | 1979 | 1980 | 1981 | 1982 | 1983 | 1984 (till Sept.) |
|---|---|---|---|---|---|---|---|---|---|---|---|
| Andhra Pradesh | 61 | 61 | 51 | 27 | 17 | 17 | 42 | 39 | 26 | 63 | 38 |
| Assam | 9 | 9 | 6 | 2 | 1 | 2 | 5 | 4 | 1 | 22 | 4 |
| Bihar | 24 | 15 | 17 | 16 | 12 | 3 | 4 | 10 | 9 | 29 | 17 |
| Gujarat | 89 | 97 | 83 | 60 | 46 | 48 | 85 | 79 | 69 | 115 | 66 |
| Haryana | 61 | 63 | 27 | 23 | 13 | 16 | 20 | 21 | 21 | 59 | 38 |
| Karnataka | 66 | 64 | 43 | 45 | 26 | 24 | 40 | 25 | 34 | 65 | 40 |
| Kerala | 19 | 25 | 25 | 16 | 7 | 11 | 11 | 15 | 9 | 22 | 19 |
| Madhya Pradesh | 45 | 35 | 18 | 8 | 8 | 7 | 18 | 15 | 9 | 30 | 24 |
| Maharashtra | 265 | 255 | 143 | 150 | 101 | 111 | 107 | 114 | 95 | 171 | 105 |
| Orissa | 12 | 10 | 7 | 2 | 2 | 6 | 8 | 5 | 10 | 14 | 11 |
| Punjab | 46 | 43 | 25 | 23 | 9 | 13 | 18 | 17 | 14 | 169 | 79 |
| Rajasthan | 36 | 24 | 16 | 17 | 10 | 8 | 15 | 26 | 14 | 25 | 17 |
| Tamil Nadu | 99 | 141 | 61 | 32 | 28 | 26 | 37 | 30 | 41 | 76 | 53 |
| Uttar Pradesh | 116 | 72 | 55 | 41 | 26 | 33 | 30 | 24 | 22 | 98 | 62 |
| West Bengal | 107 | 74 | 56 | 40 | 23 | 30 | 23 | 34 | 27 | 71 | 67 |
| Other states and union territories | 44 | 39 | 29 | 16 | 19 | 10 | 12 | 18 | 31 | 46 | 39 |
| All India | 1099 | 1027 | 662 | 518 | 348 | 365 | 475 | 476 | 432 | 1075 | 679 |

*Source: Economic Review 1980–81 and 1984–85, West Bengal Government Press, Alipore, 1981, 1985.*

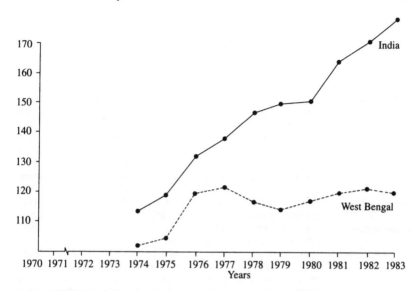

Fig. 5.1. Index of industrial production in India and West Bengal

*Source:* West Bengal, *Economic Review: Statistical Appendix, 1980–81 and 1984–85* (Alipore, West Bengal Government Press, 1981 and 1985), table 6 (a)

million in 1977–82 as against 1174.6 in 1971–76.) During these periods 141 letters of intent were converted into industrial licences for a 1927.7 million investment during 1977–82 compared with only 124 licences involving 1109 million Rupees in 1971–76.[34] The Left Front's claims of discrimination by the central government would therefore appear to be largely unfounded.

This seeming industrial expansion is deceptive. At 1970–71 prices state net domestic product in the manufacturing sector is at about the same level in 1984–85 as it was when the Left Front first came to power. In this period West Bengal fell from second to fifth place among Indian states as other states expanded their manufacturing while Bengal's position remained roughly the same (table 5.4). While second only to Maharashtra as late as 1977–78, it fell behind Tamil Nadu in the following year, and behind Gujarat and Uttar Pradesh in 1982–83. West Bengal, while maintaining its absolute position in manufacturing, is losing relative to other Indian states.

Both CPM cadre and businessmen, ironically, very often have an identity of views regarding the record of the Left Front government in labor and

[34] West Bengal State Committee, CPM, *Significant Six Years of the Left Front Government of West Bengal* (Calcutta: CPM West Bengal State Committee, September 1983), p. 58.

Table 5.4. *State domestic product (net) in manufacturing sector*

| State | 1970–71 | 1971–72 | 1972–73 | 1973–74 | 1974–75 | 1975–76 | (Rs lakh) 1976–77 |
|---|---|---|---|---|---|---|---|
| Andhra Pradesh | 22135 | 22923 | 23836 | 24691 | 27044 | 28814 | 28689 |
|  | (100.0) | (103.6) | (107.7) | (111.5) | (122.2) | (130.2) | (129.6) |
| Assam | 7020 | 7360 | 7660 | 8030 | 8370 | 8680 | 8740 |
|  | (100.0) | (104.8) | (109.1) | (114.4) | (119.2) | (123.6) | (124.5) |
| Bihar | 22177 | 22786 | 22971 | 24359 | 24393 | 25873 | 27930 |
|  | (100.0) | (102.7) | (103.6) | (109.8) | (110.0) | (116.7) | (125.9) |
| Gujarat | 34939 | 32946 | 39368 | 42791 | 43973 | 42590 | 47108 |
|  | (100.0) | (94.3) | (112.7) | (122.5) | (125.9) | (121.9) | (134.8) |
| Haryana | 8587 | 10039 | 10494 | 10814 | 12025 | 12362 | 13199 |
|  | (100.0) | (116.9) | (122.2) | (125.9) | (140.0) | (144.0) | (153.7) |
| Himachal Pradesh | 1346 | 1400 | 1263 | 1328 | 1242 | 1335 | 1395 |
|  | (100.0) | (104.0) | (93.8) | (98.7) | (92.3) | (99.2) | (103.6) |
| Jammu & Kashmir | 1335 | 1433 | 1532 | 1651 | 1675 | 1709 | 1825 |
|  | (100.0) | (107.3) | (114.8) | (123.7) | (125.5) | (128.0) | (136.7) |
| Karnataka | 28588 | 30117 | 30762 | 31855 | 32361 | 35374 | 41759 |
|  | (100.0) | (105.3) | (107.6) | (111.4) | (131.2) | (123.7) | (146.1) |
| Kerala | 15632 | 17338 | 18253 | 17974 | 17214 | 18355 | 19348 |
|  | (100.0) | (110.9) | (116.8) | (115.0) | (110.1) | (117.4) | (123.8) |
| Madhya Pradesh | 17880 | 19080 | 21110 | 25880 | 22130 | 21480 | 27500 |
|  | (100.0) | (106.7) | (118.1) | (144.7) | (123.8) | (120.1) | (153.8) |
| Maharashtra | 102777 | 105323 | 109309 | 108693 | 115718 | 124651 | 139272 |
|  | (100.0) | (102.5) | (106.4) | (105.8) | (112.6) | (121.3) | (135.5) |
| Orissa | 8331 | 6888 | 6591 | 8323 | 9166 | 7546 | 10915 |
|  | (100.0) | (82.7) | (79.1) | (100.0) | (110.0) | (91.0) | (131.0) |
| Punjab | 11494 | 11927 | 14072 | 14626 | 14856 | 17600 | 19079 |
|  | (100.0) | (103.8) | (118.0) | (127.2) | (129.3) | (153.1) | (166.0) |
| Rajasthan | 12666 | 13078 | 13322 | 13531 | 13856 | 14487 | 15259 |
|  | (100.0) | (103.3) | (105.2) | (106.8) | (109.4) | (114.4) | (120.5) |
| Tamil Nadu | 45871 | 46574 | 48059 | 46556 | 40448 | 52436 | 60626 |
|  | (100.0) | (101.5) | (104.8) | (101.5) | (88.2) | (114.3) | (132.2) |
| Uttar Pradesh | 37925 | 35838 | 38156 | 37484 | 37376 | 42862 | 45507 |
|  | (100.0) | (94.5) | (100.6) | (98.8) | (98.6) | (113.0) | (120.0) |
| West Bengal | 55587 | 56469 | 58172 | 58571 | 56786 | 57850 | 65822 |
|  | (100.0) | (101.6) | (104.7) | (105.4) | (102.2) | (104.1) | (118.4) |
| Delhi | 8588 | 9032 | 9326 | 9231 | 9478 | 10284 | 10776 |
|  | (100.0) | (105.2) | (108.6) | (107.5) | (110.4) | (119.7) | (125.5) |
| All India | 4619 | 4750 | 4954 | 5252 | 5468 | 5557 | 6040 |
|  | (100.0) | (102.8) | (107.3) | (113.7) | (118.4) | (120.3) | (130.8) |

*Table 5.4 continued*

| State | 1977–78 | 1978–79 | 1979–80 | 1980–81 | 1981–82 | 1982–83 | 1983–84 | (Rs lakh) 1984–85 |
|---|---|---|---|---|---|---|---|---|
| Andhra Pradesh | 29936 | 34499 | 36737 | 36559 | 40713 | 41314 | 41236 | 45822 |
| | (135.2) | (155.9) | (166.0) | (165.2) | (183.9) | (186.6) | (186.3) | (207.0) |
| Assam | 9220 | 9870 | 9780 | 9200 | 11600 | 12250 | 13120 | 14690 |
| | (131.3) | (140.6) | (139.3) | (131.1) | (165.2) | (174.5) | (186.9) | (209.3) |
| Bihar | 29135 | 31150 | 31157 | 34414 | 41473 | 42846 | 45575 | 47073 |
| | (131.4) | (140.5) | (140.5) | (155.2) | (187.0) | (193.2) | (205.5) | (212.3) |
| Gujarat | 53194 | 55528 | 57422 | 26989 | 60713 | 73117 | 74417 | 76406 |
| | (152.2) | (158.9) | (164.3) | (163.1) | (173.8) | (209.3) | (213.0) | (218.7) |
| Haryana | 14732 | 16236 | 17597 | 18425 | 19183 | 20044 | 21241 | 22126 |
| | (171.6) | (189.1) | (204.9) | (214.6) | (223.4) | (233.4) | (247.4) | (257.7) |
| Himachal Pradesh | 1917 | 1639 | 1232 | 1267 | 1671 | 1667 | 1716 | 1800 |
| | (142.4) | (121.8) | (91.5) | (94.1) | (124.1) | (123.8) | (127.5) | (133.7) |
| Jammu & Kashmir | 1984 | 2319 | 2210 | 2195 | 2707 | 3125 | 3553 | 3977 |
| | (148.6) | (173.7) | (165.5) | (164.4) | (202.8) | (234.1) | (266.1) | (297.9) |
| Karnataka | 46828 | 53092 | 55741 | 53395 | 54445 | 57493 | 60367 | 62603 |
| | (163.8) | (185.7) | (195.0) | (186.8) | (190.4) | (201.1) | (211.2) | (219.0) |
| Kerala | 19294 | 19710 | 21825 | 21906 | 21709 | 22010 | 21253 | 21805 |
| | (123.4) | (126.1) | (139.6) | (140.1) | (138.9) | (140.8) | (136.0) | (139.5) |
| Madhya Pradesh | 26700 | 27640 | 29360 | 31460 | 34710 | 40140 | 39500 | 41470 |
| | (149.3) | (154.6) | (164.2) | (176.0) | (194.1) | (224.5) | (220.9) | (231.9) |
| Maharashtra | 151142 | 171486 | 174364 | 175265 | 179635 | 189204 | 194298 | 203481 |
| | (147.1) | (166.9) | (169.7) | (170.5) | (174.8) | (184.1) | (190.0) | (198.0) |
| Orissa | 10879 | 12597 | 12545 | 13103 | 12831 | 14049 | 15909 | 15974 |
| | (130.6) | (151.2) | (150.6) | (157.3) | (154.0) | (168.6) | (191.0) | (191.7) |
| Punjab | 21453 | 23074 | 24326 | 25073 | 27022 | 28409 | 28868 | 29460 |
| | (186.6) | (200.7) | (211.6) | (218.1) | (235.1) | (247.2) | (251.2) | (256.3) |
| Rajasthan | 15894 | 16761 | 16677 | 14339 | 15850 | 16704 | 17430 | 17747 |
| | (125.5) | (132.2) | (131.7) | (113.2) | (125.1) | (131.9) | (137.6) | (140.1) |
| Tamil Nadu | 62468 | 69315 | 88862 | 74060 | 76718 | 74363 | 67735 | 77377 |
| | (136.2) | (151.1) | (193.7) | (161.5) | (167.2) | (162.1) | (147.7) | (168.7) |
| Uttar Pradesh | 52336 | 58796 | 56872 | 62058 | 61850 | 83292 | 86325 | 91789 |
| | (138.0) | (155.0) | (150.0) | (163.6) | (163.1) | (219.6) | (227.6) | (242.0) |
| West Bengal | 67969 | 65623 | 64533 | 67051 | 68089 | 69567 | 70184 | 67764 |
| | (122.3)' | (118.1) | (116.1) | (120.6) | (122.5) | (125.1) | (126.3) | (121.9) |
| Delhi | 12353 | 13484 | 14462 | 13556 | 15338 | 16729 | 17039 | 18021 |
| | (143.8) | (157.0) | (168.4) | (157.8) | (178.6) | (194.8) | (198.4) | (209.8) |
| All India | 6427 | 7095 | 6972 | 6923 | 7328 | 7835 | 8229 | 8673 |
| | (139.1) | (153.6) | (150.9) | (149.9) | (158.6) | (169.6) | (178.2) | (187.8) |

*Source:* Sreelekha Basu, "West Bengal's Economic Growth in All-India Perspective," *Economic and Political Weekly*, July 25, 1987, p. 1254.

management. A CPM cadre claimed his party was popular with big business, as under Congress rule the businessmen could not control their factories due to union infighting. Lack of discipline made collective bargaining impossible. Under the CPM government, mediation has become possible, as there are now organized unions with whom bargaining can be done. Discipline and production can be maintained with cooperation of the Communist government and unions.[35] The *Financial Times* reported Calcutta businessmen as saying that of all the Indian State governments the Left Front had ruled with the most integrity since 1977.[36] A senior executive of a private company expressed similar views and noted with satisfaction how Jyoti Basu had ordered agitating workers at a local factory to get back to work. The owner of Godrej, on meeting Jyoti Basu, was encouraged to open factories in the state, and a correspondence with the Chief Minister was conducted on the matter. The businessman was reported to have been favorably impressed by the Chief Minister and found all the negative things he had heard about him to be untrue.

In its *Political-Organisational Report* the CPM State Committee noted a new attitude of the business class towards the Communist government.

After our vast success in the 1977 elections there was considerable concern among trade and industry. Because they are practical realists they realised that this time there will be no repetition of 1967–69 and our government is permanent and in the new context they are trying to accommodate with the new government. They have learned from experience that CITU struggle hard for demands and stand by interests of the working class yet they implement the terms of the agreement. But the industrialists as a class, support the Congress I, in spite of that; from their own experience they realise Congress (I) unions are generally divided in different groups and have no policy, and each group wants to feather their own nest, but never implement terms of agreement.[37]

Jyoti Basu made the government policy towards business clear at the beginning of the first term of the Left Front government. "We believe in Socialism but we know it well that we have to work with the capitalists. Socialism cannot be ushered in overnight. Let the capitalists understand us – our policy and our interest; we shall also try to appreciate their point of view."[38] The economist Ashok Rudra found such attitudes disturbing. "Jyoti Basu, according to press reports, admitted that in a class ridden society *it was not always possible to avoid conflicts* – that is what the Marxist CM [Chief Minister] thinks of class struggle."[39]

---

[35] "Quiet Beginning," *Economic and Political Weekly*, July 9, 1977, p. 1079.
[36] David Housego, "Critical Election for the Marxists of West Bengal," *Financial Times*, February 5, 1979.
[37] West Bengal State Conference, *Rajnaitik-Sangathanik Report*, p. 51.
[38] *Business Standard*, June 29, 1977.
[39] Ashok Rudra, "The Left Front Government," *Economic and Political Weekly*, September 3, 1977, p. 1565.

This all-class position was formulated by E.M.S. Namboodiripad at the time
of the split, in his 1964 *A Brief Critical Note on the Programme Drafts.*

No class or stratum as a class or stratum is kept out of the front. But all those who depend
on foreign monopoly, feudal lords, social, economic and cultural backwardness etc. will
naturally take their stand against democracy. They therefore, will, in fact, keep themselves out of and even fight the democratic forces. This however happens not because
they belong to this or that class or stratum but because they oppose the anti-imperialist,
anti-feudal and democratic measures. Naturally, therefore, even those whose economic
ties are with foreign monopolists or with feudal lords, but who are patriotic and
democratic enough to support the democratic programme will have a place in the front.
Hence the "National" character of the front.[40]

Whatever the orthodox Marxists might think of E.M.S. Namboodiripad's
position, he cannot be criticized for not following his theory in practice.[41] He
has been described as Jyoti Basu's intellectual guru, and certainly Jyoti Basu
has applied this theory in the Left Front. The support he has received from the
capitalists indicates that a sufficiently moderate and businesslike attitude can
obtain the support of the bourgeoisie for the Communists. Namboodiripad, as
General Secretary of the CPM, can no longer advocate his personal position as
it deviates to some extent from official policy, however it has not prevented
Jyoti Basu putting it into practice. For this reason the ideological positions taken
at the time of the split are important because they enabled the participants to
develop their personal political stands relatively free from party restrictions and
often in a public manner.[42]

Though the CPM has consistently criticized the role of foreign capital in
India, when they came to power they found themselves encouraging foreign
investment in West Bengal.[43] This meant actively seeking foreign investment
in the State to the extent of offering soft loans and interceding on behalf of
multinational corporations with the Central government to obtain licences for
them.[44] From being a party committed to removing the multinationals from
India, the CPM Left Front government has become their spokesman, arguing
that since socialism cannot be created in one state, foreign corporations can be
used to achieve development and employment opportunities in the state. The
Left Front wanted to give the bankrupt Lily Biscuits Company to Britannia
Biscuits, a multinational, though the central government had rejected this. The
West Bengal government, through its own West Bengal Electronics

[40] E.M.S. Namboodiripad, *A Brief Critical Note on the Programme Drafts* (New Delhi: CPI,
1964), pp. 6–7.
[41] Bhupesh Gupta, *On Comrade E.M.S. Namboodiripad's "Brief Critical Note on the Programme
Drafts"* (Delhi: CPI, 1964), p. 29.
[42] *Ibid.*, pp. 22–3.
[43] West Bengal State Conference, *Rajnaitik-Sangathanik Report*, p. 50.
[44] CPI, "The Left Front Government," pp. 71–6.

Development Corporation, wanted to go into a joint project with Philips to produce Walkie Talkie transreceivers, though the central government had banned entry of foreign companies in this area. A joint sector project agreement was signed with the Indian industrialist R.P. Goenka for a Rs. 645 crore petro-chemical complex at Haldia.[45] The business community, however, was sceptical that the project would ever go into production, and if it did would ever earn a profit. The project was subsequently turned over to Tata which had a better reputation in industrial development.

The Chief Minister, Jyoti Basu, was forthright in his support for business investment in West Bengal.

I think people are feeling confident that more stress is being laid on the private sector, more responsibility is being given to them and that the industrial climate is comparatively better in West Bengal ...

Take a company like Philips or take GEC. Philips has been trying for an expansion here for a long time. They did not get it. They were discouraged by the Centre. Then I wrote on their behalf. I said that I did not see why they should not be allowed to expand here. Fortunately, they have just got their licence. And we have given them land at a very reasonable price. Similarly, GEC was not getting a licence for expansion. I wrote on their behalf too. And they have now got their licence. Similarly Tata's, whose presence was not very strong here, have come in. This is an added factor to our advantage. When well known companies come in, whether on their own or through joint sector projects, it helps us.[46]

Due to the Left Front's inability to confiscate foreign firms and their own limited finances for investment, Communists have felt compelled to encourage foreign and domestic investment in Bengal's economy.[47] According to N.K. Chandra, Professor at the Indian Institute of Management, the projects currently contemplated with multinationals

should these materialise, would become new outposts of foreign capital with the blessings of the Left Front Government ... It is no wonder that our own jute press spokesmen of international monopoly capital like the London Economist, the British Broadcasting Corporation and so on, are going head over their heels to placate the Left Front and sing its virtues. The issues at stake do not concern West Bengal alone. If the Left Front government welcomes the expansion of Multinational Foreign Corporations how can the Left Front criticise other state governments? Or, indeed Indira Gandhi and her son? ... Why must the Left Front government go out of its way and plead with the Centre for relaxing restrictions on Foreign Multinational Corporations? Was not the erstwhile Congress Ministry under SS Ray criticised for such bankrupt policies?[48]

---

[45] N.K. Chandra, "Industrialisation and the Left Movement: On Several Questions of Strategy in West Bengal," *Social Scientist*, vol. 7, no. 1/2, August–September 1978, pp. 23–4; Interview with Jyoti Basu, *Capital*, July 8–21, 1985, p. 30.

[46] *Ibid.*, p. 32.

[47] Chandra, "Industrialisation and the Left Movement," p. 23.

[48] *Ibid.*, pp. 25–9.

The CPM justified this by pointing out that other Communist governments encouraged foreign investment, but given the limitation of the CPM's power to one province with a capitalist economy the situation is hardly analogous.[49] It implied that only foreign investment in Communist ruled states in India was progressive and therefore acceptable, while those in other states served to strengthen the bourgeoisie-landlord government. To the extent that the foreign corporations could ameliorate the stagnation in West Bengal's economy, the CPM government would presumably be a beneficiary. However, in theoretical terms it puts the state party at variance with the party policy of denouncing foreign investment. It was the fundamental problem of any revolutionary party that achieved only partial control of the government in a capitalist society, and then found itself responsible for solving the problems the capitalist system had created. Suddenly "their" problems had become "our" problems, and only by encouraging capitalist development and labor tranquility could the economic situation improve. The CPM had either to undermine the old system or encourage investment in the hope that their improved performance over Congress would increase their support and legitimacy. In the first two United Fronts it had attempted the former and succeeded at least temporarily in increasing benefits for the workers and peasantry; in the Left Front government, it chose the latter strategy and succeeded in at least placating the capitalists and landed interests but did little for the lowest classes.

Though business has come forward with only limited investment, the business class perceive the Communists as much more dangerous to business in opposition than in government where they feel obliged to adopt a responsible attitude and encourage investment to create jobs. Big business has been able to capitalize on Left Front interest in job creation and party funding in order to create a climate of labor tranquility. It is the mutual interest of business and the Left Front in maintaining harmonious labor-management relations that has led to a reduction in labor unrest unprecedented in recent years. However, as the next section indicates, this has not been accompanied by a commensurate improvement in working-class living standards.

### Industrial labor

Eleven million of West Bengal's 68 million people live in Calcutta, India's second largest city. The working class centered around Calcutta is a highly diverse grouping, of whom 20 percent are refugees from East Bengal and over 25 percent migrants from other states.[50] The groups are unevenly distributed in

[49] *Ibid.*, p. 25.
[50] Harold Lubell, *Calcutta: Its Urban Development and Employment Prospects* (Geneva: International Labour Office, 1981), p. 54.

the industrial sector and have varying degrees of affinity with the Communist trade union movement.

The major industry of West Bengal was traditionally jute, which has had a predominantly non-Bengali work force, Bengalis constituting only 22.86 percent of the total as compared to 40.87 percent from Bihar state and 24.40 percent from Uttar Pradesh.[51] This industry, however, has been on the decline for some years. It was overtaken in 1959 as Bengal's leading employer by the engineering industry which has a predominantly Bengali labor force of 58.12 percent, compared to 19 percent from Bihar and 15.12 percent from Uttar Pradesh.[52] While over a third of the out-of-state Indian migrants were illiterate and took up unskilled manual labor, the refugees were the most educated group and took up skilled labor in trades and services.[53] Where heavy manual labor is involved, such as in porterage, less than 5 percent are Bengali.[54] Generally speaking the non-Bengalis took up the less-skilled work such as in jute, coarser textiles, and transport while Bengalis entered the engineering, chemical, and finer textile industries and the clerical jobs which were considered almost synonymous with Bengalis.[55] This had its political ramifications. A skilled and educated white- and blue-collar working class, many of them refugees, provided the Communists with a ready base for trade union activities. This was compounded by the higher rates of unemployment among these educated Bengalis than among the out-of-state manual labor migrants.

Among the Bengali refugees unemployment was over 35 percent.[56] "Nearly 60 percent of the unemployed persons belonged to the educated vocal sections of the community. It is unemployment among the educated persons rather than among the illiterate working classes which constitutes the crux of the problem."[57] An ILO study noted: "one special reason for concern with Calcutta's educated unemployed is that the group hardest hit is the Bengali middle class, which comprises an intellectual elite – the *bhadralok* – who have played a prominent part among the factions whose activities have disturbed political life in Calcutta."[58] The effects of this were somewhat offset by economic growth, with employment in the engineering industry increasing by 8.3 percent annually between 1959–65.[59] However, an economic slump resulted in a 2.6 percent

[51] West Bengal, Department of Labour, *Labour in West Bengal 1980* (Calcutta: West Bengal Government Press, 1981), p. 90.

[52] *Ibid.* Lubell, *Calcutta*, p. 17.

[53] *Ibid.*, p. 54.

[54] *Ibid.*, p. 62.

[55] *Ibid.*, p. 60.

[56] *Ibid.*, p. 54.

[57] S.N. Sen, *The City of Calcutta*, pp. 110–11, quoted in Lubell, *Calcutta*, p. 64.

[58] Lubell, *Calcutta*, p. 85.

[59] *Ibid.*, pp. 7–8.

annual fall in employment from 1965 to 1969 in engineering and a 2 percent decline per year in factory employment as a whole from 880,000 in 1966 to 791,000 in 1969.[60] It was precisely at this time that the Communist Party – Marxist (CPM) received its greatest growth, with the 1966 food movement and the ensuing victory of the Communists in the 1967 and 1969 state elections. Of the 840,000 workers in organized factories about 30 percent were in trade unions, with the Communist ones, particularly the CPM's CITU, being the largest.[61]

The return to power of the CPM with an unassailable majority in 1977 put their trade union movement in a dominant if awkward position. In the first two United Front governments the instability of the leftist position made militant labor agitation and *gheraos* a productive method of expanding influence, while the police were being held back from intervening by the Communist government. The 1977 victory, by contrast, gave the Communists the time and opportunity to consolidate their position by more moderate, constitutional, and administrative measures, often without militant support from the working class. Within six months of their coming to power complaints were heard about the way the trade union front was being handled.

Ever since it came to power, one of the main preoccupations of the Left Front government had been to keep the industrial workers on leash ... The total ceasefire on the trade union front that has been in operation for the last six months with the full blessing of the CPM leadership cannot be justified by any tactical considerations. While this has earned the Left Front government effusive good conduct certificates from Chambers of Commerce and other spokesmen of national and multinational big business, this has led to a certain demoralisation and disenchantment among the militant working class in West Bengal – a class which remained steadfast in its loyalty to the CPM during the party's most difficult days.[62]

As a Communist trade union their ultimate goal was to raise political consciousness of workers to the level where the working class understood the necessity of revolution and the impossibility of achieving their goals within the capitalist system. While material demands might be raised initially, this was to create a spirit of rising expectations which could not ultimately be met within the system. Such a strategy would involve numerous strikes and demonstrations by the working class, with a consequent disruption to the economy. Trade union militancy and the State's economic development in a capitalist system did not go together and it would have been unrealistic for the Left Front government to

---

[60] *Ibid.*, p. 8.
[61] Profulla Roy Choudhury, *West Bengal – A Decade (1965–1975)* (Calcutta: Boipatra, 1977), p. 9.
[62] Ajit Roy, "Substituting Reform for Revolution," *Economic and Political Weekly*, December 31, 1977, p. 2154.

pursue both options effectively. On balance the Left Front gave primacy to developing the state's economy. The operative policy has been that of conciliating the demands of labor and capital, and the impossibility of achieving success within the capitalist system appears to have been maintained as a proviso only for the benefit of its Communist bona fides.

Through use of the state government collective bargaining machinery the Communists would use their influence to achieve the maximum obtainable for the trade unions without resorting to industrial action. Only in cases of extreme provocation would strikes be resorted to.[63] In his budget speech for 1981–82 the CPM Central Committee member and Labor Minister Krishnapada Ghosh stated:

We have persistently followed a policy of encouraging collective bargaining as a mode of settlement of disputes. It is to be appreciated that conciliation and collective bargaining has beyond doubt come to stay as the most effective instrument for settlement of industrial disputes in West Bengal.[64]

The Communist Unions' role would be different now that the Communists were in power. Jyoti Basu stated that the "Organised trade union movement has displayed a rare degree of maturity and a sense of responsibility in responding to the need for industrial peace without in any way circumscribing the rights of the workers or throwing overboard their hard earned privileges."[65] From a trade union organizer, Krishnapada Ghosh became a mediator between labor and business trying to persuade the latter to adopt the demands of the former, while maintaining labor peace wherever possible. The conflict inherent in this role between the need for Communist trade union militancy and the State government's desire for economic growth was illustrated in the case of the CPM's CITU dominated Reserve Bank of India employees' agitation against a 15 percent increase in work load.[66] The local CPM trade union leaders in the RBI were informed by Promode Das Gupta that the agitation should be cooled down, as it threatened to disrupt the working of the State government which required the continued functioning of the Reserve Bank. This created resentment with the local CPM trade union leaders who were thereby placed in an awkward position. Had the agitation taken place in a non-Communist State the agitation would presumably have been allowed to progress. The result is that the Communist trade union movement adopts a more militant agitational role outside Bengal but has to curb militancy within the state.

[63] West Bengal State Conference, *Rajnaitik-Sangathanik Report*, p. 68.
[64] Krishnapada Ghosh, Minister-in-charge Labour Department, *Budget Speech in Respect of Demand No. 42*, West Bengal Legislative Assembly 25th March 1981, p. 2.
[65] Jyoti Basu, Chief Minister, *Budget Speech on Grant under Labour and Employment*, West Bengal Legislative Assembly, 11th March 1978, p. 2.
[66] *The Statesman*, June 18, 1982.

In a democratic environment, CITU could never afford to completely ignore rival unions taking more militant positions and pressing for higher demands when CITU was willing to settle for less. The CPM State Committee noted some of their unions "failed to raise the legitimate demands of workers because of fear irresponsible elements will take advantage of the situation and create problems for the government. As a result many irresponsible leaders have raised the legitimate demands of workers and misled them."[67] At the other extreme CPM unions "sometimes in competition with irresponsible unions of the Congress demand and press for unrealistic demands. In the ultimate analysis this does not help the workers and the government which intervenes in such disputes is embarrassed because demands are unrealistic."[68] Thus not only did the Communist government have to choose between economic growth and trade union militancy, but the Communist unions had to make the same choice. CITU could either support its Communist government by maintaining labor tranquility through collective bargaining, thereby facing the danger of being outflanked by more militant rival unions pressing for higher demands, or they could disrupt the economy by strikes as happened during the two United Front governments.

Since the return of the CPM to power, CITU has undoubtedly increased its strength. CITU has expanded its West Bengal membership from 477,618 in 1977 to 620,107 in 1981, reaching 709,708 in 1986, making it the largest union in the state, though its percentage increase has been less than that of some smaller unions. In West Bengal there were 875,952 workers employed in factories with more than ten workers and 1,327,653 workers in cottage and small-scale industries averaging about seven employees, giving the CPM a strong base among the working class, particularly in the larger factories and business establishments.[69] However, the State Committee noted there were many unorganized workers, mainly the non-Bengalis with whom the CPM had no contact and who were susceptible to Congress influence.[70] Though in the April 1979 resolution of the party they had decided to arrange teachers for Hindi speaking people, this political education was never undertaken.[71] This lack of effort in politicizing the substantial minority of non-Bengali people was particularly surprising given the CPM determination to penetrate the Hindi heartland where most of the migrant labor originated from. However, it helps to explain the lack of growth in the CPM in adjoining states despite its unassailable position in Bengal.

[67] West Bengal State Conference, *Rajnaitik-Sangathanik Report*, p. 46.
[68] *Ibid.*, p. 46.
[69] *Ibid.*, p. 66; West Bengal, *Economic Review 1984–85* (Alipore: West Bengal Government Press, 1985), pp. 130–1; Communist Party of India – Marxist, *Political Organisational Report*, Twelfth Congress, Calcutta, December 25–30, 1985, p. 158.
[70] West Bengal State Conference, *Rajnaitik-Sangathanik Report*, p. 43.
[71] *Ibid.*, pp. 79, 81.

Table 5.5. *Annual earnings, index numbers of money/real earnings of factory workers drawing less than Rs. 400.00 per month from 1960–75 and less than Rs. 1000.00 per month from 1976–82*

| Year | Per capita annual earnings Rupees | | Index no. of money earnings base 1960 = 100 | Index no. of earnings base 1960 = 100 |
|---|---|---|---|---|
| 1960 | 1,293.50 | | | |
| 1961 | 1,328.45 | | 102.69 | 101.67 |
| 1962 | 1,385.03 | | 107.06 | 100.06 |
| 1963 | 1,446.92 | | 111.85 | 99.87 |
| 1964 | 1,549.67 | | 119.79 | 99.00 |
| 1965 | 1,727.93 | | 133.57 | 104.35 |
| 1966 | 1,875.93 | | 145.01 | 100.00 |
| 1967 | 2,029.64 | | 156.89 | 98.67 |
| 1968 | 2,244.74 | | 173.52 | 101.48 |
| 1969 | 2,514.53 | | 194.36 | 113.66 |
| 1970 | 2,634.34 | | 203.63 | 112.50 |
| 1971 | 2,805.50 | | 223.84 | 120.99 |
| 1972 | 3,333.44 | | 257.69 | 132.83 |
| 1973 | 3,550.16 | | 274.44 | 127.06 |
| 1974 | 3,734.12 | | 288.67 | 103.47 |
| 1975 | 3,782.70 | | 292.42 | 101.53 |
| 1976 | 5,605.66 | Base 1976 | 100.00 | 100.00 |
| 1977 | 6,061.16 | = 100 | 108.12 | 98.29 |
| 1978 | 6,746.80 | | 120.36 | 107.48 |
| 1979 | 7,099.02 | | 126.64 | 106.42 |
| 1980 | 7,772.05 | | 138.65 | 107.48 |
| 1981 | 7,964.50 | | 142.08 | 101.49 |
| 1982 | 8,808.75 | | 157.14 | 104.07 |

*Source: Labour in West Bengal* (annual), Department of Labour, West Bengal, 1977, 1980, 1983.

Whether the CPM has taken maximum advantage of its position in the state government to obtain the best possible labor settlements for the working class or it has sold out for less for fear of alienating big business is difficult to determine. According to Timir Basu's articles in the *Economic and Political Weekly* the latter has been the case. This is confirmed by the veteran Communist trade union leader Biren Roy who states: "It has been the policy of CITU not to encourage class struggle even in the private sector in West Bengal since the Left Front came to power in 1977. This is causing harm to the working class movement. On the one hand, it has emboldened employers to mount an offensive; on the other it has helped anti-left forces to disrupt united movement of workers."[72]

[72] Biren Roy, "Jute Owners Offensive Goes Unopposed," *Economic and Political Weekly*, August 7, 1982, p. 1266.

The CPM counters this by arguing that:

Because the Left Front is in power and the working class is organised and politically conscious, many of the struggles of different sections of people against vested interests are settled in their favour. Taking recourse to strikes or some other forms of struggle has not become necessary in many cases. In these changed conditions one cannot measure the intensity and coverage of the class struggle through the number of strikes and resulting mandays lost, because without taking recourse to strikes they have been able to get their demands fulfilled.[73]

The CPM Labor Minister in tabling the government publication *Labour in West Bengal* drew attention to the evidence in it of improved labor conditions. "Members will kindly recall in this connection the organised industry-wide Settlements effected during the last few years in major industries like Jute, Engineering, Cotton Textile etc., providing for substantial wage increase and other benefits to *lakhs* of industrial workers in this State without much industrial unrest."[74] The publication he was tabling, however, indicated the opposite as it showed wages had increased less in the years under the Communist government, as seen from tables 5.5–7. The real wage for factory workers, calculated from the Consumer Price Index, increased from a base of 100 in 1976 to 104.07 in 1982.[75] By contrast, from 1966 to 1972 the real wage increase was even greater (100.00 to 132.83) than during the current Communist government.[76]

|                  |      | Real Earnings |             |
|------------------|------|---------------|-------------|
|                  | 1966 | 100.00        |             |
| Base 1960 – 100  | 1972 | 132.83        |             |
|                  |      |               | Money wages |
| Base 1976 – 100  | 1976 | 100.00        | 100.00      |
|                  | 1982 | 104.07        | 157.14      |

Since the Left Front came to power the real wages in the jute, cotton, and engineering industries have increased from 171, 189, and 170 respectively in 1978 to 196, 205, and 186 in 1984 (Base 1960 = 100), i.e. by 2.09, 1.21, and 1.34 annually. This is less than what the Communists achieved in opposition when real wages increased by 3.63, 5.40, and 5 percent from 1971–76.

[73] West Bengal State Conference, *Rajnaitik-Sangathanik Report*, p. 68.
[74] West Bengal, Department of Labour, *Labour in West Bengal 1980*, p. 109.
[75] West Bengal, Department of Labour, *Labour in West Bengal 1983*, p. 100.
[76] West Bengal, Department of Labour, *Labour in West Bengal 1980*, p. 120.

Table 5.6. *Index numbers of real wages for major industries – jute, cotton, and engineering (Base: year 1960 = 100)*

| Year | Jute | Cotton | Engineering |
|---|---|---|---|
| 1962 | 94 | 124 | 97 |
| 1963 | 105 | 125 | 98 |
| 1964 | 103 | 122 | 100 |
| 1965 | 106 | 125 | 109 |
| 1966 | 102 | 122 | 113 |
| 1967 | 103 | 123 | 113 |
| 1968 | 108 | 131 | 119 |
| 1969 | 129 | 142 | 123 |
| 1970 | 136 | 148 | 119 |
| 1971 | 142 | 145 | 120 |
| 1972 | 164 | 158 | 120 |
| 1973 | 164 | 176 | 135 |
| 1974 | 155 | 177 | 136 |
| 1975 | 176 | 194 | 157 |
| 1976 | 173 | 192 | 156 |
| 1977 | 168 | 186 | 151 |
| 1978 | 171 | 189 | 170 |
| 1979 | 188 | 208 | 175 |
| 1980 | 188 | 210 | 173 |
| 1981 | 187 | 209 | 172 |
| 1982 | 187 | 203 | 172 |
| 1983 | 183 | 206 | 174 |
| 1984 | 196 | 205 | 186 |
| Annual percentage increase 1971–76 | 3.63 | 5.40 | 5.00 |
| Annual percentage increase 1978–84 | 2.09 | 1.21 | 1.34 |

*Source: Labour in West Bengal* (annual), Department of Labour, West Bengal Government, 1977, 1980, 1984.

| Real wages Base 1960 – 100 | Jute | Cotton | Engineering |
|---|---|---|---|
| 1971 | 142 | 145 | 120 |
| 1976 | 173 | 192 | 156 |
| 1978 | 171 | 189 | 170 |
| 1984 | 196 | 205 | 186 |

| Annual percentage increase | Jute | Cotton | Engineering |
|---|---|---|---|
| 1971–76 | 3.63 | 5.40 | 5.00 |
| 1978–84 | 2.09 | 1.21 | 1.34 |

Table 5.7. *Index numbers of money wages for major industries – jute, cotton, and engineering (Base: Year 1960 = 100)*

| Year | Jute | Cotton | Engineering |
|------|------|--------|-------------|
| 1962 | 101 | 132 | 104 |
| 1963 | 117 | 139 | 109 |
| 1964 | 124 | 147 | 121 |
| 1965 | 136 | 160 | 140 |
| 1966 | 146 | 175 | 163 |
| 1967 | 164 | 195 | 179 |
| 1968 | 187 | 224 | 204 |
| 1969 | 221 | 243 | 210 |
| 1970 | 247 | 268 | 215 |
| 1971 | 262 | 268 | 221 |
| 1972 | 317 | 306 | 233 |
| 1973 | 355 | 381 | 292 |
| 1974 | 431 | 493 | 381 |
| 1975 | 506 | 560 | 451 |
| 1976 | 503 | 556 | 453 |
| 1977 | 534 | 593 | 481 |
| 1978 | 556 | 617 | 555 |
| 1979 | 650 | 719 | 606 |
| 1980 | 705 | 786 | 647 |
| 1981 | 760 | 850 | 700 |
| 1982 | 819 | 891 | 755 |
| 1983 | 902 | 1013 | 858 |
| 1984 | 1105 | 1155 | 1051 |
| Annual percentage increase 1971–76 | 15.33 | 17.91 | 17.49 |
| Annual percentage increase 1978–84 | 14.10 | 12.46 | 15.34 |

*Source: Labour in West Bengal* (annual) Department of Labour, West Bengal Government, 1977, 1980, 1984.

The same holds true for money wages, which in these three major industries increased from 1971 to 1976 by 15.33, 17.91, and 17.49 percent per annum while from 1978 to 1984 the percentage increase was 14.10, 12.46, and 15.34 annually.[77]

Money Wage

| Annual percentage increase | Jute | Cotton | Engineering |
|----------------------------|------|--------|-------------|
| 1971–76 | 15.33 | 17.91 | 17.49 |

[77] *Ibid.*, p. 119; West Bengal, Department of Labour, *Labour in West Bengal 1984* (Calcutta: West Bengal Government Press, 1985), p. 87.

Table 5.8. *Man-days lost in strikes and lockouts (millions)*

| Strikes | | | | Lockouts | | |
|---|---|---|---|---|---|---|
| Year | India | West Bengal | as percentage of India | India | West Bengal | as percentage of India |
| 1967 | 10.565 | 1.529 | 14.4 percent | 6.583 | 3.486 | 52.9 percent |
| 1968 | 11.078 | 3.159 | 28.5 | 6.166 | 3.562 | 57.7 |
| 1969 | 15.477 | 7.636 | 49.3 | 3.571 | 1.744 | 48.8 |
| 1970 | 14.749 | 5.777 | 39.1 | 5.814 | 3.647 | 62.7 |
| 1971 | 11.803 | 1.698 | 14.3 | 4.743 | 2.810 | 59.2 |
| 1972 | 13.748 | 0.944 | 6.8 | 6.796 | 2.672 | 39.3 |
| 1973 | 13.862 | 2.572 | 18.5 | 6.764 | 3.404 | 50.3 |
| 1974 | 33.643 | 7.334 | 21.7 | 6.619 | 3.082 | 46.5 |
| 1975 | 16.706 | 10.785 | 64.5 | 5.195 | 2.796 | 53.8 |
| 1976 | 2.799 | 0.951 | 33.9 | 9.947 | 7.522 | 75.6 |
| 1977 | 13.410 | 1.072 | 7.9 | 11.91 | 7.839 | 65.8 |
| 1978 | 15.4 | 5.118 | 33.2 | 12.9 | 6.855 | 53.1 |
| 1979 | 35.8 | 15.540 | 43.4 | 8.0 | 2.899 | 36.2 |
| 1980 | 12.0 | 1.485 | 12.3 | 9.9 | 4.695 | 47.4 |
| 1981 | 21.2 | 0.620 | 2.9 | 15.4 | 9.902 | 64.2 |
| 1982 | 54.9 | 0.309 | 0.5 | 22.5 | 15.479 | 68.7 |
| 1983 | 27.2 | 0.956 | 3.5 | 17.1 | 15.149 | 88.5 |

*Source:* Tata Services Ltd., Department of Economics and Statistics, *Statistical Outline of India 1984*, p. 138.
India, Labour Bureau, Department of Labour and Employment, Ministry of Labour and Rehabilitation, *Indian Labour Statistics 1972*.
West Bengal, Department of Labour, *Labour in West Bengal* (annual).

| Annual percentage increase | Jute | Cotton | Engineering |
|---|---|---|---|
| 1978–84 | 14.10 | 12.46 | 15.34 |

In these large scale more unionized industries real wages have increased significantly more than among factories as a whole.[78] Though benefits accruing to the working class are partly a product of the state of the economy, the improvement of the working classes' standard of living has been less under the Communist government than when the Communists were in opposition. This would seem to refute the claim by the Labor Minister of the material benefits accruing to the working class from the Communists being in power.

When compared with the two other most industrialized states, Maharashtra and Gujarat, and the country as a whole, the relative decline during the Left Front government is clearer. Using 1961 as a base of 100 for manufacturing

[78] West Bengal, Department of Labour, *Labour in West Bengal 1980*, pp. 109, 120.

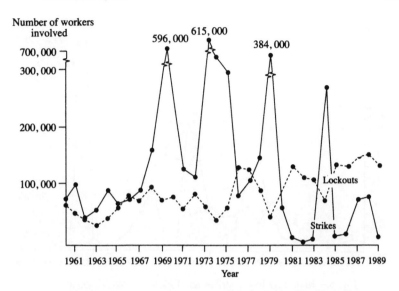

Fig. 5.2. Workers involved in strikes and lockouts in West Bengal

*Source:* West Bengal, Department of Labour, *Labour in West Bengal* (annual)

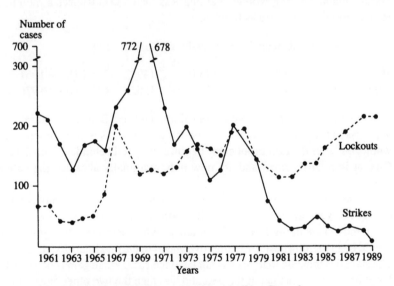

Fig. 5.3. Number of strikes and lockouts in West Bengal

*Source:* West Bengal, Department of Labour, *Labour in West Bengal* (annual)

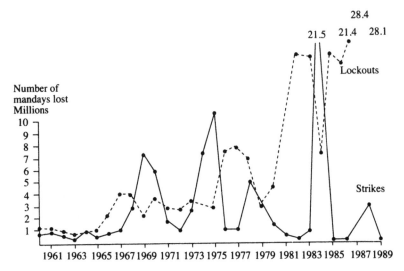

Fig. 5.4. Man-days lost in strikes and lockouts in West Bengal

industry workers earning less than 400 Rupees a month and 1976 as a base of 100 for manufacturing workers earning less than 1,000 Rupees a month, the relative money wages are as follows.[79]

|      | West Bengal | Maharashtra | Gujarat | India |
|------|-------------|-------------|---------|-------|
| 1975 | 267.8       | 195.0       | 142.5   | 205.1 (Base 1961 = 100) |
| 1981 | 142.1       | 154.2       | 155.3   | 137.5 (Base 1976 = 100) |

While the Communists were in opposition the West Bengal industrial working class surpassed the other most industrialized states and the country as a whole, but after the Left Front came to power they fell behind Maharashtra and Gujarat in relative terms and are now only marginally ahead of the national average.

It is not possible to isolate political policies as the single cause of these changes as general economic conditions affect wage levels. However, a trade union movement dominated by Communists who control the state government should be in a strong position to improve wages to the maximum extent possible. The statistics indicate that this has not been the case. Wage gains under the Left Front have been less than in the past and less than the two other most industrialized states. As seen in table 5.8, strikes have declined to only 3.5 percent of

[79] India, Labour Bureau, Ministry of Labour, *Indian Labour Statistics 1978* (Simla: Government of India, 1980), p. 76; Government of India, *India 1984*, p. 434.

the national total in man-days lost during 1983, while employer lockouts have increased to 88.5 percent of the national total. The employers have not been intimidated by the presence of a Communist government and union movement, but on the contrary appear to have taken the opportunity to reassert control over their establishments.

In spite of the slower increase in real wages the number of men involved in strikes decreased from a high of 381,515 in 1979 to 68,411 in 1980 to a long time low of only 8,114 workers in 1982 with man-days lost also showing a three-year consecutive decline.[80] All indicators for 1982 showed considerable decline, with 9- to 13-year lows in work stoppages, man-days lost and lockouts being recorded, figures the Labor Minister viewed as a mark of the Government's success.[81]

Whether this return of labor peace to West Bengal was something the Communists should be proud of depended on the role they saw for themselves in Government. That the CPM considered this labor peace a virtue in spite of a declining increase of real wages was indicative of the CPM's new moderation. Jyoti Basu wrote that:

We have maintained contact with the Chambers of Commerce and owners and have tried to help them in their difficulties. We have tried to educate them about the changed conditions in the state and how they should maintain their relations with the trade unions and workers ... We have got good results.[82]

The *Indian Express* noted that the Left Front "Government's statistics show how the entire labor community is steadily returning under the charge of employers." This was even admitted by the CITU leader, Manoranjan Roy.[83] Man-days lost through employer lockouts increased from 4,695,657 in 1980 to 16,286,763 in 1982. By contrast, man-days lost from strikes decreased from 1,485,399 in 1980 to 309,349 in 1982.[84]

It therefore appears that the return of the Communists to power has not prevented the reduction of the rate of improvement in the working class standard of living nor increased the militancy of the working class. Aside from there being less police intervention in strikes, it is doubtful if the Communist takeover of the state has brought additional material benefits to the workers. By whichever indices, whether it is improvement in standard of living or in levels of worker militancy, the results have been less impressive under the present

[80] *The Statesman*, September 20, 1982.
[81] West Bengal, Department of Labour, *Labour in West Bengal 1980*, p. 1; Ghosh, *Budget Speech*, p. 1.
[82] Basu, "Tin Bajhar," p. 18.
[83] Ashim Mukhopadhyay, "Bengal Trade Union Movement Weakening," *Indian Express*, December 21, 1982.
[84] *Link*, May 29, 1983, p. 9.

Communist government than when they were in opposition.[85] This was in marked contrast to the first two United Front governments when their short duration in power led to improvements in real and money wages, when militancy in terms of man-days lost in disputes showed a positive correlation with the Communist struggle for power. The contrast between the present Left Front and its United Front predecessors has been marked on the labor front. However, lack of both militancy and material improvements does not mean that CITU has not made organizational inroads against its competitors or broken new ground. Certainly having its own party in power has helped in its organizational expansion, though trade union registration and membership figures leveled off in the 1980s, indicating that the relatively rapid expansion of the post-Emergency period, when the Communists first returned to power, is now over.[86]

The Labor Minister's claims of success in increasing the use of tripartite conciliation to achieve settlements had not demonstrated any significant increase since the Communists came to power. The percentage figures of disputes settled through government mediation fluctuated from 25.91 percent in 1971 to 21.18 percent in 1976 to 22.88 percent in 1980 and up marginally to 26.72 percent in 1981.[87] It was difficult to find any way in which the Communist government had brought greater benefits to the working class than could have been obtained from being in opposition. If anything the reverse was the case, real wages having increased less under the Communist government than under the Congress.

A radical strategy of class confrontation would therefore seem preferable. It would avoid the Left Front's having to administer a capitalist state economy where its inexperience would be revealed. It is not up to Communists to administer capitalism, nor were they likely to prove better at it than the capitalists themselves. Even if they succeeded in running the capitalist economy, the resulting experience would probably dilute the revolutionary ideals of the party, and force it to choose between worker and employer demands. Whichever side they take on these issues they would lose. To support the workers effectively would lead to a flight of capital and growing unemployment, which had occurred under their United Front governments. To side with employers would lead to trade union alienation and the growth of non-CPM unions. Government longevity therefore meant prevarication and compromise, but above all it meant controlling the demands of its own worker constituency – the only side in management–labor relations over which it could exercise any real influence. While big business was national and even international and could

---

[85]  West Bengal, Department of Labour, *Labour in West Bengal 1980*, p. 52.
[86]  *Ibid.*, p. 52.
[87]  *Ibid.*, p. 3; West Bengal, *Economic Review 1981–82*, p. 24.

move elsewhere in India at a calculable cost, the Communist worker base had little job mobility. To attempt to stay in office over the long term therefore required a *modus operandi* with big business that ensured continued investment for maintenance of the industrial economy. To increase employment, new investment was required, which meant the granting of even more favorable terms to business than were available elsewhere in the country. Where every state was actively pursuing business investment in its own territory, a Communist government was at a natural disadvantage in the business community. The Communists were not to be outdone in this, however, and went further than other states in seeking to attract foreign investment. Jyoti Basu has defended his position saying, "I do not want my state to become an industrial desert" which it certainly could become if a confrontational approach with business was consistently followed.[88] His understanding of the economic imperatives of the Left Front position in office is more realistic than that of his leftist critics who make valid criticisms of the business policy without offering viable solutions. Once an indefinite stay in provincial office was accepted as a goal, the Left Front policy was the only practical business investment policy to follow. That it failed to arrest Bengal's continued industrial decline relative to other states, was only partly due to the Communist regime. Though it could control trade union activities, productivity and infrastructural development proved less amenable to party initiatives. The historic compromise with business could be avoided only by refusing to handle the modern economy. Since a state government did not have the power to nationalize business, the Communist government in West Bengal would have to accept business or face an economic downturn by obstructing it. Short of the Pol Pot solution of abandoning the cities – which was in any case beyond its power – there was no way it could restructure or run the industrial sector without active business cooperation. An attack on big business was therefore only possible if the government was prepared to weather a depression. This was only advisable if the Communists expected or desired their own removal from power by the central government. They could not remain in power for long without working with business, or else accepting the decline of the urban economy. Given the Communist inability to nationalize or otherwise control the business sector, there was little to be gained by pursuing policies causing a flight of capital. Far better to placate business and encourage investment by controlling industrial labor, and concentrate instead on the rural areas where the elections would be decided.

This is precisely what the Left Front did. As three quarters of the population was rural and provided the Communists with their main electoral base, their

---

[88] Ajit Roy, "Question of a Transitional Government in Marxist Terminology," *Economic and Political Weekly*, October 25, 1985, p. 1821.

plurality of the popular vote could still give them a majority of ridings. This did not follow Marxist orthodoxy, but it was the only productive strategy possible when socialist power was limited to only one province. A national government such as the Popular Unity coalition in Chile could attempt to neutralize the armed forces, control the money supply, and nationalize business, but these options did not exist at the Indian provincial level.[89] The policy options available to the West Bengal Communists were of an altogether more limited scope. They had no real choice but to follow the urban business and trade union policy they did, once they had decided to stay in office indefinitely. Though the workers did not benefit from the Communist government, the Left Front had no alternative but to sacrifice their demands in order to develop a favorable business climate. The urban policy of the Left Front was the only viable policy to follow. Short of causing an economic depression through insurrection or plant seizures, the Communists could only be reformist. As Przeworski argues "reforms are possible, but that does not mean that reformism is a viable strategy of transition to socialism."[90] Since there is no revolutionary urban industrial strategy possible at provincial government level, such a revolutionary movement must await the development of favorable forces at the national level. A provincial government can only dole out urban relief, organize people, and await national events. It is no wonder that radicals such as Ashok Rudra insisted that Marxists could not stay in power without compromising the interests of the workers.

Given the powers available to the state government, there was limited socialist restructuring possible in the urban industrial sector, which is probably why nothing significant was ever even attempted. The same, however, could not be said of the rural sector where most of the population lived. Composed largely of landless and relatively small landowners, the rural economy in its simplicity made for greater policy options. Though the state government had greater legal control over the rural sector through constitutional jurisdiction over agrarian reform, these greater policy options were primarily of an economic nature. Since all state legislation had in any case to be signed into law by the President (i.e. central government), the strict constitutional delegating of state powers was less important than the economic and political consequences of state policy decisions. Unlike the industrial sector which required sophisticated managerial and technical skills, and a level of financial investment beyond that available to a state government, the basic rural sector requirements were already at hand.

[89] J. Ann Zammit, editor, *The Chilean Road to Socialism* (Institute of Development Studies, University of Sussex, England, 1973).

[90] Adam Przeworski, *Capitalism and Social Democracy* (Cambridge: Cambridge University Press, 1985), p. 239.

A radical land redistribution need not result in any loss of production, and, with credit and inputs, might have led to production increases by the small owner-cultivators. The flight to the urban sector of rural capital belonging to village moneylenders and landowners might in the short term be prevented by popular actions, supported by state government bank employees, but alternative funding would still have to be found. Given the center's restrictions on state borrowing and the poor credit rating of a West Bengal Communist government, this could be raised only through cutbacks in government employment, an unpopular but necessary step for both efficiency and equity. Though they are common practice in Western public sectors, the Indian governments have yet to undertake these reforms. However, such steps might well prove unnecessary, as central imposition of Presidential Rule to prevent equitable land distribution by the peasant movement would forestall these cutbacks. The Communist movement would then be removed from office while at the forefront of a radical land reform movement that was holding out the prospect of benefiting the vast majority of the rural population.

The avoidance of any measures that might provoke the return of Presidential Rule is understandable, given the years in the political wilderness that had followed the previous central government repression of the Communists. It was safer to avoid provoking Presidential Rule until the threat of central intervention was removed by a national political conjuncture favorable to the Communists. The problem with such a long-term view is that there are diminishing returns from hanging on to power. Inertia, corruption, and bureaucratism would be difficult for even the most disciplined party to avoid over a prolonged period in power. Michels' "iron law of oligarchy" would gradually take effect.[91] After over a decade in office the scope for state action had not increased noticeably from the period when they first took power. The Left Front's decision to play for time till circumstances favored them was not the best approach. This do-nothing option adopted since the early 1980s is likely to run out of popular support before the nation as a whole moves in a direction favorable to the Communists. All things considered, a rural strategy of land redistribution early on in the regime when the momentum is with the new government is preferable, along with the avoidance of urban conflict that is more likely to provoke central intervention and disinvestment. Intervention by the central government would save the Communists from having to run a capitalist economy, while failure of the center to intervene would allow the land distribution to go ahead. The threat of violence is inherent in such a strategy but would not necessarily reach the scale of the earlier period, though in a worst-case scenario this could be exceeded.

[91] Roberto Michels, *Political Parties: A Sociological Study of the Oligarchical Tendencies of Modern Democracy* (New York: Collier Books), 1962.

Clearly the policy options defy easy choices and radical policies are fraught with dangers of counter-revolution. However, it would seem that drastic action is the only way forward, though choosing the right timing to avoid central intervention is critical. The best time would have been under the Janata government when the Left Front first came to power. The rise of dissident movements first in Assam and then in the Punjab offered another opportunity when the central government was occupied elsewhere. The prospects do not seem promising when looking at the policy options from the perspective of how the Left Front leadership must see their position. Both the insurrectionary and radical strategies of the early 1950s and the late 1960s having failed to win power permanently, and now with the constitutional strategy failing to achieve even the most modest reforms, the leadership is clearly in a crisis. Though they may continue to go from one Bengal election victory to another for some time, they have failed to build new bases elsewhere in the country. Only the lack of a viable alternative in West Bengal has enabled the Left Front's lacklustre performance to go unchallenged, but lack of credible opposition is not something that a Communist party, not already in full control of the state, can rely on indefinitely.

In the final analysis the policy decisions are determined by the personal philosophies of the party leadership from the limited choices available. After a lifetime of struggles and sacrifice the leaders are now faced with this last opportunity to leave an enduring legacy. The temptation to take whatever share of power is available now, knowing that complete national power will not come in their lifetimes, must be overwhelming. It is certainly easier to avoid reform and stay in office than to take the risky path of confrontation with the central government. In the circumstances there is no clearly right answer, for the outcome is ultimately unpredictable, but as Oskar Lange concludes in his essay *On the Economic Theory of Socialism*:

The economist who is called upon to advise a socialist government faces a difficult task, and the qualities needed for this task are difficult, too. For there exists only one economic policy which he can commend to a socialist government as likely to lead to success. This is a policy of *revolutionary courage*.[92]

Hardly a helpful prescription to conclude his thesis "On the Policy of Transition," but it is nevertheless the one policy the Left Front government has conspicuously failed to adopt. The Left Front has gone for the soft easy option every time, and as a result has lost its way in the labyrinth of power and administration.

When "revolutionary courage" can mean death for thousands as has hap-

---

[92] Oskar Lange, *On the Economic Theory of Socialism*, Edited by B.E. Lippincott (New York: McGraw-Hill, 1964), p. 129.

pened in the past, the safe option becomes understandable. Academic critics whose lives and careers are unaffected by the outcome, often tend to forget the human cost their radical policy suggestions would involve. The problems of academic objectivity in such a controversial ongoing experiment are many. The experiment's very relevance to regional and local governments attempting a transition to socialism makes the analysis partisan in the extreme. After all these years in office there is still no scholarly consensus on the Left Front performance. Since few social scientists know as much about the policy alternatives as the politicians and government administrators themselves, their advice is often colored more by ideological preconceptions than by political realities.

The Communist strategy in India has "been to shape policies in such a manner that, whilst the expectations of their supporters might be satisfied to a degree, care is taken to avoid specific courses of action which might provoke active opposition on the part of entrenched interests."[93] This creation of a multi-class alliance is viewed as essential to prevent the isolation of the revolutionary forces.[94] However, the entrenched interests are not only class enemies but class allies as well. There is a happy medium between the effort to encompass all potential supporters as individuals, groups or classes and the need to oppose classes or groups preventing reform, whether they be supporters or opponents of the Left. The Left Front effectively embraced all classes except for the tiny minority of the very biggest landowners, leaving no class enemies or entrenched interests to fight against. Rather it chose to struggle against the central government, complaining on the basis of largely imaginary Bengali grievances, that the state was disadvantaged in the allocation of resources. Whatever the justice of these complaints, there is no doubt that the failure of Bengal to retain its rank as the premier industrial state in the country was the result of the Bengalis' own lack of entrepreneurial inclination and of the after-effects of partition, for which the Bengali elite itself bore some responsibility. Indian states already had as much power and autonomy in administration as regional governments elsewhere in the world. Unless one insists on states having ultimate power *vis-à-vis* the center, the state government will ultimately always be at the mercy of the central government. As long as the primacy of the centre is assumed, the struggle for state autonomy will be of secondary importance to the class struggle within the state. The struggle for provincial autonomy can therefore not be a substitute for class struggle and development reform.

As has already been shown, an attack on business is not a viable option for a regional government intent on development and longevity in office. This is only

[93] Sathyamurthy, *India Since Independence*, p. 454.
[94] Biplab Dasgupta, "Gram Banglar Sreni Binyas" ("Class Relations in Rural Bengal"), *Deshhitaishee*, annual Puja issue, 1980, p. 89.

possible at the national level by a leftist central government controlling the armed forces, central bank and other state apparatus. For regional governments in industrialized countries the options in terms of revolutionary change are therefore as close to nil as makes no difference. A regional government can certainly destabilize the business class through strikes but the resulting capital flight would bring about an economic collapse. It is therefore only an option for those governments prepared to leave office in a hurry or ruin their economies. Allende's statement that "the political model toward socialism that my government is applying requires that the socio-economic revolution take place simultaneously with an uninterrupted economic expansion" was unrealistic.[95] While Noriega in Panama was prepared to allow the ruin of the economy and mass unemployment in order to retain personal power, few provincial governments would find such a long-term stagnation acceptable, even if the central government tolerated it. Such an approach can work only at a national level; at the provincial level the de-industrialization of a region would produce few opportunities for the consolidation of the Left in office. Rather it would ensure their departure. It can therefore be seen that local and regional leftist governments in advanced capitalist countries have no viable option but to introduce minor reforms and spread the welfare net further afield, hoping to get greater electoral support as a result. A peaceful revolutionary strategy is therefore impossible at the regional or local level in industrialized countries. A revolutionary provincial government can at best only be reformist in such circumstances. Social Democracy is thus the only policy for even a revolutionary provincial Communist government in advanced capitalist countries.

For developing countries such as India, however, the options are more varied. Whereas in industrialized countries the farming community is only a tiny fraction of the population, in West Bengal, as elsewhere in the Third World, most of the population subsists on agriculture. It is therefore possible to pursue a reformist strategy in the city and a revolutionary approach in the countryside, without an urban economic collapse or significant rural losses in food production. An urban strategy of improving government efficiency through financial austerity and promoting big business investment can be coupled with radical rural land reform. Something similar was done by the American occupation forces in Japan after World War II. Usually, however, locally controlled governments are too tied to landed interests to undertake such steps, which was certainly the case with the West Bengal Communists. They could argue that land reform, should it succeed, would only undermine the revolutionary fervor of the landless peasantry, giving them a stake in the status quo, which would halt further radicalization. However, the Communists, by being able

[95] Przeworski, *Capitalism*, p. 46.

to take credit for the redistribution, would not easily lose this new base, and the example in the rest of the country would certainly help to put Communist land reform on the national agenda. In this sense the Communists would be fulfilling a program of which the big bourgeoisie might approve, though lack the power or political will to undertake. The Communists would be completing the bourgeois revolution that the bourgeoisie lacks the strength to complete.

Oskar Lange, writing during the Great Depression, noted that:

As the decay of capitalism continues, there will arise many occasions when the capitalist parties will prove unable to enact reforms which are necessary even from the point of view of securing normal functioning of capitalist society ... In such cases, *if a great popular demand* for such reforms arises, the socialists may have to come to the public with a labour plan to carry out the reforms demanded and form a government pledged to put the plan into action. If they do this successfully their position will be strengthened.[96]

Lange's concept that "the capitalist parties may be utterly incapable of any action that injures the vested interests with which they are associated, even if these interests should prevent the normal functioning of the capitalist economy as a whole" was hardly new to Marxist theory.[97] The Communist requirement to complete the bourgeois revolution that the bourgeoisie was too weak to undertake is used as a justification for reformism. However, the inability of capitalist parties to carry out their own program because of the vested interests of their followers, applies equally well to the West Bengal Communists. The Communists were to prove just as unwilling as the capitalists to overcome the vested interests of their own landed supporters. As a result, the Communists refused to implement a transition to socialism, and sank into the corruptions of office.

---

[96] Lange, *On the Economic Theory*, p. 127–8.
[97] *Ibid.*, p. 128.

# 6    End of an illusion

The Left Front experiment in West Bengal is now widely regarded by knowledgeable observers as a failure. Even a Secretary of the West Bengal government when asking his IAS colleagues if they could think of a single successful program the Left Front could claim credit for, received no suggestions, though they were themselves in charge of implementing the policies. Despite some of the party faithful still claiming it a success, most veteran Communists know better. This failure was admitted in an inner party document by the Burdwan District Committee of the CPM, which the CPM leadership subsequently withdrew from internal party circulation.

the Left Front government have not been able to meet the aspirations of the people ... People feel that even the limited power at the disposal of the Left Front government has not been properly used. It will not be an exaggeration to say that procrastination and misuse in the administration are on the increase. In areas like education, health, transport, irrigation works, labour, electricity, local self-government, police administration and High Court which are all closely connected with the people, the role of the government has no impact on the masses. Even the progressive measures like taking over the vested land and cancellation of illegal *pattas* (record of right), *barga* recording ... all undertaken for the good of the people have not been properly implemented. There is considerable slackness and corrupt practices are followed in the implementation of these social programmes by the government which bring in their own complications. As a result instead of getting appreciation from the people, it is creating discontent ... The state ministers in charge of different departments are not conversant with their work and do not take the necessary initiative in implementing the social schemes under their charge. They are seen to rely more on bureaucracy. The ministers are seen to have taken a detached view and have got some hazy ideas about their charges/responsibilities. All these have clouded the minds of the people and the Left Front is losing ground. Only the group of people who are deeply committed to the Leftist ideology through hard struggle over the years stand by the Party, the others are not impressed with the performance of the Left Front government.[1]

---

[1] Burdwan District Committee, CPM, *Shamiksha Ashtam Lok Sabha Nirbachan* ("Analysis of Eighth Lok Sabha Elections"), February 28, 1985, pp. 26–7.

Even when movements have been attempted the Burdwan Committee admits they have been side-tracked by corruption and opportunism.

In organising our movement/struggle areawise we have noticed some aberrations. For example, the mentality of teaching a lesson by stopping the work of domestic help, personal enmity or to settle scores, falsely recording rights of sharecroppers, opportunist attitudes in fixing the right share of the crop to the sharecropper, lack of humility in organising strikes in small industrial units, unrealistic demands on the industry in order to retain the confidence of the workers, supporting unreasonable opportunistic demands etc etc are cases in point. Vested interests take advantage of these lapses and then help the opportunist elements to go against us.[2]

That the Left Front was a dismal failure should no longer be a matter of debate. What is more significant is the nature of its failure. This failure took three forms:
1  transformational and development reforms that failed to achieve their objectives,
2  non-policies which merely continued the status quo or followed Congress precedents and,
3  regressive policies which were more elitist than the Congress policies.

The first category of failures to achieve transformational and developmental reforms falls under the theme of agrarian reform, namely Operation Barga, land redistribution, and rural input credits. Operation Barga was largely a repeat of an earlier recording operation in the sixties under the Congress regime, and in any case proved ineffective in preventing evictions or ensuring legally specified crop shares. Under the land reform program land was redistributed but at a rate not significantly different from previous regimes and no better than what was taking place elsewhere in the country. Even what was distributed could not be supported by provision of rural credit and inputs, leaving the beneficiaries vulnerable to loss of newly acquired assets.

Under the category of non-policies, were those policies that a Communist government might have been expected to promote in order to advance the class struggle, namely mobilization and legislation in favor of Scheduled Castes and Tribes, and agricultural and industrial labor. In the case of Scheduled Castes and Tribes the Left Front was content merely to implement largely centrally initiated and funded programs, though much of this remained only on paper. Labor policy consisted of avoiding class conflict and promoting labor tranquility to the point where no economic gains were directly attributable to the Left Front government.

Most surprising of all were the regressive Left Front policies, namely demanding lower agricultural taxation and going along with the central CPM policy of higher food prices. Agricultural taxation was initially sponsored as a

[2] *Ibid.*, pp. 31–2.

progressive form of taxation but was watered down in Select Committee till it was virtually non-existent. Likewise the state CPM despite initial misgivings went along with the policy of higher food prices which the central party was demanding as a means of enlisting the support of the rural rich, at the expense of the poor.

Given this record of failed reforms, non-reforms, and regressive policies, the question remains as to how such a singularly unsuccessful government was able to achieve the world record for being the longest ruling democratically elected Communist government in history. This was the result of a fourth set of policies which could be termed "party political" objectives. This was the only set of policies the Left Front followed with single-minded devotion and as its top priority it achieved a fair measure of success. The policy was premised on the desire to stay in power at all costs, regardless of the compromises that might be required to do so. In this it was no different from any other political party which, to remain in power, adopts policies designed to win the next election rather than implement needed reforms. Its most detrimental effect was to stop all attempts at reform in their tracks when confronted with the possibility of a rural rich blacklash, business disinvestment, or trade union opposition to discipline and productivity. All these reforms ultimately posed a threat to CPM constituencies, which the Left Front felt it depended upon for re-election. Unfortunately for West Bengal, the Left Front political objective of re-election was in at least short-term conflict with development transformation because the Left Front supporters were in many cases the most serious obstacles to needed reforms.

One of the most important examples of the CPM base being the greatest obstacle to reform was its own trade union membership, fostered on years of agitation against increases in productivity which had resulted in absenteeism and indiscipline. As a result, the urban sector was caught in a low equilibrium inefficiency trap. High absenteeism and poor maintenance resulted in transport bottlenecks and power generation shortfalls which made working conditions for government employees and the public hardly conducive to efficiency. These poor working conditions lowered productivity, which resulted in further declines in maintenance and work attendance. As both transport and electricity were largely state controlled, a turn around in these two sectors alone would have greatly improved working conditions for the urban public and enabled the Left Front to retain the support of its traditional urban *bhadralok* following. Having failed to achieve this turn around among its own supporters in the public sector, the Left Front urban support was bound to wane. By failing to take the tough option within its own administration, the Left Front was unable to break the traditional malaise which the urban middle-class public had hoped might change under a Communist government. The resulting political alienation was almost inevitable as the West Bengal urban electorate had given up hope of obtaining significant civic improvement under the Communists.

The reason the Left Front chose not to tone up the public sector lay not in constitutional restraints, the Supreme Court having ruled that employees could be dismissed to increase efficiency, but because the trade unions felt bound to oppose increases in workloads and productivity.[3] Faced with opposition from trade union locals the Left Front decided to soft-pedal reforms at the workplace. The Left Front therefore failed to break the low equilibrium of inefficiency in the public services, and administrative reform remained a dead letter.

The failure of urban reform in the face of trade union opposition might have been offset by an innovative rural reform program. However, here too reform was opposed by a grouping of class interests heavily represented in the Left Front constituency. As in the urban areas, party political necessities took precedence over needed reforms. In the rural areas the party politics were such that the CPM leadership would not confront the dominant rural elite. For all the Communist talk about their base among the rural poor, this was only manifest at election time. The party organization and the Left Front Panchayats were controlled by the rural middle and upper classes, whose own political and financial interests were threatened by any independent mobilization of the lower classes. Therefore it was in the political interests of the CPM to maintain a multi-class alliance dominated by the rural elite, which could be maintained only by soft-pedalling redistributive reforms. The election of Panchayats on party slates was actually a party political objective rather than a developmental reform and as such was successful in helping the party penetrate the villages and deliver the rural vote. However, it did not change the balance of power in the villages in favor of the poor, and, as a developmental channel, proved to be no better than the district administration in helping the lower classes.

The most damaging result of the Left Front government, however, was not that it simply blocked or failed to implement needed reform, but that in pursuing party political objectives it made the possibility of future reforms more remote. In pandering to its most influential constituencies, namely state government employees and rural food surplus farmers, it entrenched their position and privileges, making the need for reform both more urgent and more difficult. To obtain the support of government employees the state salary bill was increased over threefold under the Left Front, leaving relatively little for developmental expenditure and making a cut or freezing of salaries politically difficult.[4] Despite this largesse to state employees the Left Front support has been eroded. According to the Burdwan District Committee of the CPM "the voting pattern shows that the middle level employees have voted against us although, in terms

---

[3] *The Times of India*, July 25, 1985, p. 1.
[4] Indranil Banerjie, "A Bankrupt State," *India Today*, April 15, 1985.

of benefits, this class of employees got the maximum from the Left Front government. Their support for the Left Front is progressively diminishing."[5] In the villages the creation of party Panchayats and distribution of development aid through them enhances the power of the locally dominant elite which distributes the largesse. It is difficult to see how these elites can be mobilized in a struggle of the lower classes against the elites to which they themselves belong. In this respect the CPM followed the same pattern as the Congress, but has been more successful in establishing a village level party infrastructure, manned in part by opportunists who jumped on the CPM bandwagon after the party came to power.

Through this assiduous cultivating of its relatively privileged urban and rural constituencies, the CPM party political objectives were largely achieved, enabling it to win re-election. These constituencies, though strategically important, are only a small proportion of the electorate, most of whom have received little or nothing from the Left Front. In this respect, however, the Left Front has been able to achieve gratuitous victories due to the bitter factionalism of the state Congress opposition, which has long been held in even greater disrepute than the Left Front. When faced with the two alternatives, many voters still feel the Left Front to be the better government. Thus despite sacrificing developmental transformation and the class struggle to party political interests, the Left Front continued in power by default, from lack of a credible alternative.

Though party political objectives have not meshed with the need for a developmental strategy, this is only a short-term contradiction. In the long-term the Left Front would have a much stronger base if the lower classes were mobilized by the Communists in pursuit of their own class interests rather than those of the various privileged groups. The current lack of reform only served to disillusion the rising expectations the Communists helped to foster when they were in opposition.

The impetus for reform, which the victory of the Left Front in 1977 seemed to herald, ceased after a brief flurry. "Rumour went around in early 1982, that in face of the state elections the government or the minister in charge had internally directed the officers in the field to stop Operation Barga until after the election."[6] By 1982 the Left Front programs aimed at rural socio-economic change were being wound down at the behest of the Left Front leadership. Though this was never put in writing it was confirmed by the IAS officers in charge of these programs. They claimed the Marxists feared a backlash from the landed interests at election time and only by slowing down the confrontational class demands and programs could this be avoided.

---

[5] Burdwan District Committee, *Shamiksha*, p. 33.
[6] Theodor Bergmann, *Agrarian Reform in India* (New Delhi: Agricole Publishing Academy, 1984), p. 152.

Though both revolutionary and reformist options are now a dead letter with the CPM, it would be a mistake to think that this was an inevitable outcome. Had the power struggle within the CPM been resolved in favor of the radicals rather than the centrists, a more radical option might have been attempted.

Even if the Left Front considered land equalization impractical given the constitutional constraints on state government, it could still have gone ahead with fuller implementation of existing legislation. It might be expected that national programs designed for the poor would have the best implementation records in West Bengal, rather than in more conservative states. However, the comparative data available indicates Bengal program implementation has been average at best, and more often lower than in most other Indian states. This situation indicates the end of major reforms in West Bengal.

Though there are still radicals within the CPM, relatively few are in top leadership positions. Nor are further waves of radical recruits likely. As the Burdwan District Committee of the CPM noted in its internal document:

The youth are no longer carried away by the Communist movement at the international and national level. The call to Communism has considerably waned among the youth. Not only that, the self-sacrifice, idealism, honesty, simplicity and intellectual acumen of our great Communist leaders and workers in the past attracted the youth to Communism. This situation no longer exists. The Communist party is no longer seen as a totally different party from other political parties. For the last few years in our role as government, our party workers and leadership have been in close contact with the different levels of bureaucracy. All the aberrations of *petit bourgeois* class have pervaded our party today. The relentless struggle which we should have launched against such aberrations is no longer to be seen. Our image before the people is blurred. The reaction is most noticeable among our youth. There is some thinking among the party at different levels that the *petit bourgeois* mentality and aberrations have only affected the party workers at the lower levels. There is no basis for such thinking. Apart from the lower levels, even the tested leadership is not free from this. If we have to fight this menace, we must start from the top.[7]

Such a purge of the leadership is difficult to foresee, as the younger generation of members is if anything generally more opportunist than the older Communists. The trend could therefore be towards greater conservatism rather than radicalization. If support for the Left Front erodes it may eventually face defeat at the polls; however, as Congress is unlikely to do a better job, in time they could again return to power. There would thus be a rotation of parties in power in which neither party attempts significant reforms. In this rotation the policy differences would probably be even less than those between alternating conservative and social democratic governments in Europe. There would then be a circulation of government elites rather than any change of class alignments.

[7] Burdwan District Committee, *Shamiksha*, pp. 31–2.

The CPM would not be destroyed but would remain a regional party, Communist only in name, as an alternative party of the Bengali establishment. This is quite a change for a party founded only in 1964 as a revolutionary splinter from the "revisionist" CPI, which had itself been founded in the Soviet Union as a revolutionary party. The transformation is now so complete that the present parties are unrecognizable from their origins. They are Third World examples analogous to Michels' oligarchic German Social Democrats whom Lenin denounced as revisionist.[8] The transformation into reformism of the Social Democratic Party may have been less sweeping, however, than what the CPI and later the CPM experienced. It is to the advantage of the Indian establishment that it gave sufficient freedom of action to the Communists to enable them finally to emasculate themselves of any revolutionary thrust. "Even the Communists, who in the early years of independence appeared credible challengers of the system, have been tamed, divided, and coopted."[9] The Left Front experiment in West Bengal was the definitive proof of this process. There are observers who see this as a positive development for Indian democracy because of the institutionalization of the left within constitutional norms of conduct. However, even if the left is brought within the constitutional system, if Indian democracy does not meet the demands of the lowest classes, it will be unrepresentative of the majority of India's people. A democracy that does not have a powerful constitutional party representing the class interests of most of its people is fundamentally flawed. Even though these class interests have not been effectively represented and promoted, quiescence should not be equated with stability. The integration of the Communists within the system is only as permanent as the passivity of the people. Given the right leadership and a popular following, these constitutional limits may still be broken again, if not by the mainstream parties then by new political formations. The long-term danger for the ruling elite is that, as the majority of the Indian population has been left without any national party willing to pursue its class interests predominantly, there is still a political vacuum encompassing most of the population. This political vacuum has yet to be filled, and if it is, the Indian establishment will face its greatest threat. However, the immediate dangers are from divisive communal and regional forces, on which the left will have only a marginal impact.

With neither socialism nor capitalism developing, West Bengal fell economically behind more dynamic business-oriented states. Communist work methods

---

[8] Peter Gay, *The Dilemma of Democratic Socialism* (New York: Collier Books, 1962); Carl E. Schorske, *German Social Democracy: 1905–1917* (New York: Harper & Row, 1972); Roberto Michels, *Political Parties: A Sociological Study of the Oligarchical Tendencies of Modern Democracy* (New York: Collier Books, 1962).

[9] Mohammed Ayoob, "The Primacy of the Political: South Asian Regional Cooperation (SARC) in Comparative Perspective," *Asian Survey*, vol. 25, no. 4, April 1985, p. 450.

had undermined socialist and capitalist development, both of which required productivity reforms and efficient allocation of resources, rather than electoral patronage. The Bengali Left Front experiment failed to implement a transition to socialism, and in promoting capitalism proved less effective than governments of other Indian states.

# Bibliography

NON-GOVERNMENT SOURCES

Adhikari, G. *Documents of the History of the Communist Party of India*, vol. I, 1917–1922, New Delhi: People's Publishing House, October 1971

Alavi, Hamza. "Peasants and Revolution" reprinted from *The Socialist Register 1965*, Boston: New England Press

Althusser, *Essays in Self-Criticism*, London: New Left Book, 1976

Ayoob, Mohammed. "The Primacy of the Political: South Asian Regional Cooperation (SARC) in Comparative Perspective," *Asian Survey*, vol. 25, no. 4, April 1985, pp. 443–57

Bandyopadhyay, D. "Road to Effective Land Reform," mimeographed, 1979

Bandyopadhyaya, Nripen. "Evaluation of Land Reform Measures in West Bengal: A Report," Calcutta: mimeographed by the Centre for Studies in Social Sciences, 1983

Banerjee, Saumitra. "CPI(M) Maintains Supremacy," *Sunday*, June 12–18, 1983, p. 52.

Banerjee, Sumanta. *In the Wake of Naxalbari*, Calcutta: Subarnarekha, 1980

Banerjie, Indranil. "A Bankrupt State," *India Today*, April 15, 1985

Bardhan, Pranab K. *Land, Labour and Rural Poverty*, Delhi: Oxford University Press, 1984

Bardhan, Pranab and Ashok Rudra. *Agrarian Relations in West Bengal: Results of Two Surveys*, Bombay: Somaiya Publications Ltd., 1983

"Types of Labour Attachment in Agriculture: Results of a Survey in West Bengal, 1979," *Economic and Political Weekly*, August 20, 1980, p. 1483

"Labour Employment and Wages in Agriculture: Results of a Survey in West Bengal, 1970," *Economic and Political Weekly*, November 8–15, 1980, p. 1945

Barman, Ashis. "New Challenges for Left," *Link*, January 26, 1983, p. 38

Basu, Amrita. "Democratic Centralism in the Home and the World: Bengali Women and the Communist Movement" in *Promissory Notes: Women in the Transition to Socialism*, New York: Monthly Review Press, 1989

Basu, Jyoti. "Interview," *Capital*, July 8–21, 1985, p. 30

Basu, Kalipada. *West Bengal Economy: Past, Present and Future*, Calcutta: Firma KLM Ltd., 1989

Basu, Timir. *Bhumi Sanskarer Swarup* ("A Picture of Land Reforms"), Calcutta: Abaniranjan Rai, February 1982

Bergmann, Theodor. *Agrarian Reform in India*, New Delhi: Agricole Publishing Academy, 1984

Berwick, Dennison. "Sacred and Profane," *The Sunday Times Magazine*, July 1, 1990

Bhattacharya, Ratna. *Administrators in a Developing Society. West Bengal: A Study of the Problems of the Administrators in Role Performance*, Bombay: Himalaya Publishing House, 1989

Bhattacharyya, Asit Kumar. "An examination of Land Reforms with Special Reference to West Bengal" in *Land Reform in Eastern India*, edited by Manjula Bose, Calcutta: Jadavpur University, 1981

Bird, Richard M. *Taxing Agricultural Land in Developing Countries*, Cambridge, Mass.: Harvard University Press, 1974

Biswas, Atharobaki. "Why Dandakaranya a Failure, Why Mass Exodus, Where Solution?," *The Oppressed Indian*, July, 1982

Bose, Arun. *India's Social Crisis*, Delhi: Oxford University Press, 1989

Bouton, Marshall M. *Agrarian Radicalism in South India*, Princeton: Princeton University Press, 1985

Boyce, James K. "Agricultural Growth in Bangladesh and West Bengal," Oxford University, D. Phil thesis, 1984

Brass, Paul R. *The Politics of India Since Independence: The New Cambridge History of India IV.1*, Cambridge: Cambridge University Press, 1990

Broomfield, J.H. *Elite Conflict in a Plural Society: Twentieth-Century Bengal*, Berkeley: University of California Press, 1968

Carras, Mary C. *The Dynamics of Indian Political Factions*, Cambridge: Cambridge University Press, 1972

Carter, Anthony T. *Elite Politics in Rural India*, Cambridge: Cambridge University Press, 1974

Chakrabarti, Ashis. "Muddle in Academic Field," *The Statesman*, August 25, 1982

Chakrabarty, Saroj. *With West Bengal Chief Ministers: Memoirs 1962 to 1977*, Calcutta: Orient Longman, 1978

Chandra, N.K. "Industrialisation and the Left Movement: On Several Questions of Strategy in West Bengal", *Social Scientist*, vol. 7, no. 1/2, August–September 1978, pp. 23–4

Chatterjee, Partha. *Bengal 1920–1947: The Land Question*, Calcutta: K.P. Bagchi and Co., 1984, vol. I.

Chattopadhyay, Gouranga. *Ranjana: A Village in West Bengal*, Calcutta: Bookland Private Ltd, 1964

Chaudhuri, Kalyan. "Disturbed Industrial Situation," *Economic and Political Weekly*, May 1, 1976

"Victims of Their Leaders Making," *Economic and Political Weekly*, July 8, 1978

Choudhury, Benoy. *Banglar Bhumibyabasthar Ruprekha* ("Outline of the Land Settlement of Bengal"), Calcutta: National Book Agency, 1981

Danda, Ajit K. and Dipali G. Danda. *Development and Change in Basudha*, Hyderabad: National Institute of Community Development, 1971

Das Gupta, Piyash. "CPI(M) Sangramer Madhye Janma O Briddi, Mahakaraner Kanke Prabesh O Siddi" ("The Birth and Expansion of CPI(M) – Formation of Government and its Fulfilment"), *Bartaman*, December 7, 1985

Dasgupta, Biplab. "Gram Banglar Sreni Binyas ("Class Relations in Rural Bengal"), *Deshhitaishee*, annual Puja issue, 1980, p. 89

"Agricultural Labour under Colonial, Semi-Capitalist and Capitalist Conditions: A Case Study of West Bengal," *Economic and Political Weekly*, September 29, 1984, p. A146

"Some Aspects of Land Reform in West Bengal" in *Land Reform: Land Settlement Cooperatives*, no. 1/2, United Nations Food and Agriculture Organization: 1982

Dasgupta, Satadal. *Caste Kinship and Community: Social System of a Bengal Caste*, Madras: Universities Press, 1986

Dasgupta, Satadal and Rajat Subhra Mukhopadhyay. "Party Politics, Panchayat and Conflict in a West Bengal Village," *Man in India*, vol. 69, no. 1, March 1989, pp. 23–41

Datta, Prabhat Kumar. *Land Reforms Administration in West Bengal*, Delhi: Daya Publishing House, 1988

Davis, Marvin. *Rank and Rivalry*, Cambridge: Cambridge University Press, 1983

Dreze, Jean. "Poverty in India and the IRDP Delusion," *Economic and Political Weekly*, vol. 39, September 29, 1990, pp. A95–104

Editorial, "A Look at Power Plants," *The Statesman*, August 18, 1982

"Words and Action," *The Statesman*, December 31, 1982

"Neglecting Adults," *The Statesman*, February 23, 1983

Franda, Marcus. *Radical Politics in West Bengal*, Cambridge, Mass.: The MIT Press, 1971

*India's Rural Development*, Bloomington: Indiana University Press, 1979

Freeman, James M. *Untouchable: An Indian Life History*, Stanford: Stanford University Press, 1979

Gay, Peter. *The Dilemma of Democratic Socialism*, New York: Collier Books, 1962

Ghose, Ajit Kumar. *Agrarian Reform in West Bengal*, Geneva: International Labour Organisation, 1980

Ghosh, Anjali. *Peaceful Transition in Power*, Calcutta: Firma KLM, 1981

Ghosh, Arun. *West Bengal Landscapes*, Calcutta: K.P. Bagchi and Co., 1989

Ghosh, S.K. "Land and Agricultural Development" in *Land Reforms in Eastern India*, edited by Manjula Bose, Calcutta: Jadavpur University, 1981

Ghosh, Sankar. *The Disinherited State: A Study of West Bengal 1967–70*, Calcutta: Orient Longman, 1971

Ghosh, Tushar Kanti. *Operation Barga and Land Reforms*, Delhi: B.R. Publishing Corporation, 1986

Gough, Kathleen. *Rural Society in Southeast India*, Cambridge: Cambridge University Press, 1981

Gould, Harold A. "Changing Political Behaviour in Rural Indian Society," *Economic and Political Weekly*, Special Number, August 1967, pp. 1515–22

Griffin, Keith. *The Political Economy of Agrarian Change*, London: Macmillan Press, 1974

Gupta, Ranjit Kumar. *Agrarian West Bengal, Three Field Studies*, Calcutta: Institute of Social Research and Applied Anthropology, 1977

*Essays in Economic Anthropology*, Calcutta: Institute of Social Research and Applied Anthropology, 1979

Gupta, S.K. *The Scheduled Castes in Modern Indian Politics: Their Emergence as a Political Power*, New Delhi: Munshiram Manoharlal, 1985

Hanson, James A. and Samuel S. Lieberman. *India: Poverty, Employment, and Social Services*, Washington, DC: The World Bank 1989

Herring, Ronald J. *Land to the Tiller: The Political Economy of Agrarian Reform in South Asia*, London: Yale University Press, 1983

Hindess, B. and P.Q. Hirst, *Pre-Capitalist Modes of Production*, London: Routledge & Kegan Paul, 1975

*Mode of Production and Social Formation*, London: Macmillan, 1977

Hobsbawm, E.J. *Primitive Rebels*, New York: W.W. Norton, 1965

Housego, David. "Critical Election for the Marxists of West Bengal," *Financial Times*, February 5, 1979

Institute for Financial Management and Research, *An Economic Assessment of Poverty Eradication and Rural Unemployment Alleviation Programmes and their Prospects*, Parts I & III, Madras: Institute for Financial Management and Research, 1984

Jain, L.C. *et al. Grass Without Roots: Rural Development Under Government Auspices*, New Delhi: Sage, 1985

Jobert, Bruno. "Populism and Health Policy: The Case of Community Health Volunteers in India," *Social Science and Medicine*, vol. 20, no. 1, 1985, pp. 1–28

Jose, A.V. "Real Wages, Employment, and Income of Agricultural Labourers," *Economic and Political Weekly*, Review of Agriculture, March 1979, p. A16

"Agricultural Wages in India," *Economic and Political Weekly*, Review of Agriculture, June 25, 1988

Juergensmeyer, Mark. *Religion as Social Vision: The Movement Against Untouchability in 20th-Century Punjab*, Berkeley: University of California Press, 1982

K., S. "Diminishing Returns from Blaming the Centre," *Economic and Political Weekly*, April 13, 1985, p. 633

Kamble, J.R. *Rise and Awakening of Depressed Classes in India*, New Delhi: National Publishing House, 1979

Kaviraj, Sudipta. "The Split in the Communist Movement in India," Jawaharlal Nehru University, Ph.D. thesis, 1979

Klass, Morton. *From Field to Factory: Community Structure and Industrialization in West Bengal*, Philadelphia: Institute of the Study of Human Issues, 1978

Kohli, Atul. *The State and Poverty in India*, Cambridge: Cambridge University Press, 1987

"From Elite Activism to Democratic Consolidation: The Rise of Reform Communism in West Bengal" in *Dominance and State Power in Modern India: Decline of a Social Order*, vol. II, Delhi: Oxford University Press, 1990

"Parliamentary Communism and Agrarian Reform," *Asian Survey*, vol. 23, no. 7, July 1983, p. 794

Konar, Harekrishna. *Agrarian Problems of India*, Calcutta: Gour Sabha, 1977

Kothari, Rajni. "Party Politics and Political Development," *Economic and Political Weekly*, Annual Number 1967

Krishnaji, N. "Wages of Agricultural Labour," *Economic and Political Weekly*, Review of Agriculture, September 1971, pp. A149–A151

Kumar, T.M. Vinod and Jatin De. *Basic Needs and the Provision of Government Services: An Areas Study of Ranaghat Block in West Bengal*, Geneva: International Labour Organisation, 1980

Lahiri, Ranjit Kumar. "Land Reform in West Bengal – Some Implications" in *Land Reforms in Eastern India*, edited by Manjula Bose, Calcutta: Jadavpur University, 1981

Lange, Oskar. *On the Economic Theory of Socialism*, edited by B.E. Lippincott, New York: McGraw-Hill, 1964

Lele, Jayant. *Elite Pluralism and Class Rule*, Toronto: Toronto University Press, 1981

Lelyveld, Joseph. *Calcutta*, Hong Kong: The Perennial Press, 1975

Lubell, Harold. *Calcutta: Its Urban Development and Employment Prospects*, Geneva: International Labour Office, 1981

M., B. "Agricultural Prices and the Left," *Economic and Political Weekly*, October 23, 1982, p. 1722

Maitra, Tares. *Expansion of Employment Through Local Resource Mobilisation*, Bangkok: Asian Employment Programme, International Labour Organisation, 1982

Majumder, Arun. *Poverty, Development and Exchange Relations: A Study of Two Birbhum Villages*, New Delhi: Radiant Publishers, 1987

Mallick, Ross. *Indian Communism: Opposition, Collaboration, and Institutionalization*, Delhi: Oxford University Press, 1993

Mandal, Govinda Chandra. "Land Reforms in the Context of Agricultural Development with Special Reference to West Bengal" in *Land Reforms in Eastern India*, edited by Manjula Bose, Calcutta: Jadavpur University, 1981

Manor, James. "Tried, then Abandoned: Economic Liberalisation in India," *IDS Bulletin*, vol. 18, no. 4, 1987

  "Karnataka: Caste, Class, Dominance and Politics in a Cohesive Society" in *Dominance and State Power in Modern India: Decline of a Social Order Volume I* edited by Francine R. Frankel and M.S.A. Rao, Delhi: Oxford University Press, 1989

Michels, Roberto. *Political Parties: A Sociological Study of the Oligarchical Tendencies of Modern Democracy*, New York: Collier Books, 1962

Mitter, Swasti. *Peasant Movements in West Bengal*, Cambridge: Department of Land Economy, 1977

Mukhopadhyay, Ashim. "Bengal Trade Union Movement Weakening," *Indian Express*, December 21, 1982

Mukhopadhyay, Rajatasubhra. "Resource Distribution and Power Structure: A Case Study of a West Bengal Village," *The Eastern Anthropologist*, vol. 35, no. 1, January–March 1982, p. 70

Nathan, Dev. "On Agricultural Prices," *Economic and Political Weekly*, Review of Agriculture, December 25, 1982

Nossiter, T.J. *Marxist State Governments in India*, London: Pinter Publishers, 1988

Pandian, M.S.S. "From Muzzaffarpur to Midnapur: Story of Missing Landlords," *Economic and Political Weekly*, January 22, 1983, p. 98

Patnaik, Utsa. "Class Differentiation within the Peasantry: An Approach to Analysis of Indian Agriculture," *Economic and Political Weekly*, Review of Agriculture, September 1976, p. 193

Popkin, Samuel L. *The Rational Peasant: The Political Economy of Rural Society in Vietnam*, Berkeley: University of California Press, 1979

Przeworski, Adam. *Capitalism and Social Democracy*, Cambridge: Cambridge University Press, 1985

Rajshekar, V.T. *Dalit: The Black Untouchables of India*, Atlanta: Clarity Press, 1987

Rao, C.H. Hanumantha. "Small Farmer can be Viable and more Productive," *Link*, January 26, 1983, p. 48

Rao, V.M. "Agricultural Wages in India – A Reliability Analysis", *Indian Journal of Agricultural Economics*, vol. 27, no. 3, July–September 1972, p. 38

  "Promises on Rural Development," *Economic and Political Weekly*, December 18, 1982, p. 2045

Ray, Debidas. "The Small Lessor and the Big Lessee: Evidence from West Bengal,"

*Economic and Political Weekly*, Review of Agriculture, December 1978, p. A121

Ray, Rabindra. *The Naxalites and Their Ideology*, Delhi: Oxford University Press, 1988

Ray, Rajat Kanta. *Social Conflict and Political Unrest in Bengal: 1875–1927*, Delhi: Oxford University Press, 1984

Ray, Sally. "United Front Government and the Politics of Agrarian Struggle in West Bengal, 1967 and 1969–70," *Australian Outlook*, August 1971, p. 214

Rohner, Ronald P. and Manjusri Chaki-Sircar. *Women and Children in a Bengali Village*, Hanover: University Press of New England, 1988

Rosenthal, Donald B. *The Expansive Elite*, Berkeley: University of California Press, 1977, p. 313

Roy, Ajit. "Substituting Reform for Revolution", *Economic and Political Weekly*, December 31, 1977, p. 2154

"Question of Transitional Government in Marxist Terminology," *Economic and Political Weekly*, October 25, 1985

Roy, Biren. "Jute Owners Offensive Goes Unopposed," *Economic and Political Weekly*, August 7, 1982, p. 1266

Roy Choudhury, Profulla. *West Bengal – A Decade (1965–1975)*, Calcutta: Boipatra, 1977

*Left Experiment in West Bengal*, New Delhi: Patriot Publishers, 1985

"Land Reforms: Promise and Fulfilment," *Economic and Political Weekly*, December 27, 1980, p. 2172

Rudolph, Lloyd I. and Susanne Hoeber Rudolph, *In Pursuit of Lakshmi: The Political Economy of the Indian State*, Chicago: Chicago University Press, 1987

Rudra Ashok. *Paschim Banglar Bargadar* ("West Bengal's Bargadar"), Calcutta: Kalthasilpa, 1981

*Extraeconomic Constraints on Agricultural Labour*, Asian Employment Programme Working Papers, Bangkok: International Labour Organisation, 1982

"The Left Front Government," *Economic and Political Weekly*, September 3, 1977, p. 1565

"Agrarian Policies of Left Front Government in West Bengal," *Economic and Political Weekly*, vol. 20, no. 23, June 8, 1985, p. 1016

Samanta, Amiya K. *Left Extremist Movement in West Bengal*, Calcutta: Firma KLM, 1984

Sarkar, Bikram. *Land Reforms in India*, New Delhi: Ashish Publishing House, 1989

"Legal Aspects of Land Reform Measures in West Bengal," Calcutta University, Ph.D. thesis, 1982

Sathyamurthy, T.V. *India Since Independence – Centre–State Relations: The Case of Kerala*, vol. I, Delhi: Ajanta Publications, 1985

Schneider, Bertrand. *The Barefoot Revolution: A Report to the Club of Rome*, London: Intermediate Technology Publications, 1988

Schorske, Carl E. *German Social Democracy: 1905–1917*, New York: Harper & Row, 1972

Scott, James C. *The Moral Economy of the Peasant*, New Haven: Yale University Press, 1976

Sen, Sumanta. "Grassroot Power," *India Today*, June 15, 1983, p. 50

Sen Gupta, Bhabani. *CPI-M: Promises, Prospects, Problems*, New Delhi: Young Asia Publications, 1979

"Time to take Stock," *India Today*, December 31, 1982, p. 115

Shiviah, M., K.B. Srivastava, and A.C. Jena. *Panchayati Raj Elections in West Bengal, 1978*, Hyderabad: National Institute of Rural Development, 1980

Sikar, Ranjit Kumar. "Marichijahpi Massacre," *The Oppressed Indian*, July 1982, p. 21

Sinha, Indradeep. *The Changing Agrarian Scene: Problems and Tasks*, New Delhi: People's Publishing House, 1980

Sirkar, N.K. De. "Power Supply for the Industries in West Bengal" in *Industries in West Bengal*, vol. XXII, nos 2 and 3 of *India in Industries*, edited by Parimal Sengupta, Calcutta: Oxford Book Company, 1976

Subramanian, K.S. "The Ideological Evolution of the Indian Communist Movement in the Post-Independence Period," Karnataka University Ph.D. thesis, 1983

Sundaram, K. and Suresh D. Tendulkar. *Integrated Rural Development Programme in India*, Kuala Lumpur: The Asian and Pacific Development Centre, 1984

Swaminathan, Madhura. "Village Level Implementation of IRDP: Comparison of West Bengal and Tamil Nadu," *Economic and Political Weekly*, vol. 25, no. 13, pp. A17–27

Sweezy, Paul M. and Charles Bettelheim, *On the Transition to Socialism*, New York: Monthly Review Press, 1971

Tata Services Ltd, Department of Economics and Statistics, *Statistical Outline of India 1984*

Thomas, Clive Y. *Dependence and Transformation: The Economics of the Transition to Socialism*, New York: Monthly Review Press, 1971

Todarmal. *Land in West Bengal*, Calcutta: Anima Prakashani, 1990

Tulpule, Bagaram. "Managing Durgapur – Part I," *Economic and Political Weekly*, December 25, 1976

Vaid, K.N. *Gheraos and Labour Unrest in West Bengal*, New Delhi: Shri Ram Centre for Industrial Relations and Human Resources, 1972

Vanaik, Achin. *The Painful Transition: Bourgeois Democracy in India*, London: Verso, 1990

Visharat, Mangaldev. Laxmi Narayan Pandey and Prasannbhai Mehta, "Report on Marichjhapi Affairs," mimeographed, April 18, 1979

Westergaard, Kirsten. *People's Participation, Local Government and Rural Development: The Case of West Bengal*. Copenhagen: Centre for Development Research, 1986, CDR Research Report no. 8

Wolf, Eric R. *Peasant Wars of the Twentieth Century*, New York: Harper and Row, 1969
"On Peasant Rebellions" in *Peasants and Peasant Societies* edited by Teodor Shanin, Middlesex: Penguin Books, 1971

World Bank. *World Development Report 1990*, Oxford: Oxford University Press, 1990
*India: Poverty, Employment, and Social Services*, Washington, D.C.: The World Bank, 1989

Zagoria, Donald S. "The Social Bases of Indian Communism" in *Issues in the Future of Asia* edited by Richard Lowenthal, New York: Praeger, 1969

Zammit, J. Ann, editor. *The Chilean Road to Socialism*, Institute of Development Studies, University of Sussex, England

PARTY SOURCES

All India Agricultural Workers' Union. *Statement of Policy and Constitution*, adopted by the First Conference, Midnapore, West Bengal, November 11, 1982, New Delhi: All India Agricultural Workers' Union, 1982

All India Kisan Sabha. *General Secretary's Report*, Twenty-Fourth Conference of the 8th–11th November 1982, Midnapore, West Bengal, New Delhi: All India Kisan Sabha, 1982

    *Proceedings and Resolutions*, Twenty-Fourth Conference of the 8th–11th November 1982, Midnapore, West Bengal, New Delhi: All India Kisan Sabha, 1982

Basu, Jyoti. "Tin Bajhar Bamfront Sarkar Parichalanar Avigyata Samparkay Kichhu Baktyavba" ("Something to Say Regarding the Experience of the Running of the Left Front Government for the Last Three Years"), *Deshhitaishee*, annual Puja issue 1980

    "Party, Yukta Front O Sadharan Manush Gata Tin Dasaker Andolaner Avigyata" ("Party, United Front and Common Man: Experience of Movement for the Last Three Decades"), *Deshhitaishee*, annual Puja issue 1981

Burdwan District Committee, CPM. *Shamiksha Ashtam Lok Sabha Nirbachan* ("Analysis of Eighth Lok Sabha Elections"), February 28, 1985

Communist Party of India – Marxist (CPM). *Programme*, Calcutta: CPM, 1964

    Central Committee, *Tasks on the Kisan Front*, Calcutta: April 1967

    Central Committee, *Political-Organisational Report*, Eighth Congress, Cochin, December 23–29, 1969, Calcutta: April 1968

    Central Committee, "The Party and the Struggle of the Bangladesh People," *People's Democracy*, February 13, 1972

    Central Committee, *Resolution on Certain Agrarian Issues*, Calcutta: 1973

    *Report and Resolution on Organisation*, adopted by the Salkia Plenum, December 27–31, 1978, New Delhi: May 1979

    Central Committee, *The Peasant Upsurge and Remunerative Price Issue*, New Delhi: April 1981

    *Political Resolution*, adopted by the Eleventh Congress, Vijayawada, January 26–31, 1982, New Delhi: March 1982

    *Political-Organisational Report*, adopted at the Eleventh Congress, Vijayawada, January 26–31, 1982, New Delhi: October 1982

    *On Centre–State Relations*, Delhi: December 1983

    *Political-Organisational Report*, Twelfth Congress, Calcutta, December 25–30, 1985

    *General Secretary's Report*, Twenty-Fifth Conference, May 17–19, 1986, Patna, Delhi: May 1986

    *Towards All India Action Programme: Proceedings, General Secretary's Report and Resolutions*, April 24–26, Cuttack 1987, Delhi: June 1987

    *Role of Stalin As the CPI(M) Views It*, Delhi: National Book Centre, August 1987

    *The September Struggle A Review: Review Report, Report of the Central Secretary and Proceedings*, Trivandrum, October 25–26, 1987, New Delhi: December 1987

    *Political Organisational Report*, Thirteenth Congress, Trivandrum, December 27, 1988 to January 1, 1989

    *Political Resolution*, Thirteenth Congress, Trivandrum, December 27, 1988 to January 1, 1989

    *Central Committee Resolutions On Certain Ideological Questions On Recent Developments in the Soviet Union*, New Delhi: July 1989

    *On Recent Developments in People's Republic of China*, Delhi: September 1989

Election Manifesto of CPM, Delhi: November 1989

*Review of Lok Sabha Elections*, adopted by Central Committee, December 5–7, 1989, Delhi: December 1989

*On Certain Political-Ideological Issues Related to Developments*, adopted by Central Committee, May 28–31, 1990, Delhi: June 1990

Communist Party of India – Marxist–Leninist. Provisional Central Committee, "The Left Front Government in West Bengal: From Class Collaboration to Class Capitulation," *For A New Democracy*, December 1978–February 1979, vol. I, no. 10–12, p. 84–109

Gupta, Bhupesh. *On Comrade E.M.S. Namboodiripad's "Brief Critical Note on the Programme Drafts,"* New Delhi: Communist Party of India, 1964

Namboodiripad, E.M.S. *A Brief Critical Note on the Programme Drafts*, New Delhi: Communist Party of India, 1964

Pal, Sampad. "West Bengal Thirteen-Point Programme to Streamline Party Organisation," *People's Democracy*, March 27, 1983

Paul, Subrata. "Radical Change in Land Revenue System," *People's Democracy*, September 30, 1979, p. 5

Rana, Santosh. "Left Front Government in West Bengal: Appraisal," *For A New Democracy*, Special Issue, October–February 1981–82, Calcutta: Communist Party of India – Marxist–Leninist, 1982, p. 43

Ranadive, B.T. "Speech Introducing Draft Political Resolution" in *Main Speeches at the Eleventh Congress*, Vijayawada, January 26–31, 1982, New Delhi, CPM, July 1982, pp: 42–4

Sundarayya, P. *An Explanatory Note on the Central Committee Resolution on Certain Agrarian Issues*, adopted March 8–15, 1973, Calcutta: CPM, 1973

West Bengal State Committee (CPM). *Significant Six Years of the Left Front Government of West Bengal*, Calcutta: CPM West Bengal State Committee, September 1983

West Bengal State Conference (CPM). *Rajnaitik-Sangathanik Report* ("Political Organisational Report"), 14th Plenary Session, December 27, 1981–January 1, 1982, Calcutta: West Bengal State Committee, CPM, March 1982

## GOVERNMENT SOURCES

(a) GOVERNMENT OF INDIA

Ministry of Agriculture and Irrigation. *Report of the Committee on Panchayat Raj Institutions*, New Delhi: 1978

Ministry of Agriculture. Directorate of Economics and Statistics. *Agricultural Wages in India* (Periodical)

Department of Rural Development. *Concurrent Evaluation of IRDP: The Main Findings of the Survey for January 1987–December 1987*, New Delhi: Department of Rural Development, August 1988

*Credit for Integrated Rural Development Programme: A Compendium of Important Instructions*, New Delhi: February 1984

*Proceedings of the Conference of State Secretaries in Charge of IRDP*, held at New Delhi on July 4–5, 1985. New Delhi: Government of India Press, 1985

*Thoughts on Rural Development*, Proceedings of the Seminar on "Poverty Alleviation–Policy Options" held in New Delhi on August 26, 1985, New Delhi: 1985

*Report of the Committee to Review the Existing Administrative Arrangements for Rural Development and Poverty Alleviation Programmes* (CAARD), New Delhi: December 1985

National Rural Employment Programme (NREP) and Rural Landless Employment Guarantee Programme (RLEGP), *Manual*, New Delhi: October 1986

"Background Material for Workshop on IRDP", January 29–31, 1987, edited by M.L. Sharma and T.M. Dak (mimeo)

Ministry of Finance, Department of Economic Affairs. *Report of the Taxation Enquiry Commission 1953–54*, New Delhi: GOI Press, vol. III

*Direct Taxes Enquiry Committee Final Report*, New Delhi: GOI, 1971

Ministry of Home Affairs, *Second Report of the Commission for Scheduled Castes and Tribes*, April 1979–March 1980, Delhi: GOI, Controller of Publications, 1981

*Third Report of the Commission for Scheduled Castes and Scheduled Tribes*, Delhi: GOI, Controller of Publications, 1983

*Selected Statistics on Scheduled Castes*, Occasional Papers on Development of Scheduled Castes (2), New Delhi: GOI Press, June 1984

Ministry of Information and Broadcasting, *India 1984*, New Delhi: Publications Division, March 1985

Ministry of Labour. Labour Bureau, *Agricultural Labour in India: A Compendium of Basic Facts*

*Indian Labour Statistics 1978*. Simla: GOI, 1980

National Sample Survey Organisation. *National Sample Survey*, August 1956–August 1957, 11th and 12th rounds

*National Sample Survey*, July 1971–June 1972, 26th round, report no. 239, "Consumer Expenditure for Cultivator Households, Rural"

*National Sample Survey*, 26th round, report no. 215, "West Bengal", vol. I

"Survey of 32nd Round on Employment and Unemployment started July 1977 and completed June 1978," *Sarvekshana*, April 1979, p. S590

Planning Commission, *First Five Year Plan*, New Delhi: 1953

*Draft Five Year Plan*, 1978–83, vol. II

Programme Evaluation Organisation, *Evaluation of Food for Work Programme, Final Report*, New Delhi: GOI Press, 1981

*Report of the Expert Group on Programmes for Alleviation of Poverty*, New Delhi: GOI Press, February 1982

*Report of the Working Group on the Development of Scheduled Castes during the Seventh Five Year Plan 1985–90*, New Delhi: mimeographed, February 1985

*Evaluation Report on the Integrated Rural Development Programme*, New Delhi: mimeographed, May 1985

*Sixth Five Year Plan 1980–85*, New Delhi: GOI Press

Power and Energy Division, *Review of Performance of State Electricity Boards in the Sixth Five Year Plan Period*, New Delhi: June 1985

Registrar General and Census Commissioner, *Census of India*, 1981, *Provisional Population Totals: Workers and Non-Workers*, series – I, paper 3, 1981

Taxation Enquiry Commission, *Report of the Taxation Enquiry Commission 1953–54*, vol. III

(b) GOVERNMENT OF WEST BENGAL

Bandyopadhyay, D. Land Reforms Commisssioner, *Land Reforms in West Bengal*,

Calcutta: Information and Cultural Affairs Department, WBG, 1980
Basu, Jyoti. Chief Minister, *Budget Speech on Grant under Labour and Employment*, West Bengal Legislative Assembly, 11 March 1978
Basu, Jyoti. Chief Minister, *Left Front Government's Industrial Policy: Some Aspects*, Calcutta: Information and Cultural Affairs Department, 1985
Commerce and Industries Department, *A Review of Industrial Growth in West Bengal*, Calcutta: WBG Press, March 1979
Comprehensive Area Development Corporation of West Bengal, "Comprehensive Area Development Project, Ratua-II P.O. Sambalpurtal, Malda", mimeographed
Department of Labour, *Labour in West Bengal 1980*, Calcutta: WBG Press, 1981
   *Labour in West Bengal 1983*, Calcutta: WBG Press, 1984
   *Labour in West Bengal 1984*, Calcutta: WBG Press, 1985
   *Labour in West Bengal 1989*, Calcutta: WBG Press, 1990
Department of Information and Cultural Affairs, *Left Front Government in West Bengal*. Calcutta: WBG, 1984
   *Reply to Questionnaire: Commission on Centre–State Relations*, Calcutta: WBG, July 1984
   *Left Front Government in West Bengal: Eight Years*, Calcutta: September 1985
   *School Education in West Bengal 1984*, Calcutta: Director of Information, 1985
   *Towards Formation of the Darjeeling Gorkha Hill Council*, Calcutta: 1988
   *A Reply to the Lie-Campaign*, Calcutta: March 1989
   *12 Years of Left Front Government in West Bengal*, Calcutta: June 1989
Development and Planning Department, *West Bengal Draft Five Year Plan 1978–83*, Calcutta: WBG
   *Draft Seventh Five Year Plan 1985–90 and Annual Plan 1985–86*, Volume I, Calcutta: mimeographed, January 1985
Director of Information, *Gorkhaland Agitation, The Issues: An Information Document*, Calcutta: 1986
   *Gorkhaland Agitation, Facts and Issues*: Information Document II, Calcutta: 1987
Dutta, P.K. *Statistics of Bargadars and Extent of Barga Cultivation in West Bengal*, Calcutta: Directorate of Land Records and Survey, May 1981
*Economic Review 1977–78*, Calcutta: WBG Press, 1978
   1980–81, Calcutta: WBG Press, 1981
   1980–81: Statistical Appendix, Calcutta: WBG Press, 1981
   1981–82, Calcutta: WBG Press, 1982
   1984–85, Alipore: WBG Press, 1985
   1984–85: Statistical Appendix, Calcutta: WBG Press, 1985
   1989–90, Calcutta: West Bengal State Planning Board, 1990
   1989–90: Statistical Appendix, Calcutta: State Planning Board, 1990
Ghosh, Krishnapada. Minister-in-charge Labour Department, *Budget Speech in Respect of Demand No. 42*, West Bengal Legislative Assembly, 25 March 1981
Ghosh, Tushar Kanti. Directorate of Land Records and Surveys, "Operation Barga in West Bengal's Land Reforms," mimeographed, 1980
Land Reforms Office (Management and Settlement Wings). Burdwan, *Land Reforms in the District of Burdwan*, Burdwan: WBG, mimeographed, 1980.
Land Reforms Offices. *Bargadars in West Bengal and an Assessment of their position in the Field*, mimeographed, August 1985

Legislative Department, *The West Bengal Panchayat Act, 1973 as modified up to November 1980*, Alipore: WBG Press, 1980

Mukherji, B.C. "The Impact of Panchayats on Socio-Economic Development of Rural Bengal", in *Panchayats in West Bengal From 1978–79 to 1980–81: A Review*, Calcutta: Department of Panchayats and Community Development, WBG, January 1982

Panchayats, Directorate of *Panchayats in West Bengal*, Calcutta: Director of Panchayats, 1981.

Panchayats and Community Development, Department of *The Working of Panchayat System in West Bengal, A Review of Main Events and Activities*, Calcutta: Department of Panchayats and Community Development, March 1980.

   *Panchayats in West Bengal from 1978–79 to 1980–81: A Review*, Calcutta: Department of Panchayats and Community Development, WBG, January 1982

Refugee Relief and Rehabilitation Department, Letter from Deputy Secretary to Zonal Director, Ministry of Home Affairs, on "Problems of Refugees from Dandakaranya to West Bengal", No. 3223-Rehab/DNK-6/79.

Revenue, Board of and Directorate of Agriculture (Socio-Economic and Evaluation Branch), *Agricultural Census 1976–77*, Calcutta: WBG, 1979

Revenue, Board of and Land Utilisation and Reforms and Land and Land Revenue Department Combined Statistical Cell, *Bank Loan and West Bengal: A Statistical Report*, Calcutta: WBG Press, 1979

Revenue, Board of, *Dynamics of the Rural Situation in West Bengal – Panchayat Raj*, Calcutta: WBG Press, 1979

   *Compendium of Instructions on Land Reforms*, vol. II, Kadapara: WBG Press, 1980

   Statistical Cell, *An Evaluation of Land Reforms in West Bengal*, Calcutta: WBG, 1981.

   Statistical Cell, *Land Reforms in West Bengal: Statistical Report-IV*, Calcutta: WBG Press, 1980

   *Guidelines for Bank Financing to Share-croppers and Patta Holders*, Calcutta: WBG, 1981

   Supreme Court Judgement dated the 9th May 1990 Upholding Ceiling on Land Prescribed under the West Bengal Land Reforms Act, 1955, Calcutta: WBG, 1981

   Statistical Cell, *Land Reforms in West Bengal, Statistical Report I*, Calcutta: WBG, 1979.

   Statistical Cell, *Land Reforms in West Bengal, Statistical Report V*, Calcutta: WBG, 1981

   Statistical Cell, *Land Reforms in West Bengal, Statistical Report VI*, Calcutta: WBG, 1981

   Statistical Cell, *Land Reforms in West Bengal, Statistical Report VII*, Calcutta: WBG, 1982

   *Workshop on Land Reforms: A Few Operational Decisions*, June 23–24, 1978, Calcutta: WBG, 1978

   *Workshop on Land Reforms II: Operational Decisions*, May 4–5, 1979, Calcutta: WBG, 1979

   *Third Workshop on Land Reforms: Operational Decisions*, September 15–16, 1980, Calcutta: WBG, 1980

   *Fourth Workshop on Land Reforms: Operational Decisions*, June 23–24, 1981, Calcutta: WBG, 1981

Sarkar, B.K. and R.K. Prasannan. *What Happened to the Vested Land?*, Calcutta: Directorate of Land Records and Surveys, WBG, March 1976.

Sarkar, B.K., Director of Land Records and Surveys, West Bengal, "A Note on Barga Recording in West Bengal", October 23, 1979, Typewritten.

"Statement of Vested Agricultural Land Hit by Injunction up to 31st December, 1984," mimeographed.

# Index

# Cambridge South Asian Studies

These monographs are published by the Syndics of Cambridge University Press in association with the Cambridge University Centre for South Asian Studies. The following books have been published in this series:

1 S. Gopal: *British Policy in India. 1858–1905*
2 J.A.B. Palmer: *The Mutiny Outbreak at Meerut in 1857*
3 A. Das Gupta: *Malabar in Asian Trade, 1740–1800*
4 G. Obeyesekere: *Land Tenure in Village Ceylon*
5 H.L. Erdman: *The Swatantra Party and Indian Conservatism*
6 S.N. Mukherjee: *Sir William Jones: A Study in Eighteenth-Century British Attitudes to India*
7 Abdul Majed Khan: *The Transition of Bengal. 1756–1775: A Study of Saiyid Muhammad Reza Khan*
8 Radhe Shyam Rungta: *The Rise of Business Corporations in India.1851–1900*
9 Pamela Nightingale: *Trade and Empire in Western India, 1784–1806*
10 Amiya Kumar Bagchi: *Private Investment in India, 1900–1939*
11 Judith M. Brown: *Gandhi's Rise to Power: Indian Politics, 1915–1922*
12 Mary C. Carras: *The Dynamics of Indian Political Factions*
13 P. Hardy: *The Muslims of British India*
14 Gordon Johnson: *Provincial Politics and Indian Nationalism*
15 Marguerite S. Robinson: *Political Structure in a Changing Sinhalese Village*
16 Francis Robinson: *Separation among Indian Muslims: The Politics of the United Provinces' Muslims, 1860–1923*
17 Christopher John Baker: *The Politics of South India, 1920–1936*
18 David Washbrook: *The Emergence of Provincial Politics: The Madras Presidency, 1870–1920*
19 Deepak Nayyar: *India's Exports and Export Policies in the 1960s*
20 Mark Holmström: *South Indian Factory Workers: Their Life and Their World*
21 S. Ambirajan: *Classical Political Economy and British Policy in India*
22 M.M. Islam: *Bengal Agriculture 1920–1946: A Quantitative Study*

Cambridge South Asian Studies

For EU product safety concerns, contact us at Calle de José Abascal, 56–1°,
28003 Madrid, Spain or eugpsr@cambridge.org.

www.ingramcontent.com/pod-product-compliance
Ingram Content Group UK Ltd.
Pitfield, Milton Keynes, MK11 3LW, UK
UKHW010039140625
459647UK00012BA/1490